GW00975927

COMMENDATIONS

Mouneer Hanna Anis Bishop of Egypt with North Africa and the Horn of Africa; Chairman, Global South Anglican Network

In this outstanding book Stephen Noll pours out all of his tremendous experience in the Anglican Communion. As we read it we can easily feel his passion for the Church and its future.

Phil Ashey President & CEO, American Anglican Council; Author of *Anglican Conciliarism*

Steve Noll weaves a vivid tapestry of the crisis of false teaching at the highest levels of the Anglican Communion from 1993 to the present. He makes a compelling case from the Bible, our Reformational Anglican roots, theology and history that we are in a *kairos* moment where a new "Global Anglican Communion" covenant is essential to keep biblically faithful Anglicans in the Global South and Gafcon together. The Psalmist asks: *"When the foundations are being destroyed, what can the righteous do?"* With rich documentation and critical thinking, Dr. Noll answers that question.

Bill Atwood Bishop, International Diocese (ACNA); General Secretary, Ekklesia Society

I have watched and worked with Stephen Noll for more than twenty-five years, and he has consistently shown keen analysis and made powerful arguments about how to move forward without surrendering Biblical authority. What makes this book quite remarkable is that it includes contemporary information and writings from over the years that were done in the heat of the battle. They have been gathered together to make the case for a Biblically orthodox Anglican witness.

Foley Beach Archbishop and Primate, Anglican Church in North America

In a time when the world-wide Anglican Communion is facing the tremendous onslaught of secularism and pluralism,

The Global Anglican Communion is a refreshing examination of where we are today in defending and promoting the Gospel of Jesus Christ as expressed in the Holy Scripture and the long-standing tradition of the Church. Dr. Noll gives us all hope that this beacon of light amidst the dark storm clouds rolling in can indeed flourish as a light unto the nations.

Robert W. Duncan Archbishop Emeritus, Anglican Church in North America

The Global Anglican Communion is a must-read for those concerned to shape a coherent, faithful and dynamic Anglicanism for the 21st century. This collection of essays is enlightening, both as to what has gone wrong in, and what would lead to repair of, the Anglican missionary enterprise that successfully carried the Gospel of Jesus Christ into half the world.

Joseph Galgalo Professor and Vice Chancellor, St. Paul's University, Limuru, Kenya

Noll contends that the worldwide Anglican Communion is in a flux. A process of sifting, to distinguish true Anglicanism from a false one, has begun. He makes the criteria for such a process abundantly clear. 'The plumb line' has been set. True Anglicans will be known by their genuine faithfulness to the scripture and ancient formularies. Noll is passionately prophetic and understandably contentious, juxtaposing prophetic judgment with a sure hope.

Edith M. Humphrey Professor of New Testament, Pittsburgh Theological Seminary

Stephen Noll declares himself neither a prophet nor the son of a prophet as he introduces this intriguing study of the struggle for Anglicanism in the past quarter-century. This reviewer is not sure of his parentage, but wonders if the book might suggest otherwise regarding his (unofficial) office. Sometimes friends outside the Anglican Communion are tempted to ask, "Will the real Anglican please stand up?" This book provides both Anglicans and their friends with the clear witness and wisdom of an Anglican in whom there is no guile!

Jack L. Iker Third Bishop of Fort Worth (ACNA)

Stephen Noll in his new book has provided a careful and thorough analysis of the issues and events dividing the Anglican Communion over the past three decades. As a Bishop who survived these tumultuous years of what Dr. Noll aptly calls "a battle for the soul of our Anglican heritage," I commend this book to you as a helpful "vision of a renewed and reformed Global Anglican Communion."

Peter Jensen Retired Archbishop of Sydney; General Secretary of GAFCON

This is a very timely book by a scholar with a wide experience of the Anglican Communion. Professor Noll has been thinking about and participating in the debates over the nature of the Anglican Communion for a considerable time. Indeed, he has played a pivotal role at various moments of its recent history. His contribution is definitely worth reading and pondering as we seek the Lord's will for our future relations.

Grant LeMarquand Bishop for the Horn of Africa (Retired); Emeritus Professor of Biblical Studies, Trinity School for Ministry

In "Contending for Anglicanism" Steve Noll claims to be neither a prophet nor the son of a prophet. On this point he may be incorrect. The essays in this book probe, dissect, analyze, and diagnose movements within contemporary Anglicanism and their theological foundation (or lack of the same). The prognosis is both distressing and hopeful. Although Anglicanism may survive its recent upheavals, radical surgery may be required. Noll's is indeed a prophetic voice much needed.

Michael Nazir-Ali President of OXTRAD; 106th Bishop of Rochester

Professor Noll shows us how to be on the right side of a fundamental divide, and why it is so important for our own spiritual integrity and those for whom we have a responsibility. The Anglican Communion came to be through the tireless and sacrificial work of people who went with the Gospel to different lands, sometimes adamantly opposed in their mission by both local and colonial powers. Erastian Anglicanism and its colonial offshoots are dying of unprincipled liberalism. Gospel Anglicans and their churches will continue to flourish because they stand in the Great Tradition of Evangelical and Catholic Christianity. Which side are we going to be on? Stephen Noll's and the Gospel churches, or those who have a "form of godliness but lack the power thereof"?

John Ashley Null Anglican Canon; Author of *Thomas Cranmer's Doctrine of Repentance*

In an era of shrill contentiousness that sends lovers of peace understandably looking for cover, Stephen Noll is to be commended for reminding us that to proclaim the Gospel can also mean to defend it from the assaults of contemporary culture. Since Noll has been a key leader in the events he narrates, his writings have much to offer those seeking to understand these times, including future Anglican historians.

Nicholas D. Okoh Primate, Anglican Church of Nigeria; Chairman, GAFCON Primates' Council

An erudite contribution to the GAFCON cause by a trained and seasoned Christian theologian who has been there from the beginning.

James I. Packer Professor of Theology, Regent College, Vancouver; Author of *Knowing God*

These well-informed and well-crafted essays, produced over twenty-five years, have three goals in view: *first*, to uphold the authority of scripture as Anglicans have historically received it; *second*, to uphold Anglican faith and morals as these have been established over the centuries; *third*, to trace the development of Global Anglicanism in the way indicated by the GAFCON Statement and the Jerusalem Declaration. Professor Noll seems to me highly successful in each of these purposes.

COMMENDATIONS

Rennis Ponniah Bishop, Anglican Diocese of Singapore

This book contains all that we have come to appreciate about Stephen Noll: his commitment to the authority of holy Scripture, his robust loyalty to classical Anglicanism and his clarion call to fight for the Church's faithfulness to the faith once delivered. It will cause you to join the battle with clarity, tenacity and genuine love.

Patrick Henry Reardon Pastor of All Saints Antiochian Orthodox Church; Author of *Christ in the Psalms* and *Reclaiming the Atonement*

Assembled in this volume are 25 years of reflections from the fertile pen of Dr. Stephen Noll, a clear, reliable, and competent spokesman for classical Anglicanism. Even as he chronicles the ups-and-downs, the varied fortunes of the Anglican Communion in recent times, Noll bolsters his conservative case by more than 100 pages of solid biblical exegesis, a feature that enhances the book's value far beyond its targeted audience. Strongly recommended.

Vaughan Roberts Rector, St. Ebbe's Church, Oxford; Director, Proclamation Trust

This collection of essays bears witness to both the sad decline of the liberal church into ever greater false teaching and compromise in recent years, as well as the emergence of a global coalition of faithful Anglicans, determined to preserve the faith once for all entrusted to the saints. Stephen Noll has been close to the centre of the action throughout as a courageous and wise exponent of authentic Anglicanism, rooted in tradition and always submitting to scripture. His is a voice that needs to be heard, not just as a witness to the past, but as a guide for the future.

John M. Senyonyi Vice Chancellor, Uganda Christian University

I worked under Stephen Noll at Uganda Christian University and learned to respect both him as a person and his passionate defense of the Gospel *"once delivered to the saints."* This passion has continued unabated into his 'retirement.' For decades, we have watched parts of the Anglican

Communion degenerate into heresy. Evangelical Christians have been alarmed. Professor Noll's summary and exposé of the principal deviations from the doctrines of Scripture, human nature and the church are immensely helpful.

Mark Thompson Principal, Moore Theological College, Sydney

Love for the Lord, his word, and his people has led Stephen Noll to channel his considerable biblical and theological gifts into the worldwide effort to rescue the Anglican Communion from the compromise and rank apostasy that characterizes it in so many places in the West. Against extraordinary odds, and with great grief as their denomination was stolen from under them by revisionists openly rejecting the teaching of the Bible, Stephen, alongside a number of other courageous leaders mentioned at various places in this book, have maintained a clear witness to biblical faithfulness and pastoral responsibility in the service of the crucified and risen Saviour and Lord.

Philip Turner Author of *Christian Ethics and the Church*

Stephen Noll has provided a clear and comprehensive account of the publically known actions and conflicting commitments that have produced a tear in the fabric of the Anglican Communion. At the same time, he makes a proposal for a shift in the identity of the Anglican Communion that moves from a fellowship of independent provincial churches in communion with the Archbishop of Canterbury to a fellowship of independent provincial churches united by a common confession of belief and practice and ordered by conciliar forms of governance. This is a book that should be read and discussed by supporters of these actions and proposals and critics alike.

Kevin J. Vanhoozer Professor of Theology, Trinity Evangelical Divinity School; Author of *Biblical Authority After Babel*

The last twenty-five years have seen various kinds of upheaval in the Anglican Communion, and for twenty-five years Stephen Noll has been observing, praying for, and speaking prophetically from diverse locations – academy and church, North America and Uganda – into this complex situation about matters ranging from *sola scriptura* to same-sex marriage. Dr. Noll is contending for the faith and therefore minces no words in suggesting that the 'northern kingdom' (viz., the 'Mother Church' in England and her North American children) has forfeited its role, which has passed to the 'southern kingdom' (viz. GAFCON and the Global South). Together, these essays represent a clarion call for a mere Anglicanism that acknowledges the plain and canonical sense of the Bible as the authoritative Word of God for the church's faith and practice.

Eliud Wabukala Former Archbishop and Primate, the Anglican Church of Kenya

Professor Stephen Noll has written an accurate analysis on the genesis of the breakdown of order in the Anglican communion due to heresy supported and perpetuated by the ecclesiastical establishment. It's a compelling apologia for the reform and the revival of the communion.

Hector (Tito) Zavala Bishop of Chile and Former Primate of the Anglican Province of South America.

Dr. Noll gives us a clear Biblical and theological understanding of what's going on with Anglicanism during the past 25 years. And he helps us to reinforce the armor of God we had put on, so that we can stand firm in today's troubled world and confused Church.

The Global Anglican Communion

Contending for Anglicanism 1993-2018

Stephen Noll

Anglican House

Published by Anglican House Media Ministry, Inc., Newport Beach, California, a Ministry Partner of the Anglican Church in North America. You may contact us at anglicanhousemedia.org and at anglicanliturgypress.org. Printed by Asia Printing Co., Ltd., Seoul, Korea. Text set in Baskerville typeface.

ANGLICAN HOUSE

ISBN 978-0-9993910-7-5

ABOUT THE COVER PHOTO

The cover photo was taken on the "steps" of the Temple Mount during GAFCON 2008 in Jerusalem. It shows some of the 1,300 Bishops, clergy and lay people from around the world who gathered in the land of Jesus' birth to assess the opportunities and challenges for the gospel in 21st century culture, to plan for the future, and to enjoy fellowship together.

...and many peoples shall come, and say: "Come, let us go up to the mountain of the LORD, to the house of the God of Jacob, that he may teach us his ways and that we may walk in his paths." (Isaiah 2:3)

Photo courtesy of GAFCON

CONTENTS

CONTENTS

Section Three

Is There a Global Anglican Future?
The Road Ahead 2008-2018

ACKNOWLEDGMENTS

I t is hard to know how to thank so many people I have interacted with over the past 25 years. Let me begin with my colleagues on the faculty and Dean/Presidents and Board members of Trinity School for Ministry, with special note of John Rodgers, my former boss and long-time friend, to whom I am dedicating this book. Then there were many fellow workers in the run-up to Lambeth 1998 including Bill Atwood, Jim Stanton, John Guernsey, the late Diane Knippers among others.

To my friends and colleagues in Uganda – fellow workers on the faculty and staff of Uganda Christian University, my successor John Senyonyi, the bishops of the Anglican church of Uganda and the archbishops, the late Livingstone Nkoyoyo, Henry Orombi, and Stanley Ntagali, with special mention of the behind-the-scenes work of Alison Barfoot – to you I say, *Webale nnyo*.

I have valued my colleagues in the GAFCON movement, especially members of the Theological Resource Group, including Vinay Samuel, Chris Sugden, Mark Thompson, the late Mike Ovey, Ashley Null, Phil Ashey and Charles Raven. Among the leaders of the Gafcon and Global South movements, I must mention Peter Akinola, Nicholas Okoh, Eliud Wabukala, Mouneer Anis, Samson Mwaluda, Tito Zavala, Peter Walker, and Grant LeMarquand. Michael Nazir-Ali and Peter Jensen, in particular, have been theological colleagues and leaders in the movement.

Martyn Minns has been a long-time friend and coworker from my earliest parish days through all of these periods to the present. Likewise, my bishop and archbishop, Robert Duncan, has been a supporter throughout this past quarter century. I am happy to be working now with Foley Beach, who has ably continued to lead the Anglican Church in North America.

I want to thank Ron Speers and his team at Anglican House for their work in preparing this book for publication.

We have a saying in Uganda "all protocols observed" to cover the many people who have gone unnamed. Please accept my thanks to you as well.

Through all this time I owe so much to my dear wife of fifty years, Peggy. She has prayed for me, listened to me (at length), and proofread reams of my theological effusions.

Finally, I wish to thank the publishers who kindly permitted use of the following:

"Reading the Bible as the Word of God" appeared in Frederick Houk Borsch, ed., *The Bible's Authority in Today's Church: Papers on the Authority of Scripture as Presented to the Episcopal House of Bishops* (Valley Forge, PA: Trinity Press International, 1993), pages 133-167. Used by permission of Bloomsbury Publishing Plc.

Two Sexes, One Flesh: Why the Church Cannot Bless Same-Sex Marriage was originally published by Latimer Press, an imprint of Episcopalians United, Solon, OH, 1997. It was abridged and reprinted as "Two Sexes, One Flesh: Why the Church Cannot Bless Same-Sex Unions," in *Theology Matters* 6/3 (May/June 2000).

"Lambeth Diary: A Week to Remember" was originally posted on the blog of the American Anglican Council.

"Lambeth Speaks Plainly: What the Anglican Bishops Said about Sex" appeared in *Mixed Blessings: Why Same-Sex Blessings Will Divide the Church. A Response to the Episcopal Church's Standing Commission on Liturgy and Music* (Dallas, TX: American Anglican Council, July 2000), pages 30-37.

"Sea Change in the Anglican Communion" was published in Charles Raven ed., *The Truth Will Set You Free: Global Anglicanism in the 21st Century* (London: The Latimer Trust, 2013), pages 109-121.

Stephen Noll
Epiphany 2018

To

John H. Rodgers, Jr.

Happy Warrior for the Gospel

GENERAL INTRODUCTION

Hear, you mountains, the indictment of the LORD, and you enduring foundations of the earth, for the LORD has an indictment against his people, and he will contend with Israel. (Micah 6:2)

Beloved, although I was very eager to write to you about our common salvation, I found it necessary to write appealing to you to contend for the faith that was once for all delivered to the saints. (Jude 3)

I am not a prophet nor a prophet's son, but I have been a watchman of Anglican affairs over the past quarter century, first in the Episcopal Church USA, then in the wider Anglican Communion, and I do have a dispute with the Church establishment. Much of what I have observed and commented on over these years can be characterized as a battle for the soul of our Anglican heritage. Hence I have described these essays as *contending* for Anglicanism.

Being contentious does not necessarily mean being merely contrarian. Thankfully, we have the example of Martin Luther, whose Ninety-Five Theses led to a revival of Gospel faith and a reform of the church throughout Europe. Again, I am no Luther, but I do hope that my theses in these essays may build up even as they tear down. St. Paul advises: "Let love be genuine. Abhor what is evil; hold fast to what is good" (Rom 12:9). My hope is that readers will find in these essays not only warnings against false teaching but also loving witness to the one holy catholic and apostolic Church and to the Lord of the Church.

In particular, I want to commend to readers the vision of a renewed and reformed Global Anglican Communion, a communion of churches which builds on the heritage of the Church of England and represents the emerging leadership of formerly colonial Anglican churches, with the oversight of doctrine and discipline shifted from Canterbury to the Global South.

I am contending that the providential judgment of God has fallen upon the Mother Church and her North American enablers. I am not the first to foresee this eventuality. Five hundred years ago, the poet and Anglican priest George Herbert wrote of the "Church Militant":

Religion stands on tip-toe in this land,
Ready to pass over to the American strand.

And so it happened, largely propelled by marginalized English Puritans, Methodists and Baptists. Herbert went on to note:

Yet as the Church shall thither westward fly,
So Sin shall trace and dog her instantly.

Herbert may have foreseen the inevitable rise of American power and corruption, but I doubt he imagined the advent of a global Communion, which is in fact something of a miracle.

Why did the nations of the Global South not expel the Anglican churches along with the colonial governors? The reasons are complex, but one central reason is that Anglicanism, outside its external trappings, contained the Word of God in Scripture. "When the [Church Missionary Society] came, they came holding the Bible," one delegate to Lambeth 1998 argued. "Therefore, we accept the Scripture as the most authentic we should follow." This conviction lies behind the prophetic indictment of the 2008 Jerusalem Statement. Having detailed the crisis that has torn the fabric of the Communion beyond repair, it goes on to say:

> Our fellowship is not breaking away from the Anglican Communion. We, together with many other faithful Anglicans throughout the world, believe the doctrinal foundation of Anglicanism, which defines our core identity as Anglicans, is expressed in these words: *The doctrine of the Church is grounded in the Holy Scriptures and in such teachings of the ancient Fathers and Councils of the Church as are agreeable to the said Scriptures. In particular, such doctrine is to be found in the Thirty-nine Articles of Religion, the Book of Common Prayer and the Ordinal.* We intend to remain faithful to this standard, and we call on others in the Communion to reaffirm and return to it. While acknowledging the nature of Canterbury as an historic see, we do not accept that Anglican identity is determined necessarily through recognition by the Archbishop of Canterbury.

Ten years on, I believe the indictment remains true. The stubborn refusal of Canterbury to recognize GAFCON and the vicious legal pursuit of our clergy and churches in North America by the Episcopal Church confirms the judgment. They will not repent. They will not change. But neither will the bold statement I heard repeatedly while in Jerusalem change: "We are not leaving. We *are* the Anglican Communion."

I am not a prophet, nor a prophet's son, but I can refer to the prophets of old. In the late 8th century BC, Amos saw judgment coming upon the idolatrous and iniquitous kingdom of Israel:

> This is what he showed me: behold, the Lord was standing beside a wall built with a plumb line, with a plumb line in his hand. And the LORD said to me, "Amos, what do you see?" And I said, "A plumb line."

3

Then the Lord said, "Behold, I am setting a plumb line in the midst of my people Israel; I will never again pass by them; the high places of Isaac shall be made desolate, and the sanctuaries of Israel shall be laid waste, and I will rise against the house of Jeroboam with the sword." (Amos 7:7-9)

Where there is prophetic judgment, there is also prophetic hope. "The seed is the stump," says Isaiah (6:13). Western Anglicanism is being cut down to the roots; the seed of the Anglican future lies in the Global South. That seed has taken root and flourished in many ways. Will it continue to grow to revive the Communion? I cannot see the future with certainty, but I believe the opportunity is there, and the fields are ripe for harvest.

An Overview of the Book

This volume is an anthology of my writings addressing various situations and audiences over the past twenty-five years. It is not intended to be read through cover-to-cover, except by OCD-prone Anglicanophiles. Several essays were written for bishops and other church leaders (Essays 1,9,10,11, and 12). Others were presented to a non-specialist but well-informed audience (Essays 2,3,4, and 7). Still others were aimed at a more general audience (Essays 5,6, and 8). Some were previously published.

The ordering of these essays is generally but not necessarily chronological. The logic of the collection is this:

Section One

Identifies three essential doctrines – paving stones on the royal way – that have come under attack in the modern-postmodern era, and have precipitated the crisis of Anglican identity:

- The doctrine of Scripture (inspiration and interpretation);

- The doctrine of human nature (anthropology), especially of sexuality and marriage; and

- The doctrine of the church (ecclesiology).

SECTION TWO

Describes the two historic conferences in contemporary Anglican history – the 1998 Lambeth Conference and the 2008 Global Anglican Future Conference in Jerusalem; and it explains the two principal documents that emerged from each conference – Lambeth Resolution I.10 on Human Sexuality and the Jerusalem Statement and Declaration.

SECTION THREE

Examines the after-effects of the "sea change" in the Anglican Communion:

- The reform of the Communion governance, including the role of Canterbury;

- The realignment of the Global South and Gafcon movements; and

- The call to the church to contend for the faith as she awaits Jesus' coming in glory.

Readers may find parts of these essays overlapping and redundant, as I have rehearsed the history and principles of contemporary Anglicanism in different times and contexts. Some of the following essays in this volume were published previously. If there is any lesson in such repetition, perhaps it is that my vision of God's activity in the Anglican Communion has been consistent.

5

EDITORIAL COMMENTS

Here are a few editorial comments about the essays:

- Apart from the introductions to each essay, I have not sought to update the original texts in light of subsequent events. I have made a few minor edits and additions for the sake of brevity and clarity.
- These essays were written for various audiences, and I have retained the original British and American orthography and honorifics for God (He/His/Him). I have relegated footnotes to endnotes for the sake of continuity of my argument. I have the typography, terminology and references of the original essays that reflect American, British and African peculiarities.
- The term "Global South" is inexact. It is more a *cultural* than a political, economic, or even geographical marker. Hence it is most often contrasted with the "West." From this perspective, Singapore is part of the Global South, while Australia is part of the "West." While I generally follow this terminology, in some earlier essays I speak of the "Third World."
- I shall refer to the "Global South Anglican Network" or "South-to-South network" for the association of Anglican churches that has met regularly since 1994. Originally a Communion-sponsored entity, it has become increasingly independent of Canterbury, with its own governance structure. All GAFCON provinces, including the Anglican Church in North America, are also members of the Global South Anglican Network, and the leadership of both groups are working toward further unity.
- "GAFCON" originally referred to the Global Anglican Future Conference in 2008, whereas the legal entity

that emerged from it was called the Fellowship of Confessing Anglicans (FCA) and then the Global Fellowship of Confessing Anglicans (GFCA). The name "Gafcon," however ungainly, has stuck and is commonly used for the entire movement that began in Jerusalem in 2008. While most Gafcon Provinces are located in the Global South, the movement is not regionally focused and includes branches in the West.

MY ROLE

I am not a bishop, nor a bishop's son. Hence my role in the events of this period has been not that of a decision-maker but of an observer, scribe and sometime advisor.

I came to Christ - rather He came to me – as a university student, and I was baptized, confirmed, married and ordained in the Episcopal Church. I had an active five years of ministry in a charismatic renewal parish and returned for doctoral study with the hope of strengthening the renewal of the Episcopal Church through biblical and theological teaching. I was fortunate that Trinity Episcopal School for Ministry had opened in 1976 and offered me a position in 1979. I went on to be Professor of Biblical Studies and Academic Dean there.

It was in those roles at Trinity that I entered into my first skirmish in the Episcopal Church. In 1987, the Episcopal Church began drafting "inclusive language" (for God) liturgies and sought to employ the seminaries as boosters for its agenda. We at Trinity concluded that we could not in good conscience worship with these rites and were therefore excluded from the survey –"How can you critique Baal-worship if you haven't experienced it?" I did, however, write a faculty critique of the theology behind the proposed revision, arguing that biblical language for God was not revisable.

I became involved again in 1992, when the Episcopal House of Bishops Theology Committee chose four seminary professors to write position papers on the interpretation and authority of the Bible. That led to my essay "Reading the Bible as the Word of God" (Essay 1). Once again in 1997 the Episcopal House of Bishops sought guidance from the seminaries on a Resolution calling for "rites honoring love and commitment between persons of the same sex." On behalf of the Trinity faculty, I produced a book-length reply: *Two Sexes, One Flesh: Why the Church Cannot Bless Same-Sex Marriage*, excerpted here (Essay 2).

Earlier that year, I had been asked to help write legal briefs in the church trial of Bishop Walter Righter, who had knowingly ordained a practicing homosexual. The trial ended in his exoneration and coincided with the formation of a confessing body, the American Anglican Council, of which I was a founding board member. Through the AAC, I wrote articles and pamphlets leading up to and reporting from the Lambeth Conference in 1998 (Essays 5 and 6). I was also a founding member of a group of Anglican scholars – "Scholarly Engagement with Anglican Doctrine" (SEAD) – and on occasion I addressed its offspring the Mere Anglicanism Conference (Essay 4).

In 1999, my wife and I sensed a missionary call to move to Uganda, where I became the first Vice Chancellor (President) of Uganda Christian University. From 2000 to 2010, I worked closely with leaders of church and state in forming a university that was noted for its academic and professional excellence and for its unapologetic Christian character. While there, we hosted a variety of Anglican dignitaries to the campus, including Rowan Williams, George Carey and Frank Griswold.

In 2006, Archbishop Peter Akinola commissioned me, along with Archbishop Nicholas Okoh and Bishop Zac

Niringiye, to work up "The Road to Lambeth" statement. This statement, which was sent to the Archbishop of Canterbury, was the warning shot across the bow that led ultimately to the rival conferences in 2008, one in Jerusalem and one in Canterbury.

Beginning in 2007, I was a member of the Theological Resource Group that prepared materials for the Global Anglican Future Conference in Jerusalem. At the Conference I led a session with Dr. Ashley Null on Anglican Ecclesiology and served on the group that produced the conference statement, including the Jerusalem Declaration (Essays 3 and 8). At GAFCON 2013 in Nairobi, I wrote a preparatory article on Communion governance (Essay 9), moderated a session on "The Ministry of the Holy Spirit" and helped write the conference statement.

During the time in Uganda and subsequently, I participated in meetings of the Global South network: in Cairo (2005, 2016), Kigali (2006), and Singapore (2010). I have been concerned throughout this time to promote the harmony and ultimate union of these two parallel and overlapping constituencies (Essay 10). On my return to the USA in 2010, I continued to travel internationally and gave two plenary addresses in Nigeria (Essay 11).

I was present to vote with my Diocese of Pittsburgh to depart the Episcopal Church in October 2008, the very month I was awarded an honorary doctorate (Essay 12). I am now a priest of the Anglican Church in North America and Chairman of the Task Force on Marriage, the Family and the Single Life. In 2013, Archbishop Robert Duncan appointed me Special Advisor to the Archbishop on the Global Anglican Future and ACNA member of the Gafcon Theological Commission. In 2014, the Gafcon Primates authorized a "Task Force on Women in the Episcopate" to address an important issue which has divided the Communion, and I was named Convener along with the Chairman, Bishop Samson Mwaluda from Kenya. The Primates received our initial recommendations in April 2017 and authorized further consultations with regional provincial bodies leading up to GAFCON 2018.

Section One
Preparing the Way
Bible, Marriage and Church

A Roman road or *via* was known for two features; it was straight and it was well paved. Many of these Roman roads, wonders of ancient engineering and construction, are visible today. John the Baptist was a voice crying in the desert: "Prepare the way of the Lord, make his way straight" (John 1:23). John was pointing to the Lord Jesus, who says: "I am the Way, the Truth, and the Life" (John 14:6). The early church was known first as "the Way" (Acts 9:2), which spoke of the believers' single-minded commitment to the Good News of salvation in Christ and founded on the apostles' teaching and fellowship. This Good News was carried by St. Paul and other Evangelists along the Roman roads of the Mediterranean world "to the ends of the earth" (Acts 13:47).

The church in our day has been challenged to maintain that way. Since the 1960s, the Episcopal Church and other Western churches have been undermining the road, removing the ancient paving stones, and leaving behind huge potholes for people to stumble into. Three of those paving stones are *the authority of the Bible, the divine institution of marriage,* and *the doctrine and discipline of the church.* On three occasions, I found myself in the position of contending for these foundation stones of the Way.

ESSAY 1

READING THE BIBLE AS THE WORD OF GOD

(1993)

At the 1991 Episcopal General Convention, Bishop William Frey had proposed a canon that "all members of this Church shall abstain from genital relations outside of holy matrimony." The proposal failed to carry. Opponents claimed that this proposal derived from a defective "hermeneutic" of Scripture. The task of solving this defect was referred to the House of Bishops Theology Committee. The bishops appointed four writers – a liberal low-churchman (Professor Charles Price of Virginia Theological Seminary), a liberal high-churchman (Professor Richard Norris of the General Theological Seminary), a feminist liberationist (Professor Ellen Wondra of Colgate-Rochester Divinity School), and a conservative (yours truly). We were asked to define our doctrine of Scripture and interpretation and to relate it to the contemporary church and issues facing it.

In September 1992, the four writers presented their papers to the House of Bishops at their annual meeting. The bishops met and discussed the papers in table groups (this is now known as "indaba"). When the table groups reported back, they came to a happy consensus about the rich diversity of opinion in Anglicanism. Or as the Dodo puts it in *Alice in Wonderland*: "Everyone has won and all must have prizes!" In my view, this "rich diversity" fulfilled J. V. Langmead Casserley's critique of biblical criticism: "We are confronted with the paradox of a way of studying the Word of God out of which no Word of God ever seems to come." The net result of this exercise was to liberate the Episcopal leadership to do whatever they wished concerning any issue arising from the culture – and they would have no trouble finding some distinguished biblical scholar to support them.

In my essay, I chose to defend the "literal sense" of reading the Bible. Many colleagues urged me not to use this term on grounds that it would tar me as a "fundamentalist." I chose to accept that risk because to me it raised the issue of whether the Bible is God's Word written (Anglican Article XX). In my critiques, I argued that each of the other writers in one way or another claimed an alternative authority – agape, conversation, imagination – which allowed them in effect to undermine the authority of God's word in the Bible.

I argue in this essay that the "literal sense" of Scripture is not the same as a "literalist" reading. For instance, I reject the view that "if the whale did not swallow Jonah, then Jesus did not rise from the dead." I make two main clarifications of the literal sense. The first is the idea that Scripture is a threefold cord having a "truth dimension," a "poetic dimension," as well as a "salvation-historical dimension." One must consider, before pronouncing on its meaning, the genre of the Book of Jonah, Jesus' use of the "sign of Jonah" as a fulfillment of Old Testament prophecy, and the attested fact of the Empty Tomb and his resurrection from the dead (Matthew 12:38-42; 27:57-28:8).

The second clarification is that the literal meaning of Scripture "maneuvers from the truth to the whole truth" (a phrase from Meir Sternberg). The depth of God's Word means that its overarching message is available to the ordinary reader as well as to the scholar. The clarity of Scripture does not mean that every reader will come up with identical conclusions; the history of interpretation, even among those with a high view of biblical inspiration, belies this view. Having said this, Anglicans have agreed on understanding the Bible as "containing all things necessary to salvation" and as being "the rule and

14

ultimate standard of faith" (Lambeth Quadrilateral #1). They have also agreed on the unity of God's Word, "marking" this text with that text. One may debate, for instance, how precisely to understand and apply St. Paul's warning to "flee fornication" (1 Corinthians 6:18), but one cannot "imaginatively construe" it to say "free fornication" or "feel fornication"!

Let me note for the record that the GAFCON Statement Committee on which I served weighed how to formulate Anglican biblical authority and interpretation and came up with this clause for the Jerusalem Declaration:

> We believe the Holy Scriptures of the Old and New Testaments to be the Word of God written and to contain all things necessary for salvation. The Bible is to be translated, read, preached, taught and obeyed in its plain and canonical sense, respectful of the historic and consensual reading. (Jerusalem Declaration, clause 2)

I find myself in full agreement with this statement.

WORDS AND THE WORD

BIBLICAL INTERPRETATION IN CRISIS

As is now widely acknowledged, the fault lines that run through the Christian church on matters of theology and ethics, evangelism and apologetics, are manifestations of a tectonic shift in worldviews in which "hermeneutics," or biblical interpretation, plays a central role.[1] To paraphrase Abraham Lincoln's Second Inaugural Address, all interpret the same Bible, but the interpretation of all cannot be equally valid or the Bible ceases to have any coherent authority. Although hermeneutics since Schleiermacher has held out the dream of a path between ancient text and modern believer, it has produced instead a dense undergrowth of theories whose applicability to central Christian affirmations is confusing at best.

My goal in this essay is to argue that the classic way of reading scripture is in terms of its *literal sense* and that this approach remains normative and credible for the church today. I am aware of the danger involved in attempting to rehabilitate the word "literal," as its meaning is frequently caricatured or trivialized. Since the advent of the scientific revolution, "literal" has often been taken narrowly to mean "factual" or "empirically and historically verifiable."[2] Hence some fundamentalists have sought to "prove" the literal character of Genesis 1 by means of "creation science."[3] Some liberals, on the other hand, have attacked plain biblical teaching as mindless "literalism."[4] For all this potential confusion of terminology, "literal sense" has a long and honorable place in the history of interpretation. Its very scandalousness points to crucial issues of the faith that face the contemporary church.[5] Simply to grade the essays in this volume along a conservative-liberal-radical scale would miss the distinctive character of classical and modernist approaches to the Bible.[6]

I begin this chapter with a meditation on the Johannine presentation of Word and Spirit and its relevance for understanding the Bible as the inspired Word of God. I shall then survey the church's tradition of literal interpretation as a more or less consistent application of this apostolic understanding. Finally, I shall return to a restatement of the approach to the literal sense of the Bible that is faithful to the past yet aware of problematic issues in modern hermeneutics.

THE WORD OF GOD AND THE LITERAL SENSE

The literal sense of scripture can only be rightly understood as a *reflex* of the Word of God, that is, the appropriate medium of understanding that accompanies verbal revelation and inspiration. When after each lection in the liturgy we announce "the Word of the Lord," we are attesting to the authoritative character of a particular text in all its specificity, even as we are also claiming that text as a part of the whole message of salvation received and proclaimed by the church in word and sacrament.

The prologue to John's Gospel sets *Logos* as the supreme category of understanding the revelatory activity of the Triune God in his ordering of creation, his prophetic message to Israel, his incarnate Person and work, and in the believing response of the community to his revealed glory. [7]

> *In the beginning was the Word, and the Word was with God, and the Word was God.* (John 1:1)

The inner-Trinitarian love of the Father and the Son is bathed in the light of the divine speech, what Athanasius called God's "intimate locution." As Pannenberg says: "The way in which Jesus speaks of the Father is the only access to knowledge of the Father, but also of the Son, for only through the Father is Jesus known as the Son (Matt. 11:27)."[8]

> *By Him all things were made...* (John 1:3)

God's Word upholds the cosmos in its orderliness, and humanity in God's image participates *mirabile dictu* in created rationality. The Word of God not only forms us after himself but makes room for our free response. Psalm 19 captures the manifold wisdom of God's Word:

> "The heavens are telling the glory of God ... the law of the Lord is perfect, reviving the soul... may the words of my mouth and the meditation of my heart be acceptable in thy sight."

God's word is embedded in the creation, revealed in his law, and returned to him in the praises of his saints.

He came to his own, but his own received him not. (John 1:11)

The Word of God entered into the space-time matrix of historic Israel, the bearer of the oracles of God. And although the Old Testament forms of the Word were shadows and types, in Israel, too, "the Word of God was mediated in such a way that a divinely prepared form of obedient response was included within it."9 Israel's response was above all embodied in the hymns and psalms of the Royal Servant who must suffer rejection by Israel, his most intimate enemy (Ps. 41:9; Isa. 53:3; Zech. 13:7).

And the Word became flesh and dwelt among us... full of grace and truth, (John 1:14)

The Word of God, fragmented in creation and history, becomes united once for all in the God-Man Jesus Christ. In him the Word not only takes on human garb but is crucified for our sake, and the gospel becomes forever "the word of the Cross," which is folly to worldly wisdom but grace and truth to those who believe. In his incarnate and risen glory he makes known ("exegetes") the hidden Father.

...and we beheld his glory, glory ...as of the only Son from the Father. (John 1:14)

The incarnation of the Word is not left without witness. The apostolic "we" is included in the revelation of his glory. In the incarnate I AM, being and knowing are united and offered as light and life to those who are born of his Spirit. And the proper mode of knowing the in-breaking truth of the gospel is faith in the name of Jesus Christ the only-begotten Son (John 20:30-31; Acts 4:12).

In what way can we draw an analogy between the Incarnate Word and the written words of the Bible? In one sense scripture is not identical with the Divine Word or an object rivaling him in glory or calling for worship (Rev. 19:10-11). Jesus Christ is both the Form and Object of the biblical witness; his royal image is the stamp impressed in the substance of scripture. In this age the written words are the mirror in which we see him; when the perfect comes, we shall see him face to face (1 Cor. 13:12).[10] But there is no getting behind (or in front of) the verbal testimony of scripture. The Divine Essence in its Personal relations is "Logical," and his revelation comes in words and in deeds interpreted by words (John 14:11). This revelation is received by his rational creatures, irrationally rejected, and finally enfleshed in the Person of the Son, whose grace calls forth a new people with ears to hear his gospel.

As the literal sense of scripture is the reflex of the saving Word entering our world, so also it is the *inspired letter* of God, the work of the Holy Spirit (2 Tim. 3:16; 2 Pet. 1:20-21). Thus the Prayer Book Catechism says that we call the scriptures the Word of God "because God inspired their human authors and still speaks to us through the Bible." Once again, John emphasizes the Trinitarian context of the inspiration of scripture.

> *These things I have spoken to you while I am still with you. But the Counselor, the Holy Spirit, whom the Father will send in my name, he will teach you all things and bring to your remembrance all that I have said to you.* (John 14:25-26)

The words of the incarnate Son, his commandments, are the substance of scripture; it is the role of the Spirit to recall and exegete these words. The Spirit brings no new revelation but speaks through the apostolic word:

> *He will bear witness to me, and you also are witnesses...*
> (John 15:26,27)

19

At the crisis point of history, the Lord Jesus promises that the Spirit will come and reveal the truth of his words and work through the gospel.

He will convict the world... (John 16:8)

The gap between appearance and reality – Koheleth's chase after wind, the flickering shadows of Socrates' cave – is closed by the Spirit of Truth, who no longer speaks in figures but transparently of the Father (John 16:12-13, 25-30). The Spirit, who is Author of the created forms of human speech, now opens these categories to the incarnate Truth of God, evoking faith as the only way of knowing.

The epistemological role of the Spirit is crucial to understanding scripture as literal truth. Paul's rhetorical contrast of letter and Spirit in 2 Corinthians 3-4 has often been misunderstood in this regard. In an elaborate midrash on Exodus 34, Paul identifies the "letter" with the Mosaic Torah, which despite its divine origin operates within the sign-world of human command (2 Cor. 3:7-11). By contrast the apostolic "statement of the truth" (4:2) breaks forth as new light from the Creator God, and this unveiled gospel is received not by compulsion but in a receptive freedom which is itself a work of the Spirit (3:17-18). Paul's denigration of the letter is not about the mode of verbal revelation; on the contrary, he sees an enhanced role of the inspired word in converting hardened hearts. Thus the word of God can now be called the "sword of the Spirit" (Eph. 6:17; Heb. 4:12).

THE LITERAL SENSE AND THE TRADITION OF INTERPRETATION

In coming to his own, the Word of God emerges from, yet transcends, the tradition of Israel and the church. The very idea of tradition itself presupposes a determinate sense of scripture, since tradition by definition passes on something other than itself. Jewish interpreters, for all their exegetical virtuosity, regarded the letter of scripture as normative for life in the covenant and in the age to come.[11] Early Christian apologetics toward Judaism assumed a common sky under which the truth of God could be disputed. The great challenge faced by the apostles was to reconcile the interpretation of the Old Testament with the fulfilling revelatory event of Jesus Christ. In one of the earliest records of apostolic tradition, Paul states that Jesus' saving death and resurrection happened "according to the Scriptures" (1 Cor. 15:1-11). Paul's tradition undoubtedly employed specific Old Testament *testimonia*, an exegetical method fully at home in the Jewish milieu.[12] At the same time, the gospel was proclaimed as a new covenant of the Spirit that could not be simply poured out from the carnal wineskins of Jewish exegesis.

Gnosticism proved to be a snare to early Christians because it appeared to carry the common distinction between carnal and spiritual senses to its logical conclusion. But the Gnostics radically reinterpreted the New Testament sense of flesh and spirit. Gnostics rewrote scripture in such a way that its literal referents (God, creation, and law) were seen to be essentially demonic.[13] As can be seen by contrast with Christian gnostic texts, the apostolic development of historical allegory, or typology, was not a departure from literal interpretation but a reorientation of the corpus of scripture from the perspective of the gospel (1 Pet. 1:10-12), a move that would lead inevitably to the twofold testament of the Christian Bible.

The Rule of Faith, that summary of doctrine that the Fathers used in their combat with heresy, presupposes a literal meaning of scripture.[14] At the same time the Rule of Faith gave a "theological" focus to Christian hermeneutics that could embrace such diverse exegetes as Origen and Theodore of Mopsuestia.[15] The debate between the schools of Alexandria and Antioch temporarily restricted the literal sense to the "carnal" and "narrative" dimension of scripture.[16] Augustine, however, restored the normative balance of the letter as a key to the spiritual meaning of the text.[17] The Augustinian synthesis soon unraveled, however, into the medieval distinction of levels of meaning. Thus the literal sense once again was seen as being *transcended* in allegory or *supplemented* in the scholastic distinction of a "double literal sense."[18]

The outbreak of exegetical theology in the sixteenth century worked to restore the fullness of the literal sense of scripture. The Reformers' use of typology or "figural reading" was not a quaint holdover of medieval allegory but a vigorous reassertion of the unity of the testaments and of the narrative and doctrinal dimensions of scripture. Although the Reformers were united in their basic approach, each emphasized particular elements of scripture as the inspired Word. Luther saw the gospel of Christ as the hermeneutical focus of both testaments, in its role as promise to be received by faith.[19] For Calvin the key to scriptural interpretation was the activity of the Holy Spirit, who inspired the words and gave inner testimony to the believer.[20] Richard Hooker emphasized the role of "right reason" in correlating the truths of nature and biblical revelation with regard to the proper ends of each, the latter being eternal salvation in Christ.[21]

The modern grammatical-historical approach, or "higher criticism," represents both continuity and crisis for the literal sense. The Reformation attention to the grammar and logic of the text was developed through painstaking application of the emerging disciplines of philology and the social sciences. At the same time exegesis of a text focused on the reconstructed intention of an original author whose life-setting and aims were often seen as radically discontinuous with those of later redactors. The schism of canonical text and original author was a kind of Cartesian stake driven into the heart of the literal sense. While a boon to research in ancient Near Eastern and Greco-Roman culture, the historical method presents immense difficulties for reading and preaching the Bible in the faith community.[22] It would be fair to say that all subsequent theories of interpretation have had to grapple with the loss of innocence in literal reading caused by higher criticism.

In reacting to historical criticism, with its distancing of author, text, and reader, "romantic" hermeneutics has attempted to recover the power of the biblical word by abandoning the notion of literal reference.[23] The interpreter begins with the grammar of the text and then makes an intuitive leap into the consciousness of the author (Schleiermacher), or is called to authentic existence by the "Word" (Bultmann), or identifies with a paradigmatic experience of oppression (liberation theology), or enters into the "world of the text" (Ricoeur). Contemporary hermeneutics descending from Schleiermacher is founded on the dogma of historicism and its corollary, the "hermeneutical circle," which teach that human consciousness cannot transcend its own time-bound milieu.[24] Hence *experience* replaces literal content as the locus of biblical authority.[25] Philosophically, this position has never been able to escape the charge of logical absurdity. "Historicism thrives on the fact that it inconsistently exempts itself from its own verdict about all human thought."[26] Historicists insist that their theory – and theirs alone – be taken literally and for all time. Historicism thus wrongly absolutizes the difficulty of human communication from person to person and age to age.[27]

Another attempt to reestablish the literal sense of the Bible without ignoring the work of higher criticism is the "canonical approach" of Brevard Childs. Childs's project is a massive one: providing new forms of biblical introduction, critical commentary, and integrative biblical theology. What is sometimes overlooked is his call to recover a form of the literal sense of scripture as a necessary aspect of the canon.[28] "Canonical intentionality" is that cooperative inspiring work of the Holy Spirit and traditioning work of the community of faith which produces a final text of scripture normative for all future generations of believers. The aim of literal interpretation in the postcritical age will be the same as that of previous generations but with a greater consciousness of the diachronic witness of the biblical text. Childs, along with other conservative postmodern theologians, seeks to reestablish the "grammar" of the faith tradition of the church.[29] Whether he does justice to the referentiality of the text is another matter.

The reaction to the higher critical method among evangelicals has been ongoing since the eighteenth century and has focused on defending the literal sense of the Bible in terms of verbal inerrancy. This defense is often philosophically rigorous and exegetically sensitive to the variety of genres found in scripture.[30] While affirming the variety of biblical forms and imagery, J. I. Packer nevertheless emphasizes that the Bible is a "corpus of God-given instruction relating to Jesus Christ." For Packer, scripture is accommodated divine speech: "God has put His words into the mouths, and caused them to be written in the writings, of persons whose individuality, as people of their time, was in no way lessened by the fact of their being thus overruled."[31]

Other evangelicals would question the paradigm of "divine speaking" as the key to the literal sense. They would emphasize the freedom, under the overarching sovereignty of God, of the authors and editors to respond to God's revelatory deeds and oracles.[32] For them, inerrancy, if the term is retained, is not an architectonic principle of inspiration, but "simply means that the Bible can be trusted in what it teaches and affirms."[33] If the inerrancy view is overly deterministic, this latter view may be in danger of introducing the dichotomy between verbal revelation and experiential inspiration that has been the bane of modern hermeneutics.[34]

All exegetes and theologians have had the task of "rightly dividing the word of truth," of moving from the letter of the biblical text to its sense or meaning. Thus interpretation is inevitably dialectical, involving text (words), reference (Word), and reader (significance). Dialectic, like a dance, requires a lead partner. In classic hermeneutics, the literal sense of the Word leads the dance of interpretation; in modern (and gnostic) views, the consciousness of the interpreter or interpreting community governs the final sense of scripture.[35]

A PRELIMINARY DEFINITION

The literal sense is that meaning appropriate to the nature of the Bible as the Word of God in the words of men. As the Word of God, scripture is imprinted by the gospel, that obedient movement of the divine Son Jesus Christ from the transcendent Father to his own sinful people and back to him to the praise of his glory (Phil.

2:1, 6-11).[36] As an inspired human word, it participates in natural forms of speech and the historical traditions of the communities of Israel and the church, even as it summons people to faith and new life in Christ.

Three implications follow from this definition. The first is the *referentiality* of the text. Scripture "means what it says," and the "what" must refer to something else outside the text. Hence translation and exegesis necessarily accompany exposition and homiletics. It is a basic misunderstanding of the literal sense to miss the organic link between literal sign and the "thing signified." Fundamentalists often treat the words of scripture as "steno-symbols," having one and only one reference, but this move is defensive and rationalistic. Since the referent can be something visible or invisible, or both, the literal sense is the natural basis for figuration, allegory, and ambiguity.[37] Ironically, when language is seen to be essentially metaphorical, as it is in many contemporary theories, it can no longer mean anything in particular and becomes a kind of verbal black hole.[38]

The second implication of the literal sense is the existence of an *authorial purpose*. When I first wrote these words, I hoped to convey to the Episcopal bishops a particular meaning. In this version I have rephrased my argument in order to respond to criticism and to address a wider audience.[39] I have chosen to speak of authorial purpose rather than "intentionality" because *intention* is often confused with a state of mind, whereas *purpose* looks to the end or design of a writing. Purpose also leaves open the possibility that an author's design could be further elaborated by others.

The divine inspiration of scripture raises a special set of questions. Who is the true author of a particular book of the Bible? Is it possible for the human author to mean one thing and God something totally different? While the idea of human and divine authors working at cross-purposes may be accepted as theoretically possible (Gen. 50:20), it goes against God's character as truthful (2 Tim. 3:16). Like iconographers, biblical writers and editors experienced inspiration within a tradition. Prophets who claim to be direct recipients of revelation present their new word by a creative synthesis of tradition, and their disciples reorder their oracles into a shape consonant with the overall shape of the faith.[40] Jesus defined his mission by appropriating in unexpected ways the figures of the Suffering Servant and the Son of Man (Mark 10:45). Thus the *sensus plenior* [or "fuller sense"] of scripture is a function of God speaking "at many times and in many ways" through the partial purposes of his agents and gathering them together into one great canonical Design. It is in this sense that one can speak of a "canonical intentionality."[41]

The final implication of the literal sense is the *clarity* of scripture. While the Bible declares the mysteries of God, it does not do so esoterically. Traditionally theologians have distinguished between the external and internal clarity of the Bible. Meir Sternberg refers to the Bible's particular external clarity as that of "foolproof composition":

> Biblical narrative is virtually impossible to counterread. The essentials are made transparent to all comers: the story line, the world order, the value system. The old and new controversies among exegetes, spreading to every possible topic, must not blind us (as it usually does them) to the measure of agreement in this regard. The bedrock agreement is neither accidental nor self-evident. Not accidental, because it derives from the Bible's overarching

principle of composition, its strategy of strategies, maneuvering between the truth and the whole truth; nor self-evident, because such a principle does not often govern literature operating at the Bible's level of sophistication and interpretive drama.[42]

The relevance of biblical clarity is especially important given the global context of the church's mission. The diversity of language, culture, and education among those who hear the gospel demands a plain sense of the biblical offer of salvation. American Episcopalians, with their perception of the overwhelming difficulty of cross-cultural communication, can learn something from the "naive" confidence of African, Hispanic, and Asian Anglican evangelists and catechists that the Word of God can go out to all the earth.

The Bible's external clarity does not mean that all who read will obey.[43] Internal clarity is the work of the Triune God, evoking faith in the heart: "For it is the God who said, 'Let light shine out of darkness,' who has shone in our hearts to give the light of the knowledge of the glory of God in the face of Christ" (2 Cor. 4:6). The focusing of the rays of God's word in the gospel of Christ is a new creative act, "what eye hath not seen nor ear heard," and this act marvelously includes those who are being saved and bestows on his saints "hearing with faith" (1 Cor. 1:18, 2:9; Gal. 3:2). There is no ground for boasting about our knowledge of God's word because "no one comprehends the thoughts of God except the Spirit of God" (1 Cor. 2:11).

THE FULLNESS OF SCRIPTURE AS GOD'S WORD

THREE DIMENSIONS OF SCRIPTURE

Contrary to the opinion that literalism involves a narrowing of biblical meaning, a proper literal sense is rich and complex, reflecting the very character of God, out of whose fullness we have received grace upon grace. A literal sense actually guarantees the *possibility* of multiple meanings (or "allegories" in the broadest sense). One might draw a limited analogy to a dictionary entry, in which one word has a number of distinct though overlapping senses. Meaning, of course, is not only lexical but syntactic, which further enriches the tapestry. Finally, biblical language claims to be a vehicle of revelation, by which words can come to say something new in the service of the in-breaking Word of God.

The inspired letter of scripture, far from being flat, is spacious, encompassing *poetic, truth, and salvation-historical dimensions.* Like the threefold cord that is not easily broken (Eccles. 4:12), any biblical text will reflect its own particular configuration of these three dimensions.

THE POETIC DIMENSION

I am using "poetic" in the broadest sense of human artistry as the self-effacing activity of the Word of God coming to us in fully human words. When God speaks, he lisps in human language forms, and the Spirit guides the biblical writers in speaking of him (2 Pet. 1:21). Literal interpretation thus requires careful attention to the syntax of a particular biblical passage: word usage, grammatical structure, literary devices, and genre. Since the Bible is ancient literature, it is important to employ historical tools of comparative linguistics and higher criticism along with literary analysis of the text itself.

Literal sense is "genre-related." We must constantly ask: what kind of writing is this? Form and genre criticism have heightened our awareness of the diversity of biblical revelation as it comes to us through legend, novella, chronicle, testament, hymn and lament, admonition and proverb, dialogue and love song, judgment and salvation oracle, gospel, epistle and apocalypse. The

29

distinctness of biblical literary forms is a witness to God's involvement in the whole life of his people and also in the various affections of the individual soul.[45] The whole Bible is thus a resource book for the believer, "a mass of strange delights," as the poet George Herbert describes it, "where we may wish and take." Put another way, scripture is like a musical score: only as the words and melody are performed do we hear the creation of the Author.[46]

THE TRUTH DIMENSION

The truth dimension of scripture refers to its claim to participate in the speech of God. Truth, which derives from the universal sovereignty of God, is the basis for the authority of the biblical word that stands firm even if heaven and earth should pass away (Mark 13:31; Rom. 3:4). At the same time, truth is apprehended not by mystical absorption into God but through the structures of reality, things visible and invisible, and through the analogical nature of language (Ps. 33:4-9).

Truth is attested to in both *propositional* and *representational* form. As propositions, the words of scripture can also be called God's "commandments" (Deut. 4:2-9; John 14:21-24). Like the two tables of the Law, these commandments include matters of belief about God and obedience to his moral will. The primacy of Torah ("teaching") reminds us of explicit doctrines and commands to be heeded. While the teaching of Jesus transforms the commandments of the Mosaic Torah, it retains their normative form: discipleship involves single-minded adherence to his words (Matt. 5:17-20; 7:24).

Representational truth, or *mimesis*, operates by verisimilitude, or truth-likeness.[47] Mimesis is not thereby artificial or purely formal: it is Lady Wisdom, the force of truth, of nature, drawing the soul to understanding.[48] Mimetic truth operates differently from propositional truth. It is grasped by the imagination, and it draws on common experience and creates new experience.[49] It is the fruit of a conversation in which no "answer" is given but a relationship affirmed. When God proudly displays to Job his creature Leviathan, who is "king over all the sons of pride" (Job 41:34), Job is satisfied, knowing himself even in his quandary to be loved as a royal son.

It is a mistake to identify biblical truth with either propositions or mimesis exclusively, as in the reduction of scripture by fundamentalists to a set of lessons or by liberals to "the play of metaphor." A proposition such as "the Lord Reigns" can be represented narratively by means of the "omniscient" viewpoint of the biblical narrator and in the "omnipotent" outworking of God's will, as when Hushai bests the counsel of Ahitophel (2 Sam. 17:14).[50] On the other hand, a well-chosen proof-text or allusion can summarize a wealth of biblical experience and imagery, as in Peter's appeal:

> Come to him, to that living stone, rejected by men but in God's sight chosen and precious; and like living stones be yourselves built into a spiritual house, to be a holy priesthood, to offer spiritual sacrifices acceptable to God through Jesus Christ. (1 Pet. 2:4-5)

The interplay of propositional and mimetic truth accounts for the Bible's "history-like" character, which has been at the center of the knotty question: Is biblical narrative history or fiction?[51] Propositional truth asserts the actuality of an event, mimesis only its plausibility. Several years ago, when I wrote a brief commentary on the Book of Esther, the editors wished me to assert the essential historicity of the events it describes, but I found it impossible to separate with any certainty the elements of history, liturgy, and fiction.[52] While our modern sensibility insists on deciding the issue, biblical writers seemed confident that fact and fiction can be mixed and remain a witness to a transcendent order not of our own making.

THE SALVATION-HISTORICAL DIMENSION

In speaking of the third or *salvation-historical dimension*, I am using "historical" in the theological sense of God's sovereign revelatory activity with its insistent eschatological thrust. A corollary to this historicality is the scandal of particularity: as Wesley says, "'Tis mystery all, the Immortal dies." The saving activity of God is a mystery that cannot be deduced from the truth of God or the laws of history (Eph. 1:9-10). The literal word, historically considered, breaks in as the preaching of Christ and forms faith in the hearer (Rom. 10:17). Christology thus becomes the lens through which the special history of Israel and the church is read.

What role then does historic Israel play in this scenario? Philosophical hermeneutics, from Origen to Bultmann, have foundered on the "problem of Israel." It was the genius of Luther to recover from Pauline theology a "literal-prophetic" sense of God's word of promise which united the hopes of Israel with the faith of the church.[53] *Typology* is the characteristic interpretative activity that honors the original situation of the oracles of God while pressing on to enunciate their fulfillment in Christ.

The "historicity" or background of the Bible, both in matters of natural and human history, is the context, the home, into which the Word comes. Higher criticism has given a wealth of data to illuminate this history, although its direct relevance to the text of scripture has at times been overstated.[54] Unfortunately, skeptics and defenders of orthodoxy have chosen to skirmish in the historical underbrush. By asking a different set of questions of the biblical data ("Did it really happen that way?"), they have obscured the more eschatological concern of biblical narrators ("Where is it all headed?" – Luke 24:13-27). On the other hand, some postmodern literary critics, in recovering the literary unity of the biblical text, have neglected the historical context that is an accidental property of God's revelatory activity.[55]

The salvation-historical dimension of scripture works to unify not only events but genres, as can be seen in the grouping of biblical books under the authorship of Moses, David, Solomon, or Paul, and beyond that in the equating of "all scripture" with prophecy (Luke 24:44). Implicitly, the biblical authors assume the position of omniscient access to God's will and purposes in creation and history.[56] Whereas higher critics have excelled in dissecting the text into its formal units, premodern commentators, with their focus on its inspired unity, often saw it as of one genre: hence the different typographic conventions of King James and modern versions. The mosaic unity of the Bible, as Northrop Frye calls it, constitutes the "world of the text" that recent critics have rediscovered.[57]

Likewise propositional and mimetic truth are ultimately reconciled by eschatological hope. In the same breath, the Psalmist proclaims that the Lord reigns and cries out, "How long, O Lord?" Even after the deepest probing of the mysteries of life, the sages return to affirm God's ways (Job 42:1-8; Eccles. 12:13).[58] To set our mind on things above and let the word of Christ dwell richly within us gives a perspective from which to enter into the problems and ambiguities of living in fallen structures of society

(Colossians 3-4). The world awaits the coming of the Lamb to reveal its purpose, and when he opens "the scroll written within and without," its rationality is not destroyed but redeemed by a reordering of its priorities (Revelation 4-5).[59]

The unifying movement of salvation history is never simply complete. As the short ending of Mark suggests, the essential work of the Son of God is done, but the story breaks off here so that the reader may paint himself into the picture. It is in this sense that one can speak of scripture as an "open parable":[60] the church down to the end of the age is called on to participate in the divine plan of salvation (Eph. 2:9-10).

AUTHORITY: TAKING GOD AT HIS WORD
THE PRIMACY OF SCRIPTURE

Anglicanism has gladly joined with the Reformation in its affirmation of the scripture principle – the primacy and sufficiency of the Bible – as its norm in matters of doctrine, discipline, and devotion.[61] This primacy is acknowledged explicitly in the Anglican formularies, such as the Thirty-Nine Articles of Religion.

Article 6 Of The Sufficiency Of The Holy Scriptures For Salvation

Holy Scripture containeth all things necessary to salvation; so that whatsoever is not read therein, nor may be proved thereby, is not to be required of any man, that it should be believed as an article of the Faith, or be thought requisite or necessary to salvation.

Article 20 Of The Authority Of The Church

The Church hath power to decree Rites and Ceremonies, and authority in Controversies of Faith; and yet it is not lawful for the Church to ordain anything that is contrary to God's Word written, neither may it expound one place of Scripture, that it may be repugnant to another.

While some may question the authority of the *Thirty-nine Articles* in the American church, J. Robert Wright has demonstrated that they are the theological basis for the Episcopal ordination oath: "I do believe the Holy Scriptures of the Old and New Testament to be the Word of God, and to contain all things necessary to salvation."[62] The portrait one gets in these formularies is of a church and clergy reading, expounding, and believing scripture as "God's word written." This view is also implicit in the assignment of scripture reading in every service of the Prayer Book.[63]

The classic stance of Anglicanism has not gone without question or qualification. Many Anglicans, fearing bibliolatry, see an absolute disjunction between Christ as the Word and scripture as the witness to the Word.[64] Another current view sees scripture as the "repository of the Church's symbols of life and faith,"[65] from which the church draws new light in every age, a view that I would less politely call the "grab-bag approach." Finally, among many Anglican writers the perspective of the Knower (reader) has come to take priority over the determinacy of the Known (literal text), so that the "inerrant truth" of the Bible becomes the "experience" that we share with religious people of all ages.[66]

I have argued that literal sense remains the most credible approach to interpreting the Bible. I likewise maintain that only in the light of its referentiality, purposiveness, and clarity can scripture function as prime authority in the church. In accordance with Jesus' teaching that "man cannot serve two masters," approaches that treat scripture as one authority among others inevitably end up granting autonomy to the individual conscience or the collective conscience of the church.[67]

The appropriate response to biblical primacy is hermeneutical submissiveness. The church and the individual are to receive the gospel in the spirit of the Blessed Virgin: "Behold the handmaid of the Lord; let it be to me according to your word." In the fascinating liberal-evangelical dialogue between David Edwards and John Stott, the extent of this submission to scripture is the central issue.[68] Edwards argues that for all Christians the Bible, in some sense, is or becomes or conveys "the word of God." Its history is, in some sense, "salvation history." Its great images are signs pointing to our salvation, from the Garden of Eden to the final City of God. That seems – to understate its value for our salvation – sufficient (pp. 43-44).

Edwards defines the term *sufficient* to mean "minimally necessary," thus creating a vast space in which his reason can pick and choose as to which biblical teachings are authoritative. Stott's reply focuses on whether such minimalism is finally coherent:

> Sometimes you seem anxious to demonstrate that your position is more biblical than mine. I wonder why? I mean, if you could prove this to me, I would want to change my mind and position at once. But if I could show you that my position is more biblical than yours, would you be willing to change?... In later chapters you reject traditional Christian teaching about the atonement, miracles, homosexual partnerships, and the awful reality of hell, not only on the ground that you consider them unbiblical, but because on other grounds you find it unacceptable. Does this not mean that in the end you accord supremacy to your reason rather than to Scripture? (pp. 104-5)

"Searching the scriptures" requires both access to the whole Bible and willingness to follow wherever it leads (Acts 17:11; John 5:39). In what I have called the grab-bag approach, scripture is seen as a resource from which we choose the "correct" and omit the "incorrect" elements in preaching and theology. This view, mentioned above, is implicit in the 1979 Prayer Book Lectionary, and explicit in any sample of Episcopal preaching. When the grab-bag method is used, the choice and use of the texts usually end up conforming to the priorities of the late twentieth-century enlightened consciousness. I do not deny that every interpreter brings a certain bias, or that there is a legitimate canonical focus on central texts, or that different kinds of scripture function authoritatively in different ways.[69] Nevertheless, the Christian who reads the Bible literally must be attentive to every text, comparing scripture with scripture as a check against one-sided reading.

TRANSFORMED BY THE WORD

Before addressing the specific assigned topics for application, let me begin with a meditation on the means of spiritual transformation inherent in a literal reading of the Bible. The meditation follows the lines of Cranmer's collect: "Blessed Lord, who hast caused all holy Scriptures to be written for our learning..."

Grant us to hear and read them

The first aim for the church's disciplines of preaching and teaching, worship and prayer, is a literate congregation of believers (Matt. 28:20; Acts 2:42). In the apostolic church, this was done through public reading and preaching and memorization; since the print revolution, private Bible reading has become a major devotion for Christian discipleship. The disappearance of reading in the twentieth century is not simply due to lack of time but reflects the hermeneutical crisis of Western thought.[70] Even if they have never heard of the deconstructionist theory that texts are self-immolating, people are daunted by the welter of experts advocating opposite opinions on every subject. With its classic approach to literal and plain sense, the church has a compelling reason to promote literacy among its own and in the society at large.

...mark and learn them

Reading must be accompanied by critical analysis and synthesis. It is characteristic of the Bible that it invites exegesis.[71] The advent of higher criticism has greatly increased our awareness of the genre differences and the diachronic character of the biblical text. What has often been lost, on lay person and scholar alike, is the theological unity of scripture, which is a key assumption of its authority (Ps. 119:160; Article 20). I would like to commend the lost art of proof-texting as a remedy to the fragmentation of the biblical text.[72] Good proof-texting is a foundation not only for biblical theology but for systematic theology and preaching as well, as it forces one to ponder the literal sense of a passage and its intertextual connections with other passages. Just as one would wish to understand the thought of a politician, writer, or philosopher by apt quotations from his works and accurate footnotes, so proof-texting seeks to justify generalizations and applications of the word of God by means of literary reference.

... and inwardly digest them

A further step in this process is the drawing of analogies between the biblical texts and our context. While there are appropriate rules for contextualization, the process of reading and marking the words of scripture is an activity of the Spirit forming a Christian personality and worldview.[73] Classic African-American preaching, for instance, assumes the authority of the Bible as a whole but exhibits a freedom of movement from text to text with a creative retelling of the story, interpreting the experience of slavery and racism in a "Bibleistic way."[74] Truly digesting the word is difficult for modern readers because we have all imbibed the "hermeneutics of suspicion" in regarding all argument as propaganda. We need to learn not only to approve those judgments of scripture that confirm our views but to expect judgments that find us guilty, trusting that in those judgments we will find our true life (Mark 8:34-38; John 6:68).[75] It has never been easy to emulate the prophet who ate the scroll of God's word and found it sweet to the tongue but bitter in the stomach (Ezek. 3:3; Rev. 10:10).

RESURRECTION AND VIRGIN BIRTH

A mind formed by the literal sense of scripture finds denial of Jesus' bodily resurrection and virgin birth unthinkable. Virtually all responsible biblical exegetes would admit that *as a whole and in its final form* the New Testament proclaims that Jesus rose bodily from the dead and reigns eternally in heaven; that he is uniquely Son of man and Son of God; and that these things are in accordance with the prophetic sense of the Old Testament scriptures. All those writings that purport to narrate Jesus' life refer to the empty tomb, and other texts (e.g., Acts 2:23-24, 31-32; 13:29-30; 1 Tim. 3:16; Heb. 12:2; 1 Pet. 3:18-19) are more consistent with the empty tomb than with any other hypothesis. Likewise the two Gospels that related Jesus' human origin say that he was born of a virgin, and no other New Testament Christological statement presumes some other form of birth. Working from the canon therefore, we can appreciate the "cultural-linguistic" framework from which the credal affirmation of the virgin birth developed.

The perceived problem of the resurrection and virgin birth has to do not with whether the Bible attests to them but whether they are true, either as historical events or as necessary doctrines. At one level, this involves a philosophical debate about the possibility of miracles.[76] Even granting that miracles are possible, which is clearly the assumption underlying the literal sense of scripture, higher criticism has attempted to unwind the threefold cord by identifying earlier and later forms of tradition, different literary forms of the Gospel accounts, and the influence of the church's faith in articulating the event. This exercise has made clear the difficulty, if not the impossibility, of simply harmonizing the various infancy and resurrection accounts and has sensitized us to the kerygmatic character of the Gospel narratives.[77] But it also has obscured the integrity of the biblical witness to the truth of these mighty acts of God and the evangelical power and normative imprint of the text in shaping the believer and the church.[78]

In reporting historical events, biblical authors often *assume* that their words will be accepted as they intend them. Only occasionally do they state their canonical purpose explicitly as John does when he writes: "Now Jesus did many other signs which are not written in this book; but these are written that you may believe that Jesus is the Christ and believing you may have life in his name" (20:30-31). John is claiming contact with factual events that "Jesus did," especially the resurrection. At the same time these events have revelatory power to bring people like Thomas to faith.

In doctrinal matters as well, the truth dimension of scripture is usually tacit; but when challenged, biblical writers do make clear normative claims. When Paul confronts those who said there was no resurrection of the dead in 1 Corinthians 15, he is uncompromising in his retort. He recites the apostolic tradition that he received as absolutely reliable (15:1-11). Then he argues that this tradition has two and only two logical outcomes: either its truth confirms the coming general resurrection of the dead, or its falsity means that the gospel is blasphemy and Christians are fools and knaves (15:12-20).

With regard to the incarnation, John is equally uncompromising: "Every spirit which confesses that Jesus Christ has come in the flesh is of God, and every spirit which does not confess Jesus is not of God" (1 John 4:2-3). John is not simply asserting the existence of the historical Jesus but the divine Sonship against those who are scandalized by the particularity of God in the flesh. In one sense the virgin birth is analogous to the empty tomb in the order of teaching, that is, it is not part of the earliest kerygma (Acts 10:38-41; Rom. 1.3). However, since the virgin birth is the perfect narrative complement to New Testament teaching on the nature of Christ,[79] and since no other explanations of Jesus' birth are seriously considered by New Testament authors,[80] the incorporation of the virgin birth as an item of credal orthodoxy appears a natural deduction from scripture itself.[81]

SEXUAL MORALITY

I hardly need mention that sexual morality is the worldview battleground in late twentieth-century America, with such issues as divorce, abortion, and homosexuality featured in the media and politics. This has led in the church to a corresponding battle for the Bible, with some calling for an abandonment of biblical teaching as oppressive and others for radical reinterpretation of traditional texts. In the latter category, I would include the influential book – *Dirt, Greed, and Sex* (1988) – by William Countryman on sexual ethics.[82]

Countryman's avowed method is "to read the texts as literally as possible" (p. 2), and he does indeed engage in exegesis of a wide range of biblical texts. Because the worldview of ancient texts is, for him, so obviously irretrievable, literal reading serves to "relativize the present" and so open us to adapting our sexual ethics to new, evolving norms of modern individualism (pp. 237-40). Countryman goes to great length to show that none of the New Testament writers literally intended to proscribe physical fornication and homosexuality (p. 141), but given his approach, what difference would it make if they did? Using Jesus' declaring all foods clean (Mark 7:19) as an interpretative fulcrum, he allegorizes Jesus' specific condemnation of "fornication, adultery, and licentiousness" in the verses immediately following (pp. 84-86). Countryman's attempt to drive a wedge between "metaphorical purity" and specific moral behavior is possible only because he overlooks the foundational role of the doctrine of creation.[83] This leads to an odd kind of spiritualizing of the literal sense in a gnostic direction.

By contrast, I would suggest Mark 10:2-9 as a more central text in gaining access to Jesus' understanding of sexual morality. The pericope is the first of a series of "hard sayings" about discipleship in chapter 10. For the sake of the kingdom of God, the disciple will be utterly faithful in marriage, will manifest childlike openness to

God's will, will be ready to sell all possessions, will abandon family status and property, will drink the cup of suffering and death, and will become servant of all. All of these sayings involve a reversal of worldly expectations, giving up the normal social honors. What then does the disciple give up in marriage? Jesus' answer seems to be, divorce!

Why should giving up divorce further the aims of the kingdom? Jesus does not say directly. Jesus places his teaching above that of Moses and claims to reveal a primal design of God from the beginning. This design involves a uniting of two in one flesh and a call for utter faithfulness between them. This faithfulness, he implies, is not possible by human will because of the hardness of the human heart; but "with God all things are possible" (10:27). Grace reverses the Law and perfects nature in this parable of the New Covenant between God and his people. But grace comes at a price: sacrificing one's right to leave. Paul, who likewise speaks of marriage as a "mystery," calls for mutual submission of husband and wife; and John in the wedding of Cana links the cup of joy with the cup of sorrow. Matthew adds another hard saying of the Lord to suggest that the celibate life is an equivalent dedication to the kingdom (19:11-12).

Jesus places on the legal ordinance of marriage the honor and weight of representing his new relationship as Bridegroom with his church. The specific outworkings of this new institution in the life of the church have been somewhat variable.[84] In equating remarriage with adultery, it is not completely clear whether he intends to rule out every conceivable case or rather to challenge disciples dramatically to single-minded obedience. It is clear that he affirms the natural basis of marriage as good, but beyond that identifies marriage (and celibacy) with his own work of atoning sacrifice. Jesus may have widened the menu of food choices, but his teaching on sexual relations is narrow. Thus people, then and now, have wondered: Who can stand it? (Matt.19:10). The church has no authority to reconfigure marriage but calls men and women to offer their fallen human sexuality within marriage and in "single-minded" service of the gospel.

To know Christ's word is not to do it, but it is the first step to grace and hope. Richard Hays, who has made an especially clear exposition of Paul's understanding of homosexuality in the Epistle to the Romans,[85] has written elsewhere a moving account of a man named Gary, who was wrestling with the word:[86]

> Gary came to New Haven in the summer of 1989 to say a proper farewell. My best friend from undergraduate years at Yale was dying of AIDS.... For more than 20 years Gary had grappled with his homosexuality, experiencing it as a compulsion and affliction. Now, as he faced death, he wanted to talk it through again from the beginning, because he knew my love for him and trusted me to speak without dissembling. For Gary, there was no time to dance around the hard questions. As Dylan had urged, "Let us not talk falsely now; the hour is getting late."
>
> In particular Gary wanted to discuss the biblical passages that deal with homosexual acts. Among Gary's many gifts was his skill as a reader of texts... The more we talked the more we found our perspectives interlocking. Both of us had serious misgivings about the mounting pressure for the church to recognize homosexuality as a legitimate Christian lifestyle. As a New Testament scholar, I was concerned about certain questionable exegetical and theological strategies of the gay apologists. Gary, as a homosexual Christian, believed that their writings did justice neither to the biblical texts nor to the depressing reality of the gay

subculture that he had moved in and out of for 20 years...

Gary wrote urgently of the imperatives of discipleship:

> Are homosexuals to be excluded from the community of faith? Certainly not. But anyone who joins such a community should know that it is a place of transformation, of discipline, of learning, and not merely a place to be comforted or indulged...

In the midst of a culture that worships self-gratification, and a church that preaches a false Jesus who panders to our desires, those who seek the narrow way of obedience have a powerful word to speak. Just as Paul saw in pagan homosexuality a symbol of human fallenness, so I saw conversely in Gary, as I have seen in other homosexual friends and colleagues, a symbol of God's power made perfect in weakness (2 Corinthians 12:9) ...

That seems to be the spiritual condition Gary reached near the end of his life. He wrote this in his last letter: "Since All Saints Day I have felt myself being transformed. I no longer consider myself a homosexual. Many would say, big deal, you're 42... and are dying of AIDS. Big sacrifice. No, I didn't do this of my will, of an effort to improve myself, to make myself acceptable to God. No, he did this for me. I feel a great weight has been lifted off me."

Gary and his friend Richard, it seems to me, are examples of what it means to be servants of the Word. Gary was truthful about his own life experience but also stubbornly honest in acknowledging the possibility that scripture might judge rather than endorse that experience. His friend acted as the good pastor-teacher in sympathetically listening to him and searching the scriptures with him. The beginning of wisdom for Gary was a weighing of words that claim the authority of the Word; the end, however, was the work of the Spirit, applying the forgiveness of sins and new life in Christ from which nothing in heaven and earth can separate us.[87]

The church's submission to the word of God in scripture is nothing more than trusting in God's power and God's way of salvation on behalf of all the lost sheep of Christ's fold. When we let God be God and let God speak, then we will come to know that his word to us is not Yes and No, but finally and forever Yes in the Son of God, Jesus Christ (2 Cor. 1:18-20).

> O God, whose glory it is always to have mercy: Be gracious to all who have gone astray from your ways, and bring them again with penitent hearts and steadfast faith to embrace and hold fast the unchangeable truth of your Word, Jesus Christ your Son; who with you and the Holy Spirit lives and reigns, one God, for ever and ever. Amen.

ESSAY 2

TWO SEXES, ONE FLESH

WHY THE CHURCH CANNOT BLESS SAME-SEX MARRIAGE

(1997)

By the 1990s, homosexuality had become the hot-button issue of the Episcopal Church. The first wave of the movement had resulted in affirmations that homosexuals are children of God and entitled to full membership in the church. The second wave led to ordinations of gays and lesbians by "apostolic pioneers" like Bishops Paul Moore, Jack Spong, and Walter Righter. The third wave broke over the Church with the issue of same-sex marriage.

Homosexual practice posed an insuperable barrier for conservative Episcopalians because unlike other issues such as women's ordination and Prayer Book revision, it is specifically condemned both in the Old and New Testaments without any countervailing texts. (Not to say that revisionists didn't try to find a way to get around this. Professor Robert Gagnon, author of *Homosexuality and the Bible*, has been the Irenaeus of our day in confuting these attempts.)

By the mid-90s Episcopal revisionists had won the political battles over homosexual ordination. Marriage was another matter. Even in the secular society, same-sex marriage continued to be a no-go area, as even President Bill Clinton (reluctantly) signed the Defense of Marriage Act. It was also illegal, which meant that for the time being progressives would need a comfort station. Hence the proposal arose at the 1997 General Convention to develop rites "for the honoring of love and commitment between persons of the same sex."

In early 1997, the Episcopal Church leadership circulated a request to the seminaries to evaluate the proposal. Knowing that Trinity seminary alone would clearly oppose it, the faculty commissioned me to write a response, which evolved into a book: *Two Sexes, One Flesh: Why the Church Cannot Bless Same-Sex Marriage*. With help from Episcopalians United, the book was circulated to every bishop and delegate to the 1997 General Convention.

My main contribution to the debate was to take the measure of homosexual relationships in terms of God's design for marriage. We are not talking about some jot or tittle of Christian practice but an "estate" that God has ordained from the beginning and which our Lord Jesus Christ commended as a sign of his relationship to his Church. Some today argue that same-sex marriage is merely an expansion of God's design. I tested that proposition and found it wanting. Indeed homosexual relationships, whatever their benefits, cannot satisfy the opposite-sex character of marriage, and hence the Church cannot invoke God's blessing on them.

The General Convention in 1997 did not adopt the proposal to produce same-sex rites, but neither did it accept my conclusion of "say no now and forever." In the decade to come, same-sex marriage became one of the notable "tears" in the fabric of the Anglican Communion. In 2015, one month after the U.S. Supreme Court made same-sex marriage the law of the land, the Episcopal Church followed suit and approved same-sex liturgies for the church.

One chapter in the book that is dated is "Marriage and the Law." Twenty years ago, same-sex marriage was not legal in any of the United States and only a few countries overseas. Today it is mandated over much of the West, often accompanied by "hate speech" laws that make it a crime to follow one's Christian conscience. That said, I would continue to argue that "marriage equality" as a basis for family law is more a slogan than a coherent rationale, and the real goal of the same-sex movement is the abolition of marriage.

Also antiquated is my focus on *homosexuality*, which has now been replaced by *gender identity*. Transgenderism – the "T" in LGBT along with its mysterious mate "Q," which means whatever other gender you imagine for yourself – has now taken center stage in the culture wars. In one sense, gender identity is a logical development of Anthony Giddens's "transformation of intimacy" with this Gnostic twist: a body does not really need to meet another body comin' through the rye to have a "pure relationship." It's all about me! The absurd story of a woman who has married herself – "a fairytale without a prince" – is really not so novel. In fact, it is the ancient story about a fellow named Narcissus, who fell in love with his own reflection.

In 2000, Presbyterians for Faith, Family and Ministry asked if I might adapt my book for their journal *Theology Matters*. I am using that version, slightly altered. Sad to say, same-sex marriage has been approved by the Presbyterian Church USA and has led to many confessing Presbyterians leaving that church.

This is an essay about marriage, not about homosexuality. I do not pretend to be an expert on homosexuality. In fact, because of the politicization of the issue, it is hard to distinguish between experts and advocates.[1] What I do wish to do in the current sexuality debate in the churches is to see homoerotic relationships in the mirror of God's will for marriage. For it seems to me that unless one can justify these relationships in terms of marriage, they lose their coherence and even their dignity. We are not talking about the blessing of the hunt but the blessing of a relationship purporting to be "union" of two persons.

For this very reason, if these relationships cannot fulfill God's will for marriage, then to place them on an equal footing is to dishonor marriage (Hebrews 13:4).

1. REVISING MARRIAGE

Great love stories end with a wedding. The recent Jane Austen revival on TV and screen attests to the enduring attraction of the story of love moving toward its culmination in marriage. This culmination is particularly vivid in the final scene of the 1995 BBC version of *Pride and Prejudice*. The setting is an English parish church. The liturgy is the traditional Prayer Book service. The event is a double wedding between two virtuous sisters, Elizabeth and Jane Bennet, and their hard-won lovers, Mr. Darcy and Mr. Bingley. As the officiating minister intones the purposes of marriage over the two happy couples, the camera pans all the other couples attending, some of whom we know to be far from happy. It then jumps to the one couple whose licentiousness led to a forced marriage and to the widow whose selfishness has turned her daughter into a loveless spinster.

All these configurations of fallen and foolish people are held together by a common understanding that in holy matrimony "a man shall leave his father and mother and cleave to his wife, and the two shall become one flesh."

Now let's stop the videotape and revise the scenario. It's still a quaint parish church and a liturgy is in use, but it is now the year 2000. It's still a double wedding, but now Mr. Darcy and Mr. Bingley stand together holding hands, so also Elizabeth and Jane (same-sister marriage? – why not!). The congregation now contains a variety of couples, gay, lesbian, bisexual, and straight, all of whom have received the Church's blessing of their state of life.

Is this latter scenario possible?

Yes and no. Yes, in fact, it already is happening, as can be attested in various media shots of smiling same-sex grooms and brides. But no, it can't really happen, because marriage is God's idea, and God has ordained marriage exclusively for two sexes to be united in one flesh. This is the burden of this essay.

The mainline Protestant churches of the West are in the midst of a worldview war, pitting those who hold to the classic formulations of the Gospel of Jesus Christ against others who wish to "revision" the Gospel in terms of "liberation." The Waterloo of this war is sexuality and the prize revisionists seek is the detaching of God's blessing of sex from its exclusive association with heterosexual marriage. The push to bless same-sex relationships is not therefore an isolated issue. The decision on this issue will signal how the Church defines the Gospel.

SEXUALITY AND THE TRANSFORMATION OF INTIMACY

Sexuality is a word that is less than two centuries old. Traditionally, sexuality has been understood in a neutral sense as "the constitutionally bipolar character of human nature," including the *biological duality* of male and female sexes as necessary for reproduction; the *psychological identity* of each person as either a man or a woman; the *erotic longing* of a woman and a man for each other; the *social construction* of gender roles within family and society; and the *sublimation* of erotic love as motive for art, philosophy, and religion.[2] This definition of sexuality mirrors God's purposes for marriage, because sexuality is a rung in the "ladder of love" that culminates in marriage.

In revisionist parlance, however, sexuality is most often associated not with marriage but with liberation from it. Sociologist Anthony Giddens recently published a history of modern sexuality under the title *The Transformation of Intimacy*.[3] Sexuality and intimacy, according to Giddens, are terms that convey a revolutionary new meaning.

- Sexuality in its modern usage means *plastic sexuality*. Giddens does not use "plastic sexuality" as a pejorative term, suggesting artificiality. On the contrary, it represents the emancipated possibilities of sex "severed from its age-old integration with reproduction, kinship and the generations." The two marks of plastic sexuality are female sexual autonomy and the flourishing of homosexuality.

- The advent of plastic sexuality makes possible *confluent love*. Confluent love is an opening of one person to another for the purpose of self-realization and self-enhancement. Specifically, confluent love makes mutual sexual satisfaction the sine qua non of an intimate relationship. "Confluent love is active, contingent love, and therefore jars with the 'for ever', 'one-and-only' qualities of the romantic love complex." Whereas romantic love fastens on one "special person," confluent love is realized in one or more "special relationships."

- The kind of relationship formed by confluent love is termed the *pure relationship*. "In the pure relationship, trust has no external supports and has to be developed on the basis of intimacy." Intimacy or commitment in this sense must continually be negotiated in what Giddens calls a "rolling contract." Lest intimacy slide into codependency, partners in a pure relationship must be willing to grow or break apart: "It is a feature of the pure relationship that it can be terminated more or less at will by either partner at any particular point."

Giddens notes that heterosexual marriage has no special claim on love and intimacy as he defines them. In fact, homosexuals are the pioneers of the dawning age of pure relationships, because "in gay relationships, male as well as female, sexuality can be witnessed in its complete separation from reproduction." Speaking as a secular prophet (or pied piper), Giddens observes that traditional marriage has lost its legitimacy and has already decayed into unstable "companionate" relationships based on friendship or utility. He expects these companionate forms to "veer towards the pure relationship, within the life experience of the individual and the society at large." He sees this evolution of marriage both as inevitable and desirable, though he admits that no one knows for the future "if sexual relationships will become a wasteland of impermanent liaisons, marked by emotional antipathy as much as by love and scarred by violence."

Writing in a more popular venue, Tim Stafford describes the same phenomena in our culture as the outworking of a new *ethic of intimacy*.[4] This ethic includes the following characteristics: an invariably positive view of sex; belief in sex as a private bodily right; a requirement of personal, repeated consent to sex; an ongoing search for "compatibility" among partners; insistence that sex has no necessary consequences; rejection of the double standard of sexual freedom of men and women; an age of "maturity" (usually age 16) as the doorway to sexual activity.

The ethic of intimacy, Stafford thinks, is the reigning norm among non-Christians and even common among

Christians. It is found both among heterosexuals and homosexuals. One major contention of this book is that the concept of same-sex marriage is so bound up with the ethic of intimacy that it cannot be adapted to the requirements of classical Christian marriage. Legitimizing the ethic of intimacy by approving same-sex marriage will further confuse Christians struggling with the allurements of contemporary culture.

STRAIGHT TALK ABOUT TERMS OF ENDEARMENT

Revisionism begins at the most basic level, by reinterpreting the meaning of words. We live in the Clintonian age, where the question of whether or not sex is sex depends on what "is" is. When I wrote the book *Two Sexes, One Flesh* in 1997, I was arguing against a resolution before the General Convention of the Episcopal Church that affirmed rites "honoring love and commitment between persons of the same sex." My response to this resolution was as follows:

> What kind of love are we considering? C. S. Lewis spoke of "Four Loves": family affection, erotic desire, friendship, and Christian compassion (agape). To a Christian coming from another culture or another century, the intended meaning of this Resolution might be obscure. "Perhaps," she might wonder, "they wish the Church to bless friendship in an age where it has lost its meaning. Maybe they want to commend the fidelity of long-term roommates or the vows of monks and nuns."
>
> To this stranger, we would have to reply: "The Church is not developing rites to honor the love of friends, companions, or soul-mates, which love has traditionally included an assumption of erotic indifference or a vow of sexual abstinence. No, this Resolution is aiming to legitimize a new relationship that

may include friendship, affection, and compassion, but which is constituted by *erotic love and genital acts between two persons...*"

So the Resolution is considering the Church's institutionalizing of a particular kind of love, *namely the erotic relationship and activity of homosexual lovers.* What will the inclusion of this kind of love mean for the character of marriage? Will it make no difference? The love spoken of in this resolution is, I conclude, more like the "confluent love" characteristic of the ethic of intimacy than the covenant love of the Church's tradition of marriage.

Presbyterians are now discussing the blessing of "unions." One can claim that the terminology of same-sex unions is fundamentally different from that of traditional marriage, but that does not make it so. The word "union" derives from the biblical definition of marriage: "the two shall become one flesh." The Westminster Confession defines Christian marriage as a "spiritual and physical *union* of one man and one woman." Clearly the language of same-sex unions intends to extend the heterosexual marital union to homosexual couples. While I have argued that homosexual "unions" cannot fulfill the design and purposes of marriage, I have no doubt that the language of union is marital language, and that "same-sex marriage" must be included within the Church's doctrine and discipline of marriage, not some other area.

Furthermore, I believe gay-rights advocates within the Church tacitly admit that this is the case. Let me cite several compelling reasons to think that we are talking about *same-sex marriage.*

- The terminology of love, blessing, holiness and union, as mentioned above, clearly fits the biblical category of holy matrimony as a "two-in-one-flesh" union of persons and clearly implies genital acts between two and only two partners.

- Homosexual advocates have never promoted partnerships on any other model of human relationships, e.g., friendship or kinship relations.

- Proponents of "holy unions" for homosexuals have not asked to have an additional holy union rite for unmarried opposite sex partners, e.g., for a cohabiting man and woman. I presume this is because they believe that marriage is the only Church-approved institution for the sexual union of opposite-sex partners.

- The same-sex rites and ceremonies that have been devised all mirror the marriage service and use marital language and not some other known rite, e.g., commissioning for service.

- Advocates of same-sex unions assume that same-sex couples should possess identical rights and privileges of married couples, including the right to adopt children.

- The debate in the broader culture is carried out in terms of "same-sex marriage."

- If same-sex marriage is legalized in one of the States, couples who have participated in a "holy union" ceremony will surely seek to have their unions recognized legally as marriage.

I titled the first chapter of my book, "What Are We Talking About?" and concluded that we are talking about *marriage, same-sex marriage.* Therefore I do not think a mere change of terminology avoids the reality that the Church's understanding of marriage is being changed.

CONCLUSION

Marriage cannot serve two masters. According to its historic definition, marriage cannot accommodate same-sex unions. In following what I have described as the ethic of intimacy, neither heterosexual nor homosexual relationships will manifest the same kind of love and commitment that characterize traditional marriage – and these relationships cannot be blessed by God because they are contrary to his express will for human sexuality.

The challenge to clarify the meaning of marriage carries with it a potential for renewal. It should lead us back to the fundamental question: *what is the Church's doctrine of marriage?* This is the question the Church must decide before it begins authorizing alternative forms. If the definition of marriage should be revised, then church bodies should not hide behind cleverly worded definitions or vaguely worded resolutions but should spell out the full implications of their new position.

2. THINKING BIBLICALLY ABOUT MARRIAGE

By grounding marriage in the creation purposes of God, the Bible views it as an institution ordained by God for all people and not as a special revelation for Jews and Christians only. At the same time, Jews look to the Torah and Christians to the Old and New Testaments to constitute their own understanding and to clarify secular understandings. Until very recently, Jews and Christians almost universally would have found the idea of same-sex marriage unthinkable. It simply would not fit their understanding of the biblical worldview. In this section, I shall argue first that although there is no text that says "No same-sex marriage," the Bible does present marriage in a form incompatible with homosexual unions and with underlying moral principle that is not susceptible to revision.

THE ARGUMENT FROM SILENCE

"The Bible has nothing to say about same-sex marriage. No single text can be adduced to prohibit or endorse such a practice." This observation, while technically correct, is superficial and deceptive, as the general moral principles of the Bible lead clearly to the proscription of same-sex marriage. This is the way the Church has *consistently* (though often *tacitly*) interpreted the Spirit's voice speaking through Scripture.

SOUNDS OF SILENCE

The force of an argument from silence depends very much on the subject matter involved. Scripture, for instance, has nothing to say about lovemaking techniques. Neither does it speak of artificial contraception. Nor about wife-beating. Each of these issues needs to be judged by the plain sense and the whole context of Scripture. In the case of same-sex marriage, the moral logic of prohibition goes like this:

1. The Bible, both Old and New Testaments, defines marriage essentially as a monogamous union of man and woman, and without exception condemns nonmarital sexual acts as immoral (Genesis 2:25; Deuteronomy 22:28-29; Hebrews 13:4; 1 Corinthians 6:9-11).

2. The Bible, both Old and New Testaments, consistently declares that homosexual acts are unnatural, illegal, and immoral (Leviticus 18:22; Romans 1:18-32).

3. Therefore, according to biblical norms, same-sex marriage is impossible and same-sex activity immoral.

4. The total absence of any treatment of same-sex marriage in the Bible *confirms* its impossibility as a Christian option, rather than opening it for dialogue.

NO WHOLESOME EXAMPLES

The Bible communicates its worldview not only by propositions but by examples. The Bible gives no examples of erotic love between persons of the same sex at all. Homosexual advocates have tried to enroll David and Jonathan and Ruth and Naomi as same-sex models. These examples actually hurt the case for same-sex marriage by showing the depth and variety of non-erotic loves possible outside marriage. David and Jonathan are two married men who are strong friends, not "lovers"; and Ruth is a woman who risks her reputation in order to preserve the family line of her husband and mother-in-law.

The Bible is not reluctant to show a variety of heterosexual marriages, which are hardly the stereotypical "Ozzie and Harriet" relationships. Strong, godly wives are found from Sarah, Rebekah, Rachel, down to Elizabeth, Priscilla and Eunice. Corrupt couples from Samson and Delilah to Ananias and Sapphira are also noted. Scripture gives examples of couples like Hannah and Elkanah, and Zechariah and Elizabeth, who experience childlessness as a loss without in any way delegitimating their marriages. Finally, the Bible commends examples of men and women who respond to a call to single abstinence or the circumstances of widowhood: Deborah, Jeremiah, Paul, and Lydia. But despite this variety, *the Bible does not even hint at the possibility that a marriage between people of the same sex could serve as a model, good or bad.*

JESUS' IMPLICIT TEACHING ON SAME-SEX MARRIAGE

Jesus himself said nothing explicitly on the subject. This is not surprising, given the fact that no one in first century Judaism was even dreaming of such an innovation. Nevertheless, Jesus set out for his disciples a method of working from the general and original principles of God to particular issues. Specifically, Jesus' way of answering the Pharisees about divorce forms a close analogy with our contemporary dispute.

> And Pharisees came up and in order to test him asked, "Is it lawful to divorce one's wife?" He answered them, "What did Moses command you?" They said, "Moses allowed a man to write a certificate of divorce, and to put her away." (Mark 10:2-4)

Jewish tradition had come to regard the "Mosaic exception" (Deuteronomy 24:1-4) as a legal principle allowing divorce at the will of the husband. Jesus refuses to accept the exception as a rule:

> "For your hardness of heart he wrote this commandment. But from the beginning of creation, 'God made them male and female.' 'For this reason a man shall leave his father and mother and be joined to his wife, and the two shall become one flesh.' So they are no longer two but one flesh. What therefore God has joined together, let not man put asunder." (Mark 10:5-9)

Jesus' reply to the Pharisees moves logically from premise to conclusion:

1. He grounds the two-sexes-in-one-flesh institution of marriage in God's original creation and thus in his changeless will for human fulfillment.

2. He reminds them that the Mosaic exception was a concession to sin, hardly justifying indiscriminate use.

3. He argues that since the marriage bond is God's institution prior to the Law, it is not subject to mere legal dissolution.

4. Basing his teaching on the unchangeable character of marriage, he forbids divorce to his disciples.

The setting of this passage in Matthew's Gospel suggests that the apostolic Church pondered carefully the implications of Jesus' marriage teaching. First of all, the apostles understood marital fidelity to be a challenge to a "higher righteousness" equivalent to the call to lifelong celibacy (Matthew 19:10-12). Secondly, they distinguished between the absolute form of Jesus' prohibition of divorce and the pastoral truth that "unchastity" breaks the marriage bond (Matthew 19:9). Thus they allowed separation or divorce in some circumstances. Finally, they understood Jesus' principle of two-sexes-in-one-flesh as abolishing polygamy, concubinage, and levirate marriage, even as Judaism continued to tolerate them (cf. Matthew 22:23-33).

The Pharisees posed the question whether one man could be married to two women. Today homosexual advocates ask: "Is it legitimate for a man to marry a man, or a woman to marry a woman for any cause?" Could we not formulate the Lord's reply by analogy with his reply to the Pharisees?

"Have you not read that he who made them from the beginning made them *male and female*, and said, 'For this reason a man shall leave his father and his mother and be joined to his wife, and the two shall become one flesh'? *So they who become one flesh are two sexes, male and female.*

Since therefore God has united distinct sexes, let no one unite the same sexes."

CAN BIBLICAL SEXUAL NORMS BE REVISED?

If it can be established that the Bible, reasonably construed, prohibits same-sex marriage, does this settle the question? What kind of authority does the Bible have over the Church's moral teaching?

THE SOURCES OF BIBLICAL AUTHORITY

Reformation confessions uniformly affirm the authority of the Bible as the "Word of God written" (Anglican Article XX). The Westminster Larger Catechism, for instance, states that "the Scriptures manifest themselves to be the word of God." To be sure, the catechism also speaks of the role of the "Spirit of God bearing witness by and with the Scriptures," but this witness involves confirmation and illumination of God's truth, not new revelation. So when the Westminster Confession declares marriage to be "spiritual and physical union of one man and one woman," it is presuming that this is the clear and incontrovertible teaching of Scripture.

REVISING BIBLICAL AUTHORITY

Revisionists begin from the assumption that "the Bible has since the eighteenth century been dethroned as a document of propositional authority."[5] The Bible, they contend, contains religious insights and metaphors, some good and some bad, strung together in a story or "narrative." The core authority of this story lies in its testimony to human liberation and the evolution of religious consciousness modeled on the radical spirituality of Jesus. Given the vast diversity of historical contexts and theological viewpoints found in the Bible, the idea of "proving" doctrine or establishing moral norms directly from specific texts of Scripture is, according to revisionists, at best naive and at worst fundamentalistic.

Contemporary revisionists employ several strategies in vitiating the plain sense of Scripture about homosexuality.

ABSTRACTING FORM FROM CONTENT

One strategy is to divorce general concepts from the concrete biblical forms in which these concepts appear. William Countryman, for instance, in his oft-cited book *Dirt, Greed, and Sex,* consistently distinguishes abstractions like purity, property, or inclusivism from their embodiment in specific teaching. He concludes that Jesus has abolished the purity code by declaring all things clean (cf. Mark 7:15). Hence, Countryman opines, "the gospel allows no rule against the following, in and of themselves: masturbation, non-vaginal heterosexual acts, bestiality, polygamy, homosexual acts, erotic art and literature" despite many specific texts to the contrary.[6]

THE SLAVERY-WOMEN-GAYS ANALOGY

One way of divorcing form and content is by *proof-analogies* (to coin a phrase). Revisionists frequently connect the decision of the Jerusalem Council to take the Gospel to the Gentiles (Acts 15) with deliberate departures from Scripture and tradition by the contemporary Church.[7] Once again, the analogy is merely formal. The Jerusalem Council did not deliberately depart from Scripture but became convinced that Paul's call and ministry fulfilled the Old Testament prophecies (Acts 15:15-18).[8]

The proof-analogy of "slavery-women-gays" is cited by many today as if it were virtually canonical. According to this analogy, the Church gradually came to see the evil of racism, then of sexism, and finally of heterosexism. The problem with the slavery-women-gays analogy is that it mixes very different institutions and practices and makes a number of unwarranted claims about what the Bible teaches.

- The Bible treats *slavery* as an evil, sometimes necessarily to be endured, but never endorses it as God's good will for human beings (Leviticus 25:39-40; cf. Esther 7:4; Philemon 16).

- The relationship of *women* and men is more complex. Marriage participates both in the original creation order and in the fallen order of sin where the husband "rules over" the wife. In contrast to slavery and certainly homosexuality, Scripture consistently commends the created structure of heterosexual marriage, even as the New Testament offers a vision of male and female redeemed in Christ (Hebrews 13:4; Ephesians 5:21-33).

- *Homosexuality* is treated in Scripture as a disordered orientation to the Creator and creation, and both homosexual and heterosexual fornication are considered immoral acts. The Gospel offers forgiveness to all who repent of immoral acts and who wrestle with the "sin that dwells within us" (Romans 7:17-23). But nowhere does Scripture give the slightest hint that the Gospel offered freely to Jew and Greek, slave and free, male and female, can legitimate a sexual relationship outside of heterosexual marriage.

The slavery-women-gays analogy is logically strained and is used more as a rhetorical weapon than a serious argument. Nevertheless, the analogy is an indicator of the difference between those who view the Gospel as an abstract principle of liberation and those who define liberation in terms the Bible itself specifies, i.e., the redemption of sinners through the atoning death of Jesus Christ on the Cross, and the restoration and transformation of the original creation order in Christ.

REJECTING BIBLICAL AUTHORITY

While some revisionist scholars try to accommodate biblical teaching to their foregone conclusions, other scholars take the more direct approach of rejecting biblical authority entirely. This approach is strikingly illustrated in a series of quotations by Presbyterian scholars and seminary professors writing in response to the 1993 call of the General Assembly for dialogue on sexuality:[9]

> It must be admitted that the standard biblical texts – seven in all – that either mention or may allude to homosexual practice are uniformly negative about it. In this negativity they reflect the heterosexist bias prevalent in the ancient Near East. Christian ethical decisions cannot, however, rest on those seven texts... (Choon Leong-Seow, page 26)

> On a fundamental level...the Old and the New Testaments have a common assumption about marriage and society. Both operate on the assumptions that persons draw their fundamental societal identity as members of a family... If this is, broadly speaking, the biblical perspective on social institutions, it differs markedly from a dominant perspective of modernity. The option to return to preindustrial, patriarchal societal norms is neither viable nor desirable for modern communities of faith... (J. Andrew Dearman, page 64)

> My goal is not to deny that Paul condemned homosexual acts but to highlight the ideological contexts in which such discussions have taken place. My goal is to dispute appeals to "what the Bible says" as a foundation for Christian ethical arguments. It really is time to cut the Gordian knot of fundamentalism. (Dale B. Martin, page 130)

What is common to all these statements is a tacit admission that the Bible says one thing, but contemporary Christians cannot responsibly choose to accept its plain teaching. Such an attitude strains the name of "exegesis," as it denies even as it expounds.

CONCLUSION

"Two sexes, one flesh" is the clear teaching of the Bible and our Lord himself in matters of human sexuality. But does that matter? We have traced two very different attitudes toward biblical authority. One attitude seeks to understand and obey the Bible as God's word to his people yesterday, today, and forever. The other attitude finds the biblical worldview embarrassing and offensive and seeks to salvage the Bible by radically reinterpreting it or simply calling it wrong. The issue of same-sex marriage poses one of the clearest examples of this clash of attitudes. Only the most strained exegesis and argumentation can lead one to conclude that the biblical authors would permit, much less endorse, same-sex marriage.

If the leaders of the Church cannot say No to this clear contradiction of biblical norms, then it is hard to believe they will ever be able to use the Bible credibly in any moral decision-making.

3. THE NATURAL DESIGN OF MARRIAGE

Cultures and religions throughout history recognized various forms of marriage. Same-sex marriage has not been one of them. Nor *can* it be. By setting forth the nature of marriage, I hope to show why homosexuals in partnerships cannot fulfill their own aims and hopes that their unions can truly be marriage.

This section looks at marriage in terms of its natural character as a creation ordinance and a universal fact of human society. The Bible begins at this very point in the first three chapters of Genesis, where God creates the human race male and female, ordains the marital bond of man and woman, and continues to provide for their relationship after sin has entered in and distorted it.

The two-sexes-in-one-flesh character of marriage is presupposed and necessary at every stage of God's original design and the subsequent history of his dealings with the human race.

THE PURPOSES OF MARRIAGE

One of the contributions of my Anglican tradition is the beautiful marriage service of the Book of Common Prayer, authored by Archbishop Thomas Cranmer. The preface to this service enumerates the "causes" or purposes of marriage as found in Scripture and particularly the Genesis account.

- First, It was ordained for the procreation of children, to be brought up in the fear and nurture of the Lord, and to the praise of his holy Name.

- Secondly, It was ordained for a remedy against sin, and to avoid fornication; that such persons as have not the gift of continency might marry, and keep themselves undefiled members of Christ's body.

- Thirdly, It was ordained for the comfort that the one ought to have of the other, both in prosperity and adversity.

In contemporary parlance, we can speak of these "goods" of marriage as the *biological*, the *erotic*, and the *social* purposes. I shall argue that each of these goods can only be fully experienced in the bodily union of a man and a woman and that they cohere as a full expression of human nature only in the institution of lifelong heterosexual marriage.

THE BIOLOGICAL PURPOSE (Genesis 1:26-28)

The first creation story looks at the creation generically, with each creature in its proper place and each living creature reproducing "according to its kind." The story comes to a climax with the creation of a new species: "So God created man in his own image, in the image of God he created him; male and female he created them." This new race has a two-in-one character, one humanity in two sexes, and its primary task is reproduction: "God blessed them, and God said to them, 'Be fruitful and multiply, and fill the earth and subdue it.'"

The first humble purpose of marriage is, simply, the survival and flourishing of the human race. This is the evolutionary success story the biologists tell of the human sperm uniting with an unlike egg, with its XX and XY chromosomes coming to reproduce distinct personalities within the immutable two-gender plan. It is the story anthropologists tell of hormones and instincts that have led males for millennia to search out desirable females, and females to attach these males to themselves and their offspring. It is the origin of the hope of having descendants and the instinctive and visceral pride of mother and father in saying: "this is our own child."

Whatever else marriage is, it begins with a biological drive, which is then crowned by divine blessing. The two-in-oneness of marriage turns necessity into a gift, if we have hearts to receive it as such. Ethicist Oliver O'Donovan expresses the spiritual dimension of the biological purpose in this way:

> Human beings come into existence with a dimorphically differentiated sexuality, clearly ordered at the biological level towards heterosexual union as the human mode of procreation. It is not possible to negotiate this fact about our common humanity; it can only be either welcomed

68

or resented. Marriage, precisely by being ordered around this fact, enables us to welcome it and to acknowledge it as a part of God's creational gift...

What marriage can do, which other relationships cannot do, is to disclose the goodness of biological nature by elevating it to its teleological fulfillment in personal relationship."[10]

THE EROTIC PURPOSE (Genesis 2:23)

The second creation account is much more personal. Its drama begins with the man (Adam) and God's observation that "it is not good for the man to be alone" (Genesis 2:18). Then follows an odd courtship ritual in which the human animal rejects all other animal flesh as fitting his desire. At the climax of the second story, God builds from Adam's own rib a "helper according to his opposite" (Hebrew *'ezer k'neg'do*). Seeing the woman, the man exclaims: "This at last is bone of my bones and flesh of my flesh" (Genesis 2:23). This response is not only a mental recognition of another human being but of the longed-for *complement*. From this recognition flows marital eros, echoed later by the lovers of the Song of Songs 2:16: "My beloved is mine and I am his."

Marriage is a union of flesh and bones. Specifically, it is the yearning the male senses for the female form, and the female receiving and returning those attentions. It is a matter of male and female members uniting to make what Shakespeare comically called "the beast with two backs." The physicality of sexual desire is a warning sign that in itself sex has no obvious or inherent spiritual significance. The desire of the flesh is for this world, participating in "life under the sun." It includes all the pleasurable activities of the human soul: the arts, wisdom, and love. The Preacher's counsel to "enjoy life with the wife whom you love, all the days of your vain life" (Ecclesiastes 9:9) is of a piece with the claim that "love is strong as death, jealousy is cruel as the grave..." (Song of Songs 8:6).

It may seem demeaning when the Book of Common Prayer speaks of marriage as "a remedy against sin, to avoid fornication." Of course, it is addressing the fallen desires of humanity, but even in its unfallen state eros is meant to be *exclusive*. As the philosopher Roger Scruton observes: "Sexual desire is itself inherently 'nuptial': it involves concentration upon the embodied existence of the other, leading through tenderness to the 'vow' of erotic love."[11] Thus jealousy is a threat and chastity a project for men and women not only before marriage but in marriage as well. The threat of adultery reminds us that married couples are not held together by some iron hand of biology; rather, they participate in a human drama, which has tragic dangers but may also lead to victory over sin and healing in life.

THE SOCIAL PURPOSE (Genesis 2:24)

The Paradise story concludes with the public institution of marriage: "Therefore a man shall leave father and mother and cleave to his wife." Marriage is the personal and historical crossroads of the love of man and woman and the love of parents and children. The verse also introduces a motif of tension, even potential tragedy. Children will leave parents and become husband and wife, whose children will leave them.

While marriage may be preceded by erotic courtship and fulfilled in sexual delight, the union of man and woman brings about a new reality, a society. In his "Wedding Sermon from a Prison Cell," Dietrich Bonhoeffer states: "In his unfathomable condescension God does add his 'Yes' to yours; but by doing so, he creates out of your love something quite new – the holy estate of matrimony."[12] This new society has a home base, captured again in the Anglican marriage prayer for the couple "that their home may be a haven of blessing and peace." The home is the place where the biological drive to procreate children finds its fulfillment in their nurture in the knowledge and love of the Lord.

THE ESSENTIAL NATURE OF MARRIAGE

Jesus draws from the creation texts a central principle: "the two will become one flesh" (Matthew 19:5; Genesis 2:24). By this he clearly meant the two opposite sexes joined in one physical union. Like all Jews, Jesus grounded his understanding of marriage in creation; however, while Jews (like Roman Catholics after them) saw descendants as the main outcome of marriage, Jesus drew attention to the coming into being of a spiritual union of husband and wife. God has put something together, he says, which man cannot put asunder.

The *two-sexes-in-one-flesh communion of man and woman* gathers together the three subsidiary purposes of marriage into one "intrinsic good." One cannot see or demonstrate the essence or intrinsic good of something, the "roseness of a rose," but that does not mean it does not exist. It was the error of earlier "natural law" teaching to see procreation as the obvious essence of marriage, thus making the marital relationship and act instrumental to the end of procreation. Recent Roman Catholic theologians have corrected this error while upholding the basic natural law tradition. According to Germain Grisez, "marriage and the marital act are not merely instrumental goods. Marriage is an intrinsically good communion of spouses, constituted by their mutual self-gift, and each marriage has this character from the moment the couple marry and begin to live together."[13]

Given the essence and purposes of marriage, one cannot help but make distinctions between what fulfills this character and what does not.

1. First of all, marriages may be *deficient* in terms of the God-given purposes and still be true marriages. A barren couple or a couple separated for years against their will, have a real but deficient marriage. To say these marriages are deficient is not to imply that they are morally inferior; indeed many such couples surpass their peers by becoming fathers and mothers by legal adoption and by spiritual adoption of others who are poor and needy.

2. *Variations* exist in the pattern of marriage found in human history. Some variations are morally neutral, such as interracial or inter-tribal marriage; some may be morally dubious, such as the marriage of an octogenarian to a teenager; others, like polygamy, are fractured and morally wrong for Christians at least.

3. Some non-marital relationships have the *potential* to become marriages. A man and woman are not married simply by having sex together, even though their souls may be marked indelibly through the union of the flesh. If the couple accepts the full meaning and purposes of their union and lives it over a number of years, their "common law" marriage may be recognized as irregular but real. In this case, both state and Church seek to have these irregular relationships publicly recognized.

4. Some relationships – and this includes homosexual partnerships – are simply *contrary* to the essence of

marriage. Unlike heterosexual relationships, they do not have the potential to fulfill the design purposes of marriage. Thus formal recognition cannot change their ontological status. Two lesbians who arrange for one partner to bear a child, engage in physical acts of love, and are recognized as a family in their community, will still not be married. Appearances notwithstanding, the two cannot be one flesh because God has provided only one design for the union of persons.

Human nature and society are, like the human body, malleable but not infinitely so. The same is true of marriage: it comes in many shapes and forms, but this fact does not mean that it can be made into something it isn't. This is why the Church *cannot* bless same-sex marriage.

MARRIAGE UNDER THE POWER OF SIN AND DEATH

The early chapters of Genesis depict marriage not only as a good and natural institution created by God, but as fallen under the power of sin and death. The third and fourth chapters of Genesis are not only an account of the Fall of human nature but the fall of human marriage. Marriage in its several purposes is infected by sin.

Biologically, the "evil imagination" of the human heart is passed on from generation to generation our physical nature: "Therefore as sin came into the world through one man and death through sin, so death spread to all men in that all sinned" (Romans 5:12). The pain of childbirth (Genesis 3:16) becomes a symbol that the family is a broken society where sin and death reign.

Erotically, the Fall distorts the relational life of man and woman. Reaching for fig leaves, Adam and Eve abandon any illusions about uninhibited sexuality. Guilty shame becomes a necessary component of sexual modesty.[14] By confining desire to the family ("your desire will be to your husband..."), God seals off sexualized mythology, erotic art, and cult prostitution as quests for meaning.

Socially, God also seals off the lonely man's tendency toward wanderlust and binds him to one wife and family. The curse of Genesis 3:16 means marriage will become at best a benevolent monarchy, at worst a tyranny ("...and he shall rule over you"). The relations of parents and children become an occasion for envy and murder in Genesis 4. Cain goes on to found the first city, where family rivalries must be restrained by laws.

Despite the deformation caused by sin, marriage retains its essence and purposes. Even in a polygamous union, the principle of two-sexes-in-one-flesh union of man and woman is preserved: each coupling of husband and wives is separate with distinct offspring. In the case of a barren couple, the procreative purpose is frustrated, but God may always "open the womb." Even with divorce, the Law insists that one marriage must be formally broken (and not renewed) when a second is instituted.

HOMOSEXUALITY AND THE PURPOSES OF MARRIAGE

Homosexual relationships are not only inconsistent with the primal "two-sexes-in-one-flesh" principle of creation, but they frustrate the three subsidiary purposes of marriage as well. The contrary character of homosexual love, most obvious with regard to procreation, is less obvious in the other two purposes. Homosexual couples can desire each other and engage in genital acts, and they can set up house. But even in these latter purposes, there are indications that appearance and reality are not one and the same.

HOMOSEXUALITY AGAINST BIOLOGY

Biologically, nature expresses the two-sexes-in-one-flesh principle. *Homo sapiens* is a sexually bipolar species. Nature has made no provision for same-sex gametes to fertilize each other. No homosexual act has ever produced a child. Any evolutionary tendency to homosexuality would be quickly frustrated by the non-reproductivity inherent in the trait. Male and female bodies are made for sexual intercourse, whereas same-sex partners can only simulate coitus. Monogamous sex is the safest and healthiest sex, whereas all other kinds of promiscuous and non-vaginal sex bring with them much higher health risks. These facts of life constitute the most obvious reason that homosexuality has been considered to involve abnormal and high-risk behavior.

DESIRE FOR THE TRULY OTHER

Erotically, biological realities control the direction of desire. The difference in male and female hormones dictates that males and females will look sexually distinct and identify the opposite sex as distinctly beautiful. The question of whether biology is destiny and whether some persons are naturally oriented as homosexuals we know is a major area of dispute today.[15] The Bible, to begin with, does not give any support for the idea that God created some people naturally to desire others of the same sex.

The biblical view is supported by the aggregate experience of the human race, as studied by anthropologists and sociologists. Their studies have uncovered no fixed form of homosexual desire that compares with the love of married partners. Sometimes homosexual activities mimic marital relations. Egalitarian homosexuality requires one partner to play the role of the opposite sex and, in some cases, to conceive of the other partner as being the opposite sex. This role-playing phenomenon helps explain the *berdache* custom of American Indians and trans-sexualism and transgender identification.

Philosophically, homosexual desire must also be seen to be derivative and distorted. The contemporary philosopher Roger Scruton, without relying explicitly on biblical norms or commands, concludes that an essential feature of mature sexual desire is "the opening of the self to the mystery of another gender":

> Desire directed toward the other gender elicits not its simulacrum but its complement. Male desire evokes the loyalty which neutralises its vagrant impulse; female desire evokes the conquering urge which overcomes its hesitations. Often, of course, this complementarity can be re-created, either momentarily, in play, or permanently, by members of the same sex.[16]

To say that complementary desire can be "re-created," however, admits a fundamental difference between a natural and an artificial impulse.

HOMOSEXUALITY WITHOUT MARRIAGE

Socially, the artificiality of homosexual relationships is reflected in their non-institutional status. What is most striking in an anthropological survey of sexuality is the occurrence of homosexual practices and the absence of a homosexual marriage institution.[17] This phenomenon is explained in part because much ancient homosexuality was practiced between elders and youths, or between male couples and female couples who had no opportunity for heterosexual relationships. The male *berdache* who put on squaw's clothing and played the role of a female could in some societies be treated as married, though many *berdaches* had specialized roles as priests and shamans. Transgendered homosexuality, as this has been called, is the exception that proves the rule: same-sex unions were accepted only insofar as they simulated heterosexual marriage.

Conclusion

Homosexual relationships, even in those cases where they are exclusive and long-term, frustrate the natural design of marriage and fail to fulfill its purposes. These natural purposes are derived from the essence of marriage as a two-sexes-in-one-flesh communion of a man and a woman. Marriage is natural in two senses: it is universally found in human societies, although frequently deficient and deformed; and it is the final cause or goal toward which all biological, erotic, and social relationships of men and women tend. There are other intimate love relationships among human beings, such as friendship and family affection, but these are neither sexual nor are they institutionalized in marriage. Homoerotic relationships, however, are *contrary* to nature, which explains the strength of the taboo which many people feel toward homosexuals. This taboo may be distorted by sin into hatred and violence, but it is not in itself irrational but rather based in a natural intuition.

4. Marriage and the Law

Marriage and its purposes derive from the original design of the Creator. This design is mediated and regulated in a fallen world through the various institutions of human law. The Church, as the guardian of Holy Scripture, and the State as the enforcer of law, have always had a joint interest in the oversight of marriage. In the West since the age of Constantine, civil society, i.e., the everyday life of citizens, has reflected the dual influence of Christian and secular traditions of marriage and family.

In this section, I shall consider the legitimacy of same-sex marriage as a matter of law. My particular thesis is that same-sex marriage, by its very ideology, is incapable of forming the basis of a new social order, Christian or secular. If institutionalized, same-sex marriage will only further corrode the place of marriage in contemporary society, and the whole liberationist project of which it is a part will eventually come to grief. For the Church to collaborate in this Babel-like experiment involves a tragic abandonment of its true prophetic responsibility to give moral guidance to the secular regime.

SAME-SEX MARRIAGE AND THE TRADITIONS OF JUSTICE

To the question, "Is same-sex marriage a justice issue?" one may reply: "Whose justice?" and "By which rationality?"[18] Without agreeing finally with Alasdair MacIntyre that moral and political discourse is utterly tradition-bound, I would insist that any claim to justice must be rooted in a coherent and historically tested worldview. Marriage has coexisted with three Western traditions of justice: the Law of the Hebrew Bible and Judaism, the law proceeding from classical political thought, and modern law proceeding from natural rights theory. Same-sex marriage is an experiment emerging from contemporary liberationism and its "ethic of intimacy." Liberationism has no historical track record of safeguarding marriage, and indeed it is hard to avoid the conclusion that the push for same-sex marriage is part of a larger project to subvert marriage as it is known in the other traditions.

THE LAW OF MOSES: PUTTING SEXUALITY BEHIND THE VEIL

St. Paul calls the Law a guardian for faith (Galatians 3:24); likewise marriage among the Jewish people served as a guardian of the good things of the Law. The First and Tenth Commandments frame the Law with two absolute prohibitions: against worshipping false gods (false religion) and coveting one's neighbor's spouse (false sexuality). The great danger of sexual desire, according to Genesis 3, is its pretension to transcendence: "you shall become like gods." The world of Israel's neighbors was filled with myths of gods and goddesses cavorting with each other. The central practices of fertility religion sought to manipulate the forces of the divine realm via sexual energy and were continuations of a prehistoric superstition supposing that spirituality could be communicated mechanically by means of the male's vital semen.

The advent of the biblical worldview constitutes an historic change, what one writer calls "Judaism's Sexual Revolution," which has spread throughout the world wherever monotheism has been established:

> When Judaism demanded that all sexual activity be channeled into marriage, it changed the world. The Torah's prohibition of non-marital sex quite simply made the creation of Western civilization possible... This revolution consisted in forcing the sexual genie into the marital bottle. It ensured that sex no longer dominated society, heightened male-female love and sexuality (and thereby almost alone created the possibility of love and eroticism within marriage), and began the arduous task of elevating the status of women.[19]

The laws against homosexuality are to be understood as part of the biblical refusal to mix sexuality and spirituality. Thus St. Paul spoke as a true son of Israel when he linked together false religion and false sexuality (Romans 1:18-32).

THE CLASSICAL TRADITION: FAMILY AND CITY

It is no secret that many Greeks engaged in homosexual acts, usually between older married men and male youths, but nowhere in the corpus of classical philosophy is same-sex marriage seen as an implication of justice. In Plato's *Republic*, Socrates leads his youthful inquirers to consider whether the most just regime *in the abstract* requires heterosexual communism, where women and men share all things in common, including children. He concludes, however, that the justice of such a regime is more a matter of speech than reality. In his concrete teaching on justice (*Laws*), Plato condemns the practice of homosexuality and affirms a private sphere for the family.

Aristotle argues that while the family is the original and necessary unit of civil society, human nature reaches its perfection in the city. The delicate interaction between private life and public life as joint schools for virtue is expressed in this way by a modern-day Aristotelian:

> Marriage, like every worthwhile institution, is also a tradition – a smooth handle on experience, which has been passed on from generation to generation, and in the passing, slowly worn itself into the shape required by human nature. It has a story attached to it: its comic and tragic aspects are a familiar part of popular culture; its hardships and joys can be anticipated and also shared; it has the respect and the understanding of others. Moreover, it translates itself into legal forms, and endeavours to reconstitute as legal rights the many and mysterious obligations which arise from domestic proximity.[20]

While homosexuals may exhibit genuine friendship and compassionate care for an unrelated person, they cannot produce the complex intergenerational reality of marriage and family as a societal unit. There simply is no role in the tradition for same-sex couples.

THE MODERN NATURAL RIGHTS TRADITION

Modern political philosophy is founded on the idea that individuals enter into political society by means of a social contract, in which they cede control to the state in return for protection of person and property. John Locke can thus regard marriage as a "voluntary compact between Man and Woman" rather than a divine institution.[21] Locke replaces the divine institution with the law of Nature's God, which he sees as the natural instinctual affection of man and woman and their desire to reproduce themselves. Locke's theory may indeed justify the state's *regulation* of marriage contracts, e.g., age of consent and conditions for divorce; but it does not mean that the state can alter the fundamental biological requirement that it is a man and woman who make a marriage.

Likewise Jean-Jacques Rousseau argued that the family is the only natural unit of society, and he made *vive la différence* the charter of the husband-wife relationship: "In everything not connected with sex, woman is man... In everything connected with sex, woman and man are in every respect related and in every respect different." Because of the natural complementarity of the sexes, "each contributes equally to the common aim, but not in the same way."[22] For Rousseau, marriage is the tiny society in which the lonely individual can overcome selfishness by falling passionately in love with someone different from himself.

American political sensibility is a marriage of Locke and Rousseau, of pragmatism and sentimentality. Alexis de Tocqueville commended American democracy on its accommodation of egalitarianism to the structures of family life: "The Americans have applied to the sexes the great principle of economy which governs the manufactures of our age, by carefully dividing the duties of man from those of woman, in order that the great work of society may be carried on."[23]

A century and a half later, sociologists Brigitte and Peter Berger defended this tradition, stating *"the family, and specifically the bourgeois family* [i.e. father, mother, children], *is the necessary social context for the emergence of the autonomous individuals who are the empirical foundation of political democracy.*" [24] The tradition has been upheld consistently by the courts. Justice Douglas, for instance, in nullifying a law allowing sterilization of criminals (*Skinner v. Oklahoma*), argued that "we are dealing here with legislation which involves one of the basic rights of man. Marriage and procreation are fundamental to the very existence and survival of the race."

The natural rights tradition is not sufficient to assure a Christian understanding of marriage; in fact, it needs the religious doctrine to create a moral climate in which rights will be responsibly exercised. The tradition has shown itself compatible with Christian marriage. For two centuries, the Christian ideal of marriage has been upheld in the United States by public consent and legal sanction, and clergy have functioned as ministers of the state as well as the Church in performing ceremonies.

LIBERATIONISM AS THE CONTEXT OF SAME-SEX MARRIAGE

The public and political movement to normalize homosexuality has a direct tie to the sexual liberation ideology that I have characterized as the ethic of intimacy. While the sexual liberation movement uses the language of rights, it draws on an analysis of society much more dependent on Marx and Engels, for whom the bourgeois family was an economic unit of history that was passing away, and Freud, who declared that monogamous marriage "cuts off a fair number of people from enjoyment and becomes the source of serious injustice."[25]

The liberationist project begins with a *deconstruction* of traditional institutions as inherently oppressive. If slavery has oppressed blacks and capitalism oppressed workers, so also marriage has oppressed women. From this deconstruction flows feminist theologian Carter Heyward's "healing commitment not to grant coupling or heterosexual marriage a privileged social status apart from other forms of relational commitment."[26] Liberationists then proceed to a *reconstruction* of consciousness in which the person is radically self-defining, with the right "to explore the character of the erotic as sacred power."

The debate among gay-rights advocates over same-sex marriage is poised between the deconstructive and reconstructive moments of liberation thought and politics. The deconstructionists fear that marriage may co-opt the liberation movement, while reconstructionists argue that same-sex marriage may serve as a means by which the entire institution may be redefined in terms of "families we choose."[27]

The $64,000 question is, what would the institutionalizing of "families we choose" do to our society's commitment to lifelong, monogamous marriage? The emphasis on "choice" differentiates the sexual liberationist from the natural rights tradition. In the latter, "rights" are conditioned by nature and binding contract; but to the liberationist, nature is itself an oppressive construct, and the untrammeled self reigns supreme.

REDEFINING THE RULES OF MARRIAGE

In the past, U.S. marriage law has provided the outer bounds of the institution (e.g., marriage and divorce regulations) while relying on religious teaching to define its inner character. But if the institution of marriage, for the first time in history, must redefine its opposite-sex character under the influence of a neo-pagan ideology, why should we not expect that it will be asked to redefine other aspects of its identity? This problem leads to questions in the three areas of *lifelong commitment, sexual chastity, and normativity.*

First of all, marriage in the Christian tradition has always been a *lifelong commitment*, and most secular marriages also use "till death do us part" language. Some gay advocates also define marriage as "an emotional commitment of two people for life." Others, however, argue that marriage vows should be "so long as love shall last." Why should a homosexual remain in a lifelong marriage if the emotion is drained from the commitment, especially when the interests of children are not involved?

Secondly, Christian marriage has always been seen as requiring *chastity*. Married partners remain chaste by maintaining exclusive sexual fidelity to the other partner; unmarried chastity involves abstinence from sex before marriage or outside marriage. Some proponents of same-sex marriage, like Bishop John Spong, are also pushing for non-marital sexual arrangements; others suggest that same-sex desire makes the "need for extramarital outlets" more acceptable for all married partners, gay and straight.[28]

Finally, marriage has held a *normative status* in society, both in public morals and in legal preferences. Mores, morals, and laws work together to promote virtue in a healthy society, and the Church has served society by giving theological justification for its moral norms. Morality must not only identify virtuous arrangements but disapprove violations of the norm through public shame.

One would think that the state and the Church would insist on coherent, agreed-upon answers to the questions of permanence, exclusivity, and normativity before jumping into the liberationist marriage project. But the debate goes on among liberationists themselves on these basic issues. The unsettled character of the discussion is no accident but is inherent in the very self-defining character of the ethic of intimacy.

CONCLUSION

The state and the Church both have a role and a stake in maintaining marriage as a two-sexes-in-one-flesh union of man and woman. The secular regime works from its own lights to establish the natural design of marriage for the sake of generational continuity and social stability. The Church grounds the institution in its understanding of God as Creator and Lawgiver and of the sacred nature of the marital union. The cooperation of natural, legal, and spiritual authorities means that heterosexual marriage has been a central institution in all civil societies, even though the particular form of marriage in any one society and the individual marriages within it have not always been just or happy.

The sexual revolution's assault on the barricades of tradition includes an attack on the justice of marriage. Liberationists accuse marriage of being unjust because it does not include same-sex partners. They claim to find in the natural rights tradition a "right to marry," which if translated into law, would force all states to put same-sex marriage on an equal footing with traditional marriage, thus diluting or dissolving marriage as the preferred unit of society.

This social experiment is so radical that it is unclear whether the liberationists will succeed in pushing their agenda through the courts. What is indefensible, and potentially tragic, is that some churches that should know better are providing moral encouragement for the project.

5. THE SACRED CHARACTER OF MARRIAGE

Pastors are frequently confronted with couples who combine a desire for a "traditional church wedding" with the vaguest notions of what the Church means by marriage. I used to devote one premarital session with the couple to talk about this very discrepancy. I would ask them what specifically made them want a church wedding. Eventually, whether out of embarrassment or out of some spiritual intuition, one of them would mention God. "Oh," I would say, "then you want a church wedding because you want God to bless your marriage?" "Well... yes," the reply would come. "Tell me," I would go on, "why do you think God is the least bit interested in blessing your marriage?" Many interesting conversations, and some commitments to Christ, would follow from this question.

Why do we think the Lord God, Creator of heaven and earth, is interested in blessing any human relationship? And if he is, are we not interested in what limits he has laid down for that relationship? Put another way, does the Church get its ordinances from God, or is it free to make up some new ones or reconfigure them to its liking at a particular point in history? These are, finally, the crucial questions at issue in the current attempt to authorize same-sex marriage.

In previous sections, I have concluded that same-sex marriage fails to fulfill the particular purposes of nature and traditions of law, which brings us back to our definitional objection that same-sex marriage – or any simulacrum – is not really marriage at all. This becomes a particularly serious issue when we come to the claims that the Church makes for marriage. *For the Church to pronounce God's blessing on a relationship that is a counterfeit of the real thing is tantamount to blasphemy.*

According to the Westminster Shorter Catechism, a sacrament is "a holy ordinance instituted by Christ, wherein, by sensible signs, Christ and the benefits of the new covenant are represented, sealed, and applied to believers." Marriage, according to the Reformers, is not a "dominical" sacrament, instituted by Christ, but in "signifying the mystery of the union between Christ and his Church," marriage certainly has a sacred, even a sacramental character. In the section that follows, I conclude that same-sex marriage cannot be sacred, either as a sign of the divine love or as a means to participate in that love.

HOLY MATRIMONY AS A SIGN OF THE GOSPEL

The Church's sacred rites are inherently typological, i.e., taking an earthly form as a sign of a heavenly reality. As same-sex marriage cannot appropriately represent the earthly pattern of two-sexes-in-one-flesh union, it also fails to communicate essential elements of "difference in unity" between Christ and his Church. If adopted, same-sex marriage would inevitably misrepresent the nature of marriage as a covenant and violate the rhetoric of marriage as a union of husband and wife found in the marriage service.

MARRIAGE AS A TYPE OF THE COVENANT

In calling marriage a "covenant," the Church, following Scripture, likens the marital bond to the greater covenant between God and his people. Monogamy operates by the same exclusive logic as monotheism. Israel cannot claim to be married to Yahweh and pursue other lovers without breaking the covenant and receiving a "divorce" from God (Hosea 2:2). God's people are capable of deluding themselves into thinking that they are married to Baal, but the prophets make clear that Israel's "intimate relationship" with Baal is nothing other than *prostitution*: "For long ago you broke your yoke and burst your bonds; and you said, 'I will not serve.' Yea, upon every high hill and under every green tree you bowed down as a harlot" (Jeremiah 2:20).

The prophets finally offer hope that Israel's one true husband, who had divorced her, will betroth her again "in faithfulness" (Hosea 2:20). As the heart of marriage is forgiveness, so also mercy and forgiveness lie at the fount of God's covenant with his people. The promise of a new marriage covenant initiated by God lies behind Paul's imagery of Christ giving himself up in love for the Church "that he might sanctify her, having cleansed her by the washing of water with the word" (Ephesians 5:26).

The relevance of the typology of the covenant is simply this: only God's chosen marriage can serve his salvific purposes, and those covenants that are not according to his design will serve as vehicles for a false spirituality. The burden of this section is to conclude that same-sex marriage is much more likely to convey a distorted rather than a true image of God's relationship to his people.

The rhetoric of the marriage service emphasizes the theme of *difference in unity*, which is central to marriage as a two-sexes-in-one-flesh union of man and woman, as repeatedly the Officiant refers to "this man and this woman" and "husband and wife."

Liturgical revisers could, of course, replace references to man and woman and husband and wife with "persons" and "spouses." The result would be not only bland aesthetically but deficient theologically in communicating the divine analogy inherent in the marriage bond. One characteristic of recent "inclusive language" liturgies has been their incipient modalism. By trying to avoid naming God as Father and Christ as Son, they speak of God as Creator, Redeemer, Sanctifier, and the like. The same error will be at work in any "inclusive" marriage rite that tries to draw the analogy between same-sex partners and the "relationality" in the Godhead.

MARRIAGE AS A MEANS OF GRACE

Holy Matrimony is not the same kind of rite as baptism and Eucharist. We are not saved through marriage. In fact, the Law intentionally separates marriage and sexuality from the religious and mythic meanings given in other cultures. The sacramental dimension of marriage therefore is not part of a general "metaphorical theology" but is specifically bound up with the Church's confession of the one God as Father, Son, and Holy Spirit.

The new iconoclasts, the prophets of the ethic of intimacy, are unabashed as they rend the veil between sexuality and spirituality. For liberationists the flow of grace does not move downward from the antitype (the Triune God) to the type (marriage) but rather upward from experience (sexuality) to theology (the "Divine"). Thus Carter Heyward can say: "I am interested not merely in a "theology of sexuality" – examining sexuality through theological lenses; but rather in probing the Sacred – exploring divine terrain – through sexual experience."[29] In Professor Heyward's platform, same-sex activity is only one plank of an entirely different construal of the Christian faith.

DISCIPLESHIP AND MARITAL DISCIPLINE

A genuine spirituality of marriage begins, not with projections of sexuality onto the divine, but with conforming our experience to our Lord's covenant of grace. The "estates" of marriage and singleness are intended as a schoolyard of discipleship. Just as Jesus' teaching on marriage and singleness in the Synoptic Gospels is rooted in the call to single-minded discipleship as the source of our identity, so in John, every love must be rooted in the love of the Father and the Son.

For this reason, marriage as a sacred rite is subordinate to baptism, and the Christian family is subordinate to God's family, the Church. Many Christians, both laity and clergy, locate their primary loyalty in personal relationships with spouses and lovers, not with brothers and sisters in Christ. When it comes to personal decisions about having sex, getting married, divorcing, and remarrying, many Christians consult the oracle of intimacy first and then call on the Church to rubber-stamp their decision. Marriages can be as much an instrument of selfishness as any other institution. Even in "successful" marriages, partners may manipulate each other, or jointly manipulate others in an air of complacent self-righteousness.

"What ought the church to teach and expect of people who profess and expect to be disciples of Christ?" Philip Turner asks.[30] The answer to this question, in the words of our Lord is, "Seek first the kingdom of God and his righteousness, and all these things will be added to you" (Matthew 6:33). To present the cost of discipleship without the grace of Christian community would be equivalent to telling beggars to "go and be warmed."

The Church in its celebration of marriage and its offer of premarital and post-marital care of members has been a real help to many lonely people in and out of marriages, including many homosexuals. It must train its pastors to help people live faithfully in the present permissive society by means of solid teaching, competent counseling, and the ministry of prayer. It must also discipline itself so that it does not lead astray one of Christ's little ones.

The need for marital discipline is particularly critical in the case of clergy. Gay rights advocates regularly remind Church leaders that they themselves have hardly upheld a sterling standard of lifelong monogamy in recent years. While there is a stinging truth in this accusation, surely the conclusion should be to strengthen the marital standards, not to loosen them. A Church that believes in the grace and power of the Gospel to change lives simply cannot succumb to such culture-bound fatalism.

SAME-SEX MARRIAGE AND THE LIFE OF THE WORLD TO COME

The Advent season is the Church's regular reminder that it lives in the shadow of the prophets of the Old Testament who looked to a day of judgment and in expectation of Jesus Christ's coming again in glory to judge the world and restore it to the fullness of its original design. Marriage exists in the tension between judgment and hope as much as any other institution.

MARRIAGE IN HEAVEN?

"Types and shadows have their endings." For all of its importance as a pattern of the end-time wedding banquet of the Lamb, marriage itself seems to be an institution for this age only. Is this not the lesson to be learned from the encounter between Jesus and the Sadducees, when they ask him a test question about a woman married to seven successive husbands?

> "In the resurrection, therefore, to which of the seven will she be wife? For they all had her." But Jesus answered them, "You are wrong, because you know neither the Scriptures nor the power of God. For in the resurrection they neither marry nor are given in marriage, but are like angels in heaven." (Matthew 22:28-30)

The Western Church has understood Jesus' teaching to mean that death brings every marriage to an end and that the love of the world to come will not include the particular love of husband and wife. The Eastern Church, on the other hand, teaches that the Christian husband and wife enter into an eternal sacramental bond. Protestants have been more reluctant to differentiate the state of the elect in heaven, although John Bunyan makes this comment about the Pilgrim's recognition of his family members entering the Heavenly City: "Since Relations are our second self, though that State [marriage] will be dissolved there, yet why may it not be rationally concluded that we shall be more glad to see them there, than to see they are wanting?"[31]

The heavenly Jerusalem is lighted by God and the Lamb, but surely their glory does not bleach out what Gerard Manley Hopkins called the "dappled" beauty of creation. And since gender is a central feature of this world order, should we not expect the heavenly world to be gendered in some recognizable way? In his science fiction novel *Perelandra*, C. S. Lewis imagined a world of gender beyond sex in which his hero Ransom overhears the divine love-songs of the principalities of Mars and Venus. Lewis goes on to explain:

> Gender is a reality, and a more fundamental reality than sex. Sex is, in fact, merely the adaptation to organic life of a fundamental polarity which divides all created beings. Female sex is simply one of the things that have feminine gender; there are many others, and Masculine and Feminine meet us on planes of reality where male and female would be simply meaningless. Masculine is not attenuated male, nor feminine attenuated female. On the contrary, the male and female of organic creatures are rather faint and blurred reflections of masculine and feminine. Their reproductive functions, their differences in strength and size, partly exhibit, but partly also confuse and misrepresent, the real polarity.[32]

If Lewis' intuition has any validity, it might help explain how married partners might experience a form of erotic unity-in-difference while being "like angels." At the same time, perhaps, same-sex friendships, purged of erotic confusion, may come to their fulfillment as well.

What all historic Christian traditions hold in common is a sense of the permanence of marriage for this age and of some sort of continuity of relational identity in the world to come. Traditional marriage is a kind of typological anchor, as it were, holding fast the Christian imagination of things to come. We see through a glass darkly, but we believe that what will be in the future will be some glorified version of the creation, the earthly city.

CONCLUSION

The Church does not hold marriage and family to be the source of salvation, but it does see in the family an image of the kingdom of God. When it prays "Our Father," it knows that there is an unbreakable bond between "the Father, from whom every family in heaven and on earth is named," and the institution he has ordained on earth. To be ashamed of the institution of marriage as it is given to us is to be ashamed of our heavenly Father. To endorse same-sex marriage is at heart a rebellion against his most gracious rule.

For two thousand years Christians have been declaring: "those whom God has joined together let no one put asunder." The Church has no authority to put asunder the sacrament of marriage as instituted by the Lord – either by revising the marriage rite to include same-sex pairs or by devising some quasi-marital sacred rite alongside it.

6. THE UNCHANGEABLE GLORY OF MARRIAGE

Dearly beloved: We have come together in the presence of God to witness and bless the joining together of this

93

man and this woman in Holy Matrimony…. The union of husband and wife in heart, body, and mind is intended by God for their mutual joy; for the help and comfort given one another in prosperity and adversity; and, when it is God's will, for the procreation of children and their nurture in the knowledge and love of the Lord. Therefore marriage is not to be entered into unadvisedly or lightly, but reverently, deliberately, and in accordance with the purposes for which it was instituted by God.[33]

All over the world, men and women have entered and will enter into Holy Matrimony with words like these ringing in their ears. But will these words still be spoken in all the churches? I hope so, but I am not sure. Those who would revise the doctrine of marriage are reminiscent of Humpty Dumpty when he said,

"There's glory for you."

"I don't know what you mean by 'glory,' " Alice said.

Humpty Dumpty smiled contemptuously. "Of course you don't – till I tell you. I meant 'there's a nice knock-down argument for you!' "

"But 'glory' doesn't mean 'a nice knock-down argument,'" Alice objected.

"When I use a word," Humpty Dumpty said, in a rather scornful tone, "it means just what I choose it to mean – neither more nor less."

I side with Alice. Clever proposals and arguments that seek to change the "glory," – that is, the essential character (1 Corinthians 15:41-42) – of Christian marriage may or may not pass church conventions. What they cannot do, by a mere act of human will, is make marriage into something else, and the folly of any attempt will eventually be revealed.

I believe that God is refining his Church and the institution of marriage by means of this present identity crisis. This refining must involve our repentance, which includes thinking more deeply about the true meaning of marriage. As a result of this repentance, God may teach us how to be better disciples and to value elements of Holy Matrimony that we have taken for granted or neglected. By rediscovering the riches of our heritage, we may even be able to speak, humbly and wisely, to our fellow citizens who are suffering from the breakdown of this divine institution.

Whatever the mysteries of God's providence, one thing is certain: for this present age marriage is based on his plan for two sexes to become one flesh. The glory of *two sexes, one flesh* will not pass away until that day when the Father summons his blessed Church to the marriage supper of the Lamb.

ESSAY 3

COMMUNING IN CHIRST

THE DOCTRINE AND DISCIPLINE OF THE CHURCH

(2008)

The "political" decisions of the Global Anglican Future conferences often garner the press headlines, but for those who actually have attended the gatherings in Jerusalem and Nairobi, the experience has been quite different. The schedule is organized around worship and teaching for all, bishops and their wives, clergy and laity, from all the regions of the church and world. It was in this setting that I shared a workshop on ecclesiology, the doctrine of church, ministry and sacraments, at GAFCON 2008, with my near namesake Ashley Null.

At GAFCON 2013, I led another "mini-conference" on the Person and Work of the Holy Spirit. Anglican churches worldwide today often find themselves in a competition of sorts with Pentecostals, who make a special claim for the power and gifts of the Spirit and whose "ecclesiology" is quite fluid and free-form. Pentecostalism may well be sounding a wake-up call to many nominal Anglicans to claim the fullness of the Spirit's presence and power. I have added a section from this later talk under "Participation in the Holy Spirit."

I trust that many people trained in Anglican theological colleges will find much of this material to be "mere Anglicanism." I, along with so many of my peers in the GAFCON movement, love our tradition dearly and would feel ourselves sojourners in any other. That is why we are alternatively heartbroken and contentious about the current condition of the Mother Church and its collaborators in the West.

The current crisis in the Communion leads me to devote a longer-than-usual discussion of church discipline. The ideal of "conformity" built into the Established Church in England had the advantage of tacitly enforcing church discipline through all levels of society, in homes, in schools, in parishes, and in government. The disadvantage lay in the "latitudinarian" danger of apathy and the substitution of "niceness" for taking up one's cross rather than calling for conversion of heart and life. The milquetoast vicars of 19th century novels were and are all too common.

Today the Western cultural establishment has repudiated Christianity, and the Church of England's leadership appears paralyzed, both at home and abroad. Having failed to discipline the Episcopal Church after Lambeth 1998, the Archbishops have gone silent on Lambeth Resolution I.10 (see Essay 10). The Windsor Report and the Anglican Communion Covenant are long on talk of unity yet fail at the very point where discipline is required for true unity to occur. This failure by the Instruments of Unity has called forth a "non-conforming" movement of Anglicans who honor the heritage of the Church of England but above all else uphold her true doctrine and discipline, "grounded in the Holy Scriptures and in such teachings of the ancient Fathers and Councils of the Church as are agreeable to the said Scriptures."

The Church is the Body of Christ; He is the Bridegroom, she is the Bride. My modest goal is not only to critique where Anglican leaders have fallen short but to reset milestones along the way to a revived church, through which "the manifold wisdom of God might now be made known to the rulers and authorities in the heavenly places" (Ephesians 3:10).

My brothers and sisters in Christ, as you know, we are here in extraordinary circumstances. The Anglican Communion stands at a crossroads and we have gathered in the Holy Land to enquire after the ancient paths so that we may discern for ourselves and the wider Church the path for the future that leads to life (Jeremiah 6:16). Let us not pretend that this Conference is not a sign of judgment, God's judgment on our unfaithfulness as a Communion.

Thirty years ago, I was working on a doctorate on the Dead Sea Scrolls, which were produced by a group of Jews who dissented from the worldly leadership of the Jerusalem priesthood and who set up a New Covenant community in the desert of Judea. They saw themselves repeating or rather continuing the Exile of 587 BC, when the nation had been overrun and a remnant sent to the waters of Babylon. The paradigm of Exile and Return is fixed in the Old Testament prophets and has been applied at critical moments in the Church's history. Martin Luther, for instance, spoke of the "Babylonian Captivity of the Church" by Rome. Each in his own way, George Herbert the Anglican, and Richard Baxter, the Puritan, sought to restore the church from the ground up, producing two classics of pastoral care: *The Country Parson* and *The Reformed Pastor.*

So today we are obliged to retrace the paths that made the Church of England and its daughter churches great so that we may, with penitent hearts, seek God's grace and guidance for the future of the Communion. In particular, I am addressing the topics of Anglican Ecclesiology, the doctrine of church, ministry and sacraments, and church discipline.

THE CHURCH:
KINGDOM OF GOD AND BODY OF CHRIST

We begin by asking about the nature of the church. Scripture gives no precise definition but rather a number of metaphors or analogies, two of which are of primary importance. The first is political, having to do with *the Church and the Kingdom of God*, as the Gospel introduces it: "Jesus came proclaiming: 'the Kingdom of God is near'" (Mark 1:15). It is hard to translate Jesus' use of "kingdom" properly; the idea of *basileia* is more a constitutional order or regime. The Kingdom of God is in one sense an eschatological reality, coming to fulfillment in the end-time, but the regime change is starting now with the community around Jesus. The apostles are the first *pupils* of the Kingdom, learning its secrets in Parables and the Sermon on the Mount. They are its *guardians*, founded on the confession of Peter and given the keys of access (Matthew 16:19); and they are its *witnesses* (Acts 1:6-8), commanded to make and baptize more disciples until the end of the age. What unifies the end-time Kingdom with the present church is the Lordship of Christ as Sovereign in this age and the age to come.

The Kingdom of God is inaugurated by Christ's death and resurrection, which seal the new Covenant in His blood and empower it through the Holy Spirit and faith. The Church is the outpost of the Kingdom, and hence St. Paul can say:

> To me, though I am the very least of all the saints, this grace was given, to preach to the Gentiles the unsearchable riches of Christ, and to make all men see what is the plan of the mystery hidden for ages in God who created all things; that through the church the manifold wisdom of God might now be made known to the principalities and powers in the heavenly places. This

was according to the eternal purpose which he has realized in Christ Jesus our Lord, in whom we have boldness and confidence of access through our faith in him. (Ephesians 3:8-12)

The second analogy of the Church is an organic one: *the Church as the Body of Christ united in the Spirit.* Again St. Paul says:

The body is a unit, though it is made up of many parts; and though all its parts are many, they form one body. So it is with Christ. For we were all baptized by one Spirit into one body – whether Jews or Greeks, slave or free – and we were all given the one Spirit to drink... Now you are the body of Christ, and each one of you is a part of it. (1 Corinthians 12:12-13, 27)

One can hardly imagine a more intimate, holistic metaphor for the relationship of Christ and the Church, although Paul uses a related one when he speaks of marriage, with Christ as the husband and the Church as the Bride (Ephesians 5:22-35). The relationships within the Triune God Himself are mirrored in His relation to the Church. The Eastern Church speaks of "theosis," of God's aim to transform our bodies and souls into His, as St. Peter confesses: "that you may become partakers (*koinonoi*) of the divine nature" (2 Peter 1:4; cf. Ephesians 1:22-23).

PARTICIPATION IN THE SPIRIT [2013]

"The grace of the Lord Jesus Christ and the love of God and the fellowship of the Holy Spirit be with you all" (2 Corinthians 13:14). I titled this talk "Communing in Christ." How often do we repeat this classic blessing without reflecting on that word "*fellowship* of the Holy Spirit"! The Greek word is *koinonia*, which can also be translated "participation" or "communion." It is characteristic of the Third Person of the Holy Trinity that he is relational. Bishop John V. Taylor referred to him as "the go-between God." St. Augustine saw him as expressing the love that unites the Persons of the Trinity. Contemporary scholar Robert Letham comments: "Communion and communication are inherent in his very being."

The fellowship of the Holy Spirit is naturally experienced in the fellowship of the Church, what Michael Nazir-Ali has called "the social dimension of the spiritual." "For in one Spirit we were all baptized into one body – Jews or Greeks, slaves or free – and all were made to drink of one Spirit" (1 Corinthians 12:13). The apostolic fellowship includes common teaching, common prayer and sharing of earthly goods (Acts 2:42-44). The Holy Eucharist is a supreme sign of that fellowship, being a "participation in the Body and Blood of Christ." While Anglicans may differ over the exact nature of Christ's presence in the Eucharistic elements, they are agreed that they are spiritual food and drink to be received spiritually by faith and that they convey spiritual blessing and benefits.

The fellowship of the Holy Spirit in the Church has, finally, an historical and political shape. Jesus' great final prayer is made on behalf of the worldwide Church of the ages:

> I do not ask for these only, but also for those who will believe in me through their word, that they may all be one, just as you, Father, are in me, and I in you, that they also may be in us, so that the world may believe that you have sent me. The glory that you have given me I have given to them, that they may be one even as we are one, I in them and you in me, that they may become perfectly one, so that the world may know that you sent me and loved them even as you loved me. (John 17:20-23)

The desire for and task of Christian unity, of ecumenism, is therefore a work of the Holy Spirit. Too often Evangelical Christians have been quick to break fellowship over matters of "truth." To be sure, the Holy Spirit is the Spirit of Truth, and the New Testament is filled with warnings of false teachers and false prophets (2 Peter 2:1-3; 1 John 4:1). Anglicans have over the centuries tended to be generous in maintaining ecclesial fellowship among those who disagree on "indifferent" matters of doctrine, discipline, or worship. The Lambeth Quadrilateral recognizes that Anglican church order, while episcopal in form, can be "locally adapted" to different national and cultural settings.

The very term Anglican *Communion* suggests a fellowship of churches united in the one Spirit. For all its weaknesses, Anglicanism has historically presented a united witness to the Gospel around the globe and has been a major ecumenical dialogue partner with other traditions. It is therefore sadly ironic that the current crisis in Anglicanism has not only split the Communion but called into question the identity of the Communion to other Christian bodies.

The goal of GAFCON is not to divide the church but to restore genuine communion in the Spirit. The Global Fellowship of Confessing Anglicans affirms the Lord's ecumenical mandate, as is stated in the Jerusalem Declaration:

11. We are committed to the unity of all those who know and love Christ and to building authentic ecumenical relationships. We recognize the orders and jurisdiction of those Anglicans who uphold orthodox faith and practice, and we encourage them to join us in this declaration.

12. We celebrate the God-given diversity among us which enriches our global fellowship, and we acknowledge freedom in secondary matters. We

103

pledge to work together to seek the mind of Christ on issues that divide us.

13. We reject the authority of those churches and leaders who have denied the orthodox faith in word or deed. We pray for them and call on them to repent and return to the Lord.

I would argue that these statements reflect accurately the Biblical understanding of the fellowship among churches. There remain, for instance, significant obstacles to full communion with Rome and other historic Christian bodies. There are theological tensions within the "three streams" of the GAFCON movement itself. None of these churches, however, has taken a position so totally opposed to Scripture and unprecedented in the historic teaching of the Church as have the Episcopal Church and the Anglican Church of Canada.

Let me conclude with this question concerning the Holy Spirit and the GAFCON movement. In the Jerusalem Statement we proclaim: "GAFCON is not just a moment in time, but a movement in the Spirit." What did we mean by that? Are we saying that the Global Fellowship of Confessing Anglicans is a true communion of churches differentiating itself from the historic body from which we emerged? If so, then what further steps must we take to solidify that movement of the Spirit? If not, then what are we? I have addressed this issue in more detail in my essay "Sea Change in the Anglican Communion" (Essay 9). If we take seriously our belief in the Holy Spirit as constituting the fellowship of the church, we must in good conscience seek to discern his hand in directing our movement.

THE NATURE OF THE CHURCH

Christian theology distinguishes between the invisible and visible church. According to Richard Hooker (*Laws* iii.1.2), the former "body mystical" cannot be "sensibly discerned by any man," consisting, as the Westminster Confession (xxv.1) puts it, "of the whole number of the elect that have been, are, or shall be gathered into one, under Christ the Head thereof." "The visible Church of Jesus Christ," Hooker continues (*Laws* iii.1.3), "is therefore one, in outward profession of those things, which supernaturally appertain to the very essence of Christianity, and are necessarily required of every Christian man." Just as the Kingdom of God is present yet imperfectly fulfilled in this age, and just as the individual Christian has received merely the first-fruits of the Spirit, so also the visible Church, the so-called Church Militant, is but a partial and imperfect manifestation of "the Holy City, the New Jerusalem, coming down out of heaven from God, prepared as a bride adorned for her husband" (Revelation 21:2). In this age, the true citizenship of the elect is "kept in heaven" (Philippians 3:20) and not identical with membership in the church or reception of the sacraments. Indeed, Jesus taught that the Kingdom is like a field sown with grain and weeds, which will only be separated at the last judgment (Matthew 13:24-30).

When we say in the Creed that we believe in *one holy catholic and apostolic church*, we acknowledge the attributes of the church in perfection that are imperfectly realized in the church as found at any one place or time. The church is *one* in the sense that it confesses one God the Father and one Lord Jesus Christ (1 Corinthians 8:6) and that this one God has only one elect communion of saints from all eternity, and "its division by discordant polities is an accident, contrary to its ideal" (H. C. G. Moule). The church is *holy* in that it is filled and transformed by the Holy Spirit. The church is *catholic* in that it is drawn from every nation, tribe, people, and language down to the end of the age (Revelation 7:9; Matthew 28:18-20). The church is *apostolic* in that it is founded on the truth of the Gospel proclaimed by the apostles in Scripture which is received by the hearing of faith (Ephesians 2:20; Romans 10:18-19) and passed on in the authentic teaching of the church (1 Corinthians 4:17; 2 Thessalonians 2:15).

THE MARKS OF THE CHURCH

The marks of the Church are, according to the Reformers, those characteristics that distinguish a true church from a heretical church. The Homily for Whitsunday has the fullest definition of the marks among the Anglican formularies:

> The true church is an universal congregation or fellowship of God's faithful and elect people, built upon the foundation of the Apostles and Prophets, Jesus Christ being the head corner-stone. And it hath always three notes or marks, whereby it is known: Pure and sound doctrine; The sacraments ministered according to Christ's holy institution; And the right use of ecclesiastical discipline.

This definition is broader than that of the Articles in that it speaks of a "universal congregation," which may include what we today might call the worldwide (visible) church. By contrast, Article 19 is focused more locally:

> The visible Church of Christ is a congregation of faithful men, in which the pure Word of God is preached and the Sacraments duly administered according to Christ's ordinance in all those things that of necessity are requisite to the same.

It seems likely Cranmer had in mind the collective society of English congregations gathered for worship. In a sense he may have anticipated the later formation of national "Provinces." The health of Christ's church cannot be measured by ecumenical dialogues, or the Instruments of Unity, or even by bishops in their cathedrals, unless it is manifested in vital, faithful congregations. Anglicans are not congregationalists, but according to the Articles we experience the congregation as the basic unit of church life.

Another emphasis of Article 19 is the centrality of Scripture, with its insistence that the "pure Word of God is preached." Anglicans rightly pride themselves on their rich lectionary of Scripture readings at every service. However, it is equally important that Scripture be practically applied to the lives of the people. The famous Scripture Collect captures this aim:

> Blessed Lord, who hast caused all holy Scriptures to be written for our learning: Grant that we may in such wise hear them, read, mark, learn, and inwardly digest them; that, by patience and comfort of your holy Word, we may embrace and ever hold fast the blessed hope of everlasting life, which you have given us in our Saviour Jesus Christ...

The people of the Church are to be *hearers and readers of Scripture*: note that the first East African converts were described as "readers" because the Bible was their first written text. Beyond that, the clergy are to help them discern the whole pattern of Scripture, the Old and New Testaments, and its culmination in the promise of salvation in Christ.

The marks of the church are not limited to preaching alone: the "due" administration of the sacraments is also necessary for the fullness of church life. It has been difficult for Anglicans to get this balance right. Evangelicals have relegated Holy Communion to an occasional service or tacked it on to a long service of preaching. Anglo-Catholics, on the other hand, have often treated preaching as no more than a grace note in crescendo to Communion.

And charismatics often allow both notes to be drowned out in endless choruses of praise music.

It will be important for the future of Anglicanism that we claim our classic inheritance of the one holy catholic and apostolic church, marked by lively biblical preaching and reverent reception of the sacraments, in the spirit of worship and praise.

Finally, the third mark of the Church – *discipline* – is stated in the Homilies and either assumed in Article 19 or subsumed under the words "faithful men" and "duly administered." Church discipline has been badly neglected in the Anglican tradition and is at the heart of the current troubles of the Communion, so I have reserved a separate section on this mark for the end of the presentation.

THE ORDAINED MINISTRY

The exalted nature of the Church as Christ's Body is accompanied by an exalted sense of the Spirit's gifts for ministry. As Paul says:

> And his gifts were that some should be apostles, some prophets, some evangelists, some pastors and teachers, to equip the saints for the work of ministry, for building up the body of Christ... (Ephesians 4:11-12)

Paul begins with certain extraordinary offices – apostles, prophets, evangelists. The first three offices have a dual reference: to the *original* apostolic generation, whose works and words we find enshrined in the New Testament; and also to *contemporary* missionary pioneers who bring the Gospel to unreached peoples and hostile territory. Sometimes this latter group arises outside the normal structures of the church; we Anglicans must find ways to deploy such people, as the Church of Nigeria is doing in sending its missionary bishops into already existing dioceses.

108

When we come to "pastors and teachers," it is probably more accurate to translate "pastor-teachers" for the ordinary role of the clergy. A pastor-teacher is involved in a personal way with his congregation, in imitation of the Good Shepherd who said: "I know my sheep and my sheep know me" (John 10:14). It is one of the great failures I have observed over almost forty years of church ministry – and this observation applies both in the West and in Africa – that clergy seldom visit their people at home any more, except in crisis situations.

The pastor is also a catechist and teacher, forming new converts and counselling the mature. In order to teach others, he must himself be educated in God's Word and other necessary disciplines. Hence a Church that fails to provide adequate theological training for its clergy is negligent indeed. The pastor should consider it his duty to provide Christian education at all levels of the laity, beginning with the children. He should work hard in his preaching and catechesis to speak in language understood by the people, both in their vernacular and with appropriate illustrations and applications.

The office of priest or presbyter, according to Article 23, must involve a "lawful" call from the Church. The vocation is a weighty one, as ordinands are reminded in the Prayer Book service:

> …that ye have in remembrance, into how high a Dignity, and to how weighty an Office and Charge ye are called: that is to say, to be Messengers, Watchmen, and Stewards of the Lord; to teach and to admonish, to feed and to provide for the Lord's family; to seek for Christ's sheep that are dispersed abroad, and for his children who are in the midst of this naughty world that they be saved through Christ for ever.

I have emphasized here the role of the parish priest and pastor as the key to church ministry. It is only when the pastorate is well-supplied that the other orders of ministry will be properly equipped. Having said this, note that the aim of the ordained is "to equip the saints for the work of ministry." Laypeople have an equal role to play in the work of the Church. This is a particular challenge for a "hierarchical" church – again I see this problem both in the West and in Africa – to recognize and empower laypeople in their roles of building up the Kingdom of God, not through quasi-clerical functions, but where they live and work – at home and in the field and office.

We come now to the office of bishop (I leave aside the role of deacon, which strikes me as needing serious rethinking). In the apostolic church, the distinction between bishop (*episkopos*) and elder (*presbyteros*) was fluid. In the patristic church bishops emerged as the heads of each "metropolitan" area, accompanied by priests, deacons and lay ministers. The Anglican Reformers retained the threefold ministry in practice but were reluctant to assign separate orders for priests and bishops as an essential mark of the church (hence the "ordination" of a priest and the "consecration" of a bishop). To be sure, bishops functioned as de facto hierarchs in the Church of England, with many seated in the House of Lords, and the Lambeth Quadrilateral makes the historic episcopate a non-negotiable element for ecumenical agreement. The English and American parish systems also evolved checks-and-balances between the authority of the bishop, parish priest and the laity.

The bishop exercises formal headship within the church, and this role has fallen exclusively to men throughout most of church history and even today across an ecumenical majority of churches. The notion that headship should be

110

reserved to men has biblical support in the family (Ephesians 5:22-24) and in the church (1 Corinthians 11:2; 1 Timothy 2:12-14), although the New Testament also raises the status of women in church and society as full partners in God's kingdom (Galatians 3:28). Biblically faithful Anglicans need to wrestle once again with God's order for the family and church; and unless there is overwhelming biblical justification and ecumenical consensus to change, we should reserve the episcopacy (at least) to men.

WORSHIP

The adage that "praying shapes believing" (*lex orandi lex credendi*) is a commonplace, with deep biblical roots, as can be seen from the presence of liturgical nuggets throughout the Scriptures and the entire Book of Psalms. The formative role of prayer and worship in the Jewish and Christian tradition is beyond question. Anglicans in particular have been blessed by the Book of Common Prayer, Thomas Cranmer's gift to the Christian world. One need only think of the great Collect for Purity, the Litany, the Prayer of Humble Access, and the General Thanksgiving to realize what a treasure we have been entrusted with. These prayers and others have been translated into numerous languages and adopted by many free churches into their orders of worship.

Another contribution of Anglicanism has been the use of the Church Year for continuous Bible reading through a lectionary of daily and Sunday readings. The Church Year is reflected in seasonal collects and feasts and fasts, observed in differing degrees by low- and high-churchmen. The due observance of Sunday is recognized formally in the main worship service of the week, but in other ways Anglicans need to recover the fullness of celebrating the

Lord's Day as a distinctive time of each week, a true Christian Sabbath.

While recognizing the importance of liturgical worship on Christian faith and spirituality, it can be equally stated that "believing shapes praying." It was Archbishop Cranmer's project to revise the traditional liturgy in accordance with the doctrine expressed in the Articles. Furthermore, he provided a variety of media by which that doctrine might be appropriated. Take, for instance, what Ashley Null calls "Thomas Cranmer's doctrine of repentance." We find the following expressions of this doctrine in the Prayer Book:

CATECHISM

What is required of those who come to the Lord's Supper? To examine themselves, whether they repent truly of their former sins, steadfastly purposing to lead a new life; have a lively faith in God's mercy through Christ, with a thankful remembrance of his death; and be in charity with all men.

EXHORTATION TO COMMUNION

Judge yourselves therefore, brethren, that ye be not judged of the Lord; repent you truly of your sins past; have a lively and steadfast faith in Christ our Saviour; amend your lives, and be in perfect charity with all men; so shall ye be partakers of these holy mysteries.

INVITATION TO COMMUNION

Ye who do truly and earnestly repent you of your sins, and are in love and charity with your neighbours, and intend to lead a new life, following the commandments of God and walking from henceforth in his holy ways: Draw near with faith and take this sacrament to your comfort; and make your humble confession to Almighty God, devoutly kneeling.

AFTER COMMUNION

And we humbly beseech thee, O heavenly Father, so to assist us with thy grace, that we may continue in that holy fellowship, and do all such good works as thou has prepared for us to walk in, through Jesus Christ our Lord...

We may question whether the Anglican Reformers recognized the power of music to supplement the verbal expressions of worship. "He who sings prays twice," it is often said. At this point, Evangelicals like Isaac Watts and Charles Wesley and Anglo-Catholics like J. M Neale came in to enrich our tradition of worship with powerful and beautiful hymns.

For all its merits, the conformity required in using the Book of Common Prayer has had its down side. From the early Puritans with their prophesyings, to the Wesleys' and Simeon's outdoor evangelism, to contemporary African "overnight prayer" services, Anglicans have felt the need to supplement formal corporate worship and said prayers.

Contemporary liturgies often provide "blended worship," with space in the formal liturgy for spontaneous prayer, for testimony, for praise choruses and for healing prayer and calls to faith. By relaxing the form of liturgy, contemporary Anglicans have responded to the allure of Pentecostalism. Nevertheless, this compromising of the traditional with the contemporary constitutes an ongoing tension.

We cannot afford to retreat into a rigid formalism nor can we embrace uncritically every latest trend in worship and music. There is a need, in my opinion, for a set core of identifiable Anglican prayer that can be memorized and is familiar to the flock worldwide.

THE SACRAMENTS

Sacramental theology has been one of the most disputed elements of church teaching from the time of the Reformation down to the present. It will be important to understand the essential teaching of the Articles in light of the wider doctrine of the Church. Archbishop Cranmer's first edition of the Articles included the following important preface: "Our Lord Jesus Christ hath knit together a company of new people with Sacraments...." This preface makes clear that sacraments are *public signs of church membership*. The Thirty-Nine Articles go on to state:

> Sacraments ordained by Christ are not only badges and tokens of Christian men's profession: but rather they are certain sure witnesses and effectual signs of grace and God's good will towards us, by which he works invisibly in us, and not only quickens but also strengthens and confirms our faith in him.

This definition positions Anglicans and Anglicanism in the midst of a spectrum of interpretations of the sacraments and sacramental grace – especially concerning the Eucharist. These four views can be classified as:

1. "Memorials", i.e., human aids to recollect or attest to Christ's work;

2. Spiritual presence, i.e., that God's grace is truly present through the "action" of baptizing and giving and taking the Communion;

3. "Real presence," i.e., Christ is truly present in the sacramental elements without changing their outer substance;

4. "Transubstantiation," i.e., that through the priest's re-enactment of Christ's sacrifice, the

elements are changed in essence to that which they signify.

In stating that sacraments "are not only badges and tokens," the Articles reject the memorialist view. They also explicitly reject as unbiblical the Roman doctrine of transubstantiation and the practices that flow from that view. Between the other two views (usually identified as "Reformed" and "Lutheran"), the judgement of the whole tradition is less clear, and probably best left open to conscience.

In the case of baptism, Article 27 states:

Baptism is not only a sign of profession and mark of difference, whereby Christian men are discerned from others that be not christened; but it is also a sign of regeneration and new birth, whereby as by an instrument they that receive baptism rightly are grafted into the church; the promise of forgiveness of sin and of our adoption to be the sons of God by the Holy Ghost are visibly signed and sealed; faith is confirmed; and grace increased by virtue of prayer unto God.

At one level, the Article rejects baptism as a mere memorial of church membership and states that baptism conveys the reality of new birth in Christ, "as by an instrument." The promissory character of the baptismal language – "seeing now that this person is regenerate and born again" – has been variously interpreted. For an adult, it gives assurance that the once for all salvation of Christ has been received by faith. In the case of an infant, this assurance is provided by the faith of the parents and godparents that must be owned by the child at confirmation or at a subsequent occasion of commitment to Christ. Assurance, however, is not to be confused with complacency, as St. Paul warns: "let him who stands beware lest he fall" (1 Corinthians 10:12; cf. Hebrews 5:11-

115

6:12). Finally, baptism conveys the communal reality of the Christian life: just as a child is born into a human family, so the baptized is "grafted into the body of Christ's church" and "received into the congregation of Christ's flock."

When we turn to the Lord's Supper, a similar balance occurs, as is captured in the familiar Prayer Book words of Administration:

> "The Body of our Lord Jesus Christ, which was given for you, preserve your body and soul unto everlasting life. Take and eat this in remembrance that Christ died for you and feed on him in your hearts by faith with thanksgiving."

The first clause, like our Lord's words of institution, sets forth an objective reality to the sacramental elements: "This is my Body; this is my Blood." The second clause captures one powerful feature of Reformed theology: the requirement that God's grace must be received by faith. The sacramental signs are effectual only when received by those who worthily receive them with penitent hearts. Yet even without faith, they are not bare signs, as they carry a negative effect on the ungodly, who "purchase to themselves damnation."

Another characteristic feature of Anglican sacramental teaching – which appears in the Lambeth Quadrilateral – is the naming of two Gospel sacraments. As Article 25 continues: "There are two Sacraments ordained by Christ our Lord in the Gospel, that is to say, Baptism and the Supper of the Lord." The specification of two and only two is of a piece with the focus of the Anglican formularies on "those things necessary for salvation." Baptism and Holy Communion are not only instituted by Jesus Christ but they signify his saving work on the Cross.

The Homilies concede a place for other sacramental rites:

But in a general acceptance, the name of a sacrament may be attributed to any thing, whereby an holy thing is signified. In which understanding of the word, the ancient writers have given this name, not only to the other five, commonly of late years taken and used for supplying the number of the seven sacraments; but also to divers and sundry other ceremonies, as to oil, washing of feet, and such like: not meaning thereby to repute them as sacraments, in the same signification that the two forenamed sacraments are. ("Of Common Prayer and Sacraments")

Taken together, I think Anglican teaching is clear that a sacrament, strictly speaking, must convey Christ's *saving* work, but that as part of the Church's liturgy and ministry, other external signs can be edifying.

CHURCH DISCIPLINE

Several years ago, I was speaking with a colleague on the phone and I overheard this conversation running in the background: "Emma, don't do that!" Then a pause: "Emma, I said, don't do that!" Then another pause, and then: "Emma, I can't believe you did that."

Immaturity and stubbornness are tolerable, even perversely adorable, in a small child. But it is not so in the church. The apostles exhorted their congregations, and especially its leaders, to put aside childish things and move up to solid food (1 Corinthians 3:2; Hebrews 5:12).

As noted above, the Anglican Reformers considered church discipline, either explicitly or tacitly, to be one of the marks of the true church. In order to do this topic justice, we need to take the broadest perspective: *discipline is of a piece with discipleship*. The Risen Christ commands his followers to "disciple the nations, baptizing them and teaching them all that I have taught you" (Matthew 28:18). Discipline has a constructive, educative end: presenting the

church blameless in Christ (Ephesians 5:27). The writer to
the Hebrews makes clear that spiritual discipline requires
believers to "lay aside every weight and sin that clings so
closely" in order to run the Christian race, and he goes on
to say that "the Lord disciplines him whom he loves"
(Hebrews 12:1,6). Likewise St. Paul describes the pastor's
calling as a matter of rigourous edifying: "preach the word,
be urgent in season and out of season, convince, rebuke,
and exhort, be unfailing in patience and in teaching" (2
Timothy 4:2).

The Anglican Prayer Book is itself a book of discipline.
It provides the believer with a regimen of morning and
evening prayer, a calendar of psalms and lessons, fast and
feast days, and a way of "learning" the prayers of the
congregation by memorizing responses and canticles. In
Africa people often do not have individual Prayer Books
and hymnals, yet even the children have the service and
hymns memorized in their local language. The catechism
in particular presents a summary of faith consistent with
the more sophisticated Articles of Religion, and
confirmation is set as a coming-of-age ritual to be taken
with great seriousness.

Penance is not a sacrament for Anglicans, but the
Prayer Book contains several exhortations to self-
examination, preparation for Communion and confession
of sin. Repentance and gratitude for Christ's forgiveness of
our sins is an ongoing way of life, not to be disconnected
from the freedom and joy of walking as children of light (1
John 1:7). It is unfortunate that many clergy today skip
over the longer forms of invitation to confession or even
omit them altogether. This goes against the whole grain of
the Prayer Book Eucharist as an act of thanksgiving for
Christ's death for our sins and offer of forgiveness and new
life.

Articles 32-36 address aspects of discipline, though they are hardly comprehensive (Cranmer intended his reform of English canon law to fill in the detail, which sadly never happened). Three of these Articles relate in some way to clerical discipline. One establishes that clergy of the Church of England are lawfully called to the office. Another provides clergy and lay readers with a syllabus of homilies to assist them in preaching and teaching. And another opens the priesthood to married men, in contrast to Rome's requirement of celibacy.

Clergy discipline is of great importance to the morale of the Church. Scripture and the historic church, along with the Anglican Ordinal, have been of one accord in insisting that discipline begins with the household of God, and that church leaders are therefore especially accountable (1 Peter 4:17). I have observed serious breakdowns in this area on both sides of the ocean, but only in the West has this been done shamelessly. In the Episcopal Church, clergy divorce has become rampant in the last 35 years. While the so-called "gay lifestyle" of some clergy in the West grabs the headlines, divorce among clergy, some with several marriages (let's call this serial polygamy) is probably the more corrosive factor in the decline of those churches. Whatever the precise meaning of a bishop being husband of one wife (1 Timothy 3:2), it seems to me to limit the highest office in the church to those who have not been divorced as Christians.

Article 34 may seem out of place in a section on discipline, as it speaks of the diversity of traditions within the church. It teaches us, on the one hand, to be slow to judge those who practice their religion differently from us. There are many customs – which we term adiaphora – which Christians may follow in good conscience. The Article goes on to state that we must follow local traditions in cases where they are the law of our church. This Article lays the foundation for obedience to canon law.

Article 33 speaks frankly of excommunicate persons who by open denunciation of the church should be shunned until they repent and are publicly reconciled. This Article complements the disciplinary rubric which allows a priest to refuse Communion to a "notorious evil-liver." For many Anglicans in the West the whole idea of excommunication seems quaint or even anathema, although the Episcopal Church USA has managed to reinvent it under the twisted rubric of "abandonment of communion," which is being used to bludgeon the orthodox. In the Church of England, for instance, a priest can be brought up on charges to the bishop if he were to refuse Holy Communion to an openly gay parishioner. Coming from this permissive culture to Africa, I was rather shocked to find there the opposite tendency: large numbers of Ugandan Anglicans absenting themselves from the Eucharist because of irregular marriages that render them excommunicate.

In Gospel texts supporting the practice of excommunication, the Lord Jesus himself entrusts to his apostles the keys to enter and remain in the church, i.e., the visible church (Matthew 16:19; John 20:22). In Matthew's Gospel, Jesus goes on to describe a process of discipline:

> "If your brother sins against you, go and tell him his fault, between you and him alone. If he listens to you, you have gained your brother. But if he does not listen, take one or two others along with you, that every word may be confirmed by the evidence of two or three witnesses. If he refuses to listen to them, tell it to the church; and if he refuses to listen even to the church, let him be to you as a Gentile and a tax collector. Truly, I say to you, whatever you bind on earth shall be bound in

heaven, and whatever you loose on earth shall be loosed in heaven." (Matthew 18:15-18)

We see here a careful process that moves from personal exhortation, to semi-private admonition, to public scandal and excommunication. St. Paul clearly understood the process in a similar way in dealing with the immoral man in Corinth (1 Corinthians 5:5) and the false teachers Alexander and Hymenaeus (1 Timothy 1:20). Note also that the laity is involved in various stages of this process.

John Calvin, perhaps the preeminent spokesman on the subject, teaches that church discipline is essential to preserve the honour and purity of the church, to protect the flock from false and wicked ideas and people, and to bring evil-doers back to Christ. On this latter aim, Calvin is the consummate pastor in advising that the aim of discipline is transformation:

> Let us not claim for ourselves more license in judgment, unless we wish to limit God's power and confine his mercy by law. For God, whenever it pleases him, changes the worst men into the best, engrafts the alien, and adopts the stranger into the church. (*Institutes* xii.9)

I wonder whether African pastors have done enough in this regard to labor to restore to fellowship those who have contracted "customary marriages." I believe many would wish to have their unions blessed if they were pursued and encouraged.

COMMUNION DISCIPLINE

The problem of church discipline is not limited to individuals: it can involve whole churches. Indeed it was at the heart of the Reformation conflict. The Anglican Reformers were all excommunicate in the eyes of Rome and many, including Thomas Cranmer, paid with their lives. But they refused to accept this judgment. Indeed,

Richard Hooker turned the charge back against Rome, saying:

> That which they call schism, we know to be our reasonable service unto God and obedience to his voice which crieth shrill in our ears, "Go out of Babylon, my people, that you be not partakers of her sins, and that ye receive not of her plagues" (*Revelation* 18:4). [from Hooker's "Sermon on Jude"]

Heresy is schismatic according to the Reformers, and hence to be labeled schismatic by Rome was a badge of honour.

Almost ten years ago, shortly after Lambeth 1998, when it became clear that the Episcopal Church was not going to heed the Resolution on Human Sexuality, I wrote an essay titled "Broken Communion: The Ultimate Sanction Against False Religion and Morality in the Episcopal Church," in which I called on faithful Episcopal bishops to declare a state of broken communion with those who openly advocated homosexual ordinations and same-sex blessings (no sitting bishop did so). Next I turned to the international church:

> If the charges against the revisionist leadership of the Episcopal Church are true, the appropriate response is for the Primates of the Communion to threaten and if necessary declare a state of broken communion with the Episcopal Church or with those leaders who have publicly endorsed the gay-rights agenda…

> Excommunicating bishops of the Episcopal Church or the Church as a whole may seem like a very long step to take. And it should be. No division of this sort should be taken lightly. On the other hand, for a church council to refuse to exercise ultimate sanctions when they are clearly called for is to undermine its own legitimacy. To put it bluntly, if the Episcopal Church calls the bluff of the Communion

and the Communion flinches, the Communion will undermine its own authority and identity.

In 2002, several Primates and theologians produced a document called *To Mend the Net*, an entirely reasonable proposal for careful Communion discipline, in which a church that finally refused to conform could be excluded. Even the Windsor Report held out the possibility that a church might choose to walk apart. But *To Mend the Net* was consigned to outer darkness by the Communion bureaucracy, and the "Windsor process" seems to have made "walking apart" an ever-retreating mirage.

We are here this week because, after ten years of patient but futile calls for repentance on the part of the majority of the world's Anglicans, the Communion, under the direction of the Archbishop of Canterbury, has flinched. Hence while it may seem that we are the ones who have excluded ourselves, the truth is, as Hooker put it, that this is our reasonable service to God.

We are not breaking the communion. The title deeds of the Church are ours, not by our own merits, but by his eternal Covenant. Our city is the Jerusalem which is above, who is our mother. Our communion is with God in Christ, who is the author of Scripture and the author of our salvation. *To Him be glory in the Church and in Christ Jesus for all generations for ever and ever. Amen.*

Section Two

From Lambeth to Jerusalem

The Road to GAFCON

1998-2008

Two milestones mark the course of late 20th and early 21st century in Anglican history: the 1998 Lambeth Conference in Canterbury and the 2008 Global Anglican Future Conference in Jerusalem. That this is so, simply note that there was another Lambeth Conference held in Canterbury in 2008. What will it be remembered for? Forty-four pages of table-group "reflections," also known as *indaba*? Snooze on! By contrast, Lambeth 1998 is already remembered for a single Resolution on Human Sexuality, and GAFCON 2008 for a concise Statement including the Jerusalem Declaration, a confession of Anglican doctrine and discipline relevant to postmodern secularism.

The theological statements of Lambeth 1998 and GAFCON 2008 were the result of political achievements in which the Global South churches broke the hammer-lock with which the Anglo-American bureaucracy had controlled Communion affairs since the 1960s.

The essays in this section span the decade between these two significant events. Essay 4 gives a running chronology of the decade; Essay 5 gives a feel for the high politics that surrounded passage of Lambeth I.10. Essays 6 and 7 are expositions of that Lambeth Resolution and Jerusalem Declaration respectively, which express clearly and simply the biblical and theological convictions of the majority of global Anglicans.

ESSAY 4
THE DECLINE AND FALL
(AND RISING AGAIN)
OF THE ANGLICAN COMMUNION
(2009)

This essay is a chronicle of the events surrounding and
following the Lambeth Conference in 1998, with a brief
look at the Communion-threatening actions in the
Episcopal Church USA before and after the Conference.
This essay is in some respects personal because I was
involved in several key events recounted. It is also a
theological analysis, as I am seeking to understand the
recent history of the Anglican Communion in terms of
Christian doctrine and discipline and God's providence in
history.

This address was first presented at the Mere
Anglicanism Conference in Charleston, South Carolina,
in January 2009. Now, almost ten years later, it requires
supplementing, as it preceded the formation of the
Anglican Church in North America in June 2009 and its
recognition by the Global Fellowship of Confessing
Anglicans in October 2009 (see Essay 9). It ends with a
plea for cooperation between those orthodox
"Communion Partners" who remained in the Episcopal
Church and those who departed for ACNA. It also leaves
open a faint hope that the Archbishop of Canterbury
might recognize the ACNA and GAFCON movements as
a necessary response to the disorder of the Communion.
Sadly, neither the plea nor the hope has been fulfilled (see
Essay 7).

Finally, I argued, briefly here and more extensively
elsewhere, that GAFCON might co-opt the idea of a

Covenant to guide its future conciliar governance (see Essay 9). This idea has not yet been accepted, but there are steps being proposed which will move toward that aim at GAFCON 2018.

This address is dedicated to my bishop, the Rt. Rev. Robert W. Duncan, the Bishop of the Diocese of Pittsburgh. I am proud to serve under his wise and courageous leadership and to contribute this token of theology for the cause of Christ.

I n Africa, it is expected that every speaker be prepared to give his testimony on request, and I am going to take this opportunity to share something of my testimony in the Episcopal Church and Anglican Communion running alongside a much more significant story: of how the judgment of God has fallen on the Communion and how the mercy of God is still operative.[1]

I do not intend to concentrate on the decline and fall of the Episcopal Church, which others like Philip Turner have documented on various occasions.[2] My story will cover the dozen years from the trial of Bishop Walter Righter to the Global Anglican Future Conference in Jerusalem in June 2008, with a brief vista of the way ahead.

THE RIGHTER TRIAL
THE END OF THE ROAD FOR THE EPISCOPAL CHURCH

The Righter Trial, as I see it, was the last serious attempt of the orthodox Episcopal hierarchy to stem the tide of radical revisionism that had been growing steadily since the 1960s with Bishop James Pike and from the 1970s on with Bishop John Spong. To give a brief review of events, Spong had ordained a practicing homosexual named Robert Williams in 1989, which caused a bare

128

majority of bishops to disassociate themselves from his action.[3] In 1991, in reaction to this clear violation of biblical and Episcopal Church norms, Bishop William Frey had proposed a canon stating that "all members of this Church shall abstain from genital relations outside of holy matrimony." The canon failed. By 1994, although the General Convention continued to mouth assent to the "traditional teaching" against homosexual practice, bishops were beginning to openly ordain homosexuals in many dioceses (three of the judges on the Righter Court had done so). Conservatives decided that the only resort feasible and conscionable was to bring a presentment against such a bishop, and since Spong's action had just passed the five-year statute of limitations, they chose his assistant bishop, Walter Righter, who had ordained Barry Stopfel, another practicing homosexual, in 1990. So in 1995 Righter was presented for trial for holding and teaching doctrine contrary to that of the Episcopal Church, and the trial was set for early 1996.

On New Year's Day 1996, I received a phone call from Bishop John Howe, one of the Presenters – a.k.a. "ten evil men" to the liberal church media – asking if I would help in writing the legal briefs. As a result, I wrote two pieces of theology, one on doctrine and one on discipline.[4]

Firstly, I laid out the substantive case to the effect that Righter's act did indeed involve "holding and teaching" a doctrine contrary to that held by the one holy catholic and apostolic church, of which the Episcopal Church claimed to be a part.[5] I summed up thus:

> There is overwhelming evidence that the Church universal, and the Episcopal Church in particular, has held and continues to hold the doctrine that "physical sexual expression is appropriate only within the lifelong monogamous commitment of husband and wife." The

corollary of this moral doctrine is that homosexual practice is contrary to the will of God and incapable of serving as an example to God's people. The fact that the affirmation of marriage and celibacy, rather than the prohibition of homosexuality, has been the dominant note in the Church's doctrine is simply a reminder that wholesome sexual love and disciplined abstinence are part of the Good News of following Jesus Christ.[6]

So much for doctrine. The second part of the Presenters' case was that, given the Church's traditional doctrine, the canons called for disciplinary action against Righter. Once again, I argued that in the case of a bishop "holding and teaching *any* doctrine contrary to that held by this church," (Canon IV.1 emphasis added) – whether that doctrine involved the doctrine of God or the doctrine of his holy will and design for human nature – that bishop has to be disciplined or the church will lose its credibility as a witness to the truth of God. I concluded the second brief thus:

A bishop who violates the clear biblical and traditional teaching of the Episcopal Church by ordaining a non-celibate homosexual undermines the Church's discipline and unity. Furthermore, a Church hierarchy that condones by silence or endorses publicly such a violation likewise will become overseers of confusion and disorder among Episcopalians, separation from our ecumenical partners within the Anglican Communion and worldwide Christianity, and public ridicule from outsiders who see that the Episcopal Church is not theologically or morally serious about anything.[7]

So much for discipline. The Righter judges did not see things this way. They gave Bishop Righter a pass on the grounds that the disciplinary canon did not really mean *any* doctrine but "core doctrine" as defined by their episcopal highnesses.[8]

130

The Righter decision was the culmination of forty years of Episcopal refusal to deal with heresy, going back to the Bayne Report of 1967, which stated that "the word 'heresy' should be abandoned except in the context of radical, creative theological controversies of the early formative years of Christian doctrine."[9] In renouncing heresy, the Episcopal Church was also renouncing discipline for heretics.[10] By refusing to identify heresy and to discipline individual heretics, the Episcopal Church made itself into a pandemoniacal body that would test the willingness of the wider Communion to exercise church discipline.[11]

After the Righter Trial, the battle for the soul of the Episcopal Church was all over but the shouting. There would never again be a serious threat to the revisionist domination of the official Episcopal Church, even though traditionalists mounted vigorous rear-guard stands at the General Conventions in 1997 and 2000.

A more important denouement came by way of two events within months of the Righter decision. The first of these was the organizational meeting of the American Anglican Council in Chicago in June 1996. I was to have a role on the founding Board of the AAC and as first editor of its newsletter *Encompass*. Again, I shall not focus on the domestic role of the AAC, which has had a mixed record of success. What is more significant historically is that the AAC became a major channel of access for orthodox Episcopalians to the Lambeth Conference in 1998.

The second event that overlapped the founding of the AAC was the calling of the "Anglican Life and Witness Conference" in September 1996 in Dallas. This Conference was sponsored by the AAC, the recently founded Ekklesia Society under Dr. Bill Atwood, and Drs. Vinay Samuel and Chris Sugden from the Oxford Centre for Mission Studies in England. To my knowledge, this meeting was the first major interchange among bishops of the Global South and North America on the looming threat to the Communion, although it drew momentum from the "Second Anglican Encounter in the South" meeting of Global South bishops at Kuala Lumpur earlier in the year.[12]

In an address to the Dallas conference titled "The Handwriting on the Wall," I argued that, to paraphrase Churchill after Dunkirk, the battle for the Episcopal Church was over, the battle for the Anglican Communion was about to begin:

> I subtitled this talk "Why the Sexuality Conflict in the Episcopal Church Is God's Word to the Anglican Communion," and I conclude with a warning that failure to deal with the crisis in the Episcopal Church will endanger the unity of the Anglican Communion. Representatives from your provinces, meeting at Kuala Lumpur, have already raised the alarm in your statement on "Anglican Reconstruction." This is a question that cannot be delayed. What will become of Anglican unity if the American church breaks into two bodies out of communion with each other, with one body officially linked to Canterbury and the other officially committed to Kuala Lumpur? If Anglican leaders look the other way in 1998, such a situation is distinctly possible.

Many of the relationships formed at this Conference carried over to the Lambeth Conference, which met less than a year later, and my address was circulated at the Lambeth Conference in booklet form.[13]

1998 LAMBETH RESOLUTION 1.10
MAKING STRAIGHT THE WAY

The story of the Lambeth Conference 1998 and the approval of Resolution 1.10 on Human Sexuality has been told by some as a case of crafty Westerners seducing Global

South bishops with offers of chicken dinners. This was hardly the case. Those of us who worked at the infamous Franciscan Centre did provide home turf where Global South bishops could meet each other and receive information to help them counteract the official propaganda put out by the Conference organizers at the Communion Office.[14] Global South bishops proved eloquent in their own behalf, and the final Resolution 1.10 proceeded from them.

The Times of London noted after the vote on 5 August 1998, that Resolution 1.10 was a "surprisingly trenchant verdict." Surely the coherence at the heart of the Resolution derives from its doctrinal claim that the Conference,

> in view of the teaching of Scripture, upholds faithfulness in marriage of a man and a woman in lifelong union, and believes that abstinence is right for those who are not called to marriage;

and its corollary:

> while rejecting homosexuality as incompatible with Scripture, calls on all our people to minister pastorally and sensitively…

I had no role in drafting the Resolution; however, I did attempt soon after to exposit the Resolution as a coherent statement of doctrine (Essay 6).[15] As I had argued in the Righter case, I maintained that morality, doctrine, and Scripture are all of a piece:

> The moral premise is made *in view of the teaching of Scripture*. The Conference intends to make clear that moral norms are based on biblical authority. *Scripture comes first.* In a separate Resolution (III.1) the Conference "reaffirms the primary authority of the Scriptures, according to their testimony and supported by our own

historic formularies." Two of these historic formularies are relevant here: Article XX of the Thirty-Nine Articles declares "it is not lawful for the Church to ordain anything that is contrary to God's Word written." The Lambeth Quadrilateral, adopted by the Lambeth Conference in 1888 as the basis of Christian unity, holds that the Bible is "the rule and standard of faith."[16]

I had made one other small contribution to the sexuality debate between the Righter Trial and Lambeth. That was a book titled *Two Sexes, One Flesh: Why the Church Cannot Bless Same-Sex Marriage* (1997).[17] In that book I tested the question whether homosexual practice can fit into the overarching biblical narrative of the human race. My conclusion was that not only is this practice incompatible with specific biblical texts (sufficient reason in itself to reject it), but it is contrary to the theme of what I called "the unchangeable glory of marriage":

> Jesus draws from the creation texts a central principle: "the two will become one flesh" (Matthew 19:5; Genesis 2:24). By this he clearly meant the two opposite sexes joined in one physical union. Like all Jews, Jesus grounded his understanding of marriage in creation; however, while Jews (like Roman Catholics after them) saw descendants as the main outcome of marriage, Jesus drew attention to the coming into being of a spiritual union of husband and wife. God has put something together, he said, which man *cannot* put asunder. It is Jesus' understanding of the mystical union of a man and woman that forms the basis for the Christian understanding of marriage as sacramental.[18]

So when Lambeth 1.10 rejects homosexual practice in the light of Scripture's teaching about marriage, it is not speaking of some jot and tittle of exegesis but rather a golden thread of truth running throughout the fabric of Scripture, one that touches on the very nature of God and his people, of the Bridegroom and the Bride. The centrality of the doctrine of marriage and its unanimous support in the biblical witness make it problematic for a bishop like Rowan Williams to "uphold" Lambeth 1.10 effectively while disagreeing with it personally.[19]

Gay rights apologists try to play off the normative clauses in the Resolution against the pastoral clause about "listening to the experience of homosexual persons." While not denying that the latter clause was added due to pressure from the liberal side to soften the blow of the normative clauses, I note that the majority bishops made clear that "those who experience themselves as having an orientation" are not ontologically so determined. The experience of homosexuals needs to be understood in order to offer appropriate care, but that need does not change the church's moral teaching. I explained this section in this way:

> In light of the biblical moral norms, this clause *challenges the Church to help those who think of themselves as homosexual to frame their self-understanding in terms set by the Gospel.* The call to listen to the experience of homosexual persons was added by amendment and accepted by the majority of bishops in the context of the whole resolution. They recognize that homosexual orientation is psychologically complex and socially constructed in such a way that the Church must consider carefully how to bring the health of the Gospel to people so oriented. While pastors are urged to listen patiently to those who think of themselves as homosexual, their call is to bring such persons to understand themselves simply as disciples of Jesus, committed to him and to his standards of holiness.[20]

Oliver O'Donovan, the finest Anglican ethicist of our day, argues further that there are things which the church can learn about human sexuality from the phenomenon of contemporary homosexuality beyond simply condemning it.

He writes:

> If the first good news for the gay Christian, then, is that the "great question," the question of the self with all its pain and its hope, can be opened illuminatingly in the light of the righteousness of Jesus Christ, there is also a second good news. There is a neighbor with whom to explore the meaning of the contemporary homosexual situation, a neighbor who also needs, for the sake of his or her own integrity to reach answers to questions which the gay Christian is especially placed to search out.... The gay Christian thus faces in a particular way the choice that constitutes the human situation universally: whether to follow the route of self-justification or to cast oneself hopefully on the creative justification that God himself will work within a community of shared belief.[21]

I agree with O'Donovan. I do not think anyone understands fully why homosexual attraction takes the particular form it does in our day, nor do I think the only proper response is to blame those who find themselves so attracted. The touching dialogue of Richard Hays with his dying friend is all too uncommon.[22] Further dialogue on the significance of homosexuality does not, however, change the evangelical norm enunciated in the St. Andrew's Day Statement that the church "assists all its members to a life of faithful witness in chastity and holiness, recognizing two forms or vocations in which that life can be lived: marriage and singleness."[23]

The Lambeth Resolution is unambiguous in stating the doctrinal norm and makes clear in its reference to Scripture that this norm is of the highest order in upholding Anglican identity. The Resolution does not specify, however, how compliance might be gained or what kind of discipline might follow for those bishops and churches that reject that norm. This lack is not a fault of the Resolution, but it did raise the question of whether the Communion had adequate structures or leadership to follow through on it.[24] Unfortunately, the answer to this question was No. Put simply, here we are, more than ten years later, after many meetings and proposals and much ink spilt and dollars wasted, and the Episcopal Church has not only gone forward with its "inclusion" project but it has been joined by the Anglican Church of Canada and other provinces.

The Resolution stands but was not to be acted upon, and the Communion has paid a high price for this inaction. Archbishop Rowan Williams has repeatedly referred to the authority of Resolution 1.10 with the qualification that it is *currently* the mind of the Communion.[25] This misstates the case. The bishops at Lambeth 1998 did not think they were giving an interim report but giving a permanent No, based on what is at all times and in all places the Church's doctrine concerning the "unchangeable standard" of marriage and sexuality.[26]

Doctrine without discipline is a dead letter; arguably it is worse than no doctrine at all. Let's put it this way: once a clear statement is made and then spurned, the authority and truth of that statement is called into question.[27] I am convinced that Lambeth 1.10 is the standard to which a faithful member of the Anglican Communion must assent *ex animo*. Every other mediating statement, every other interim body that fails to go back to the norm enunciated in 1998, draws a veil, successive veils, between speaking the truth and obeying it.

Some people take comfort from the fact that Lambeth 1.10 still stands. I am not so sure, for at the end of the day God will not be mocked.

AFTERMATH OF LAMBETH 1998
THE PROBLEM OF DISCIPLINE

The reaction to the passage of Lambeth 1.10 in the Episcopal Church was a firestorm of angry protest.[28] The General Convention of 2000 formalized its reaction in Resolution D039, which stated in a contorted way that the Episcopal Church caters for both those following the traditional teaching *and* for those contravening that teaching.[29] Resolution D039 makes no reference to the normative clauses of Lambeth 1.10 but does refer to the pastoral clauses in calling for more "conversation" on the subject.[30] In short, the Episcopal Church rejected the doctrine of the Communion and indeed moved very close to proposing a contrary doctrine.[31] So within two years, the authority of the Lambeth Conference had been formally and informally defied by the Episcopal Church. This situation exposed the larger problem for the Communion of how any discipline might be exercised across the boundaries of individual provinces.

The problem was inherent in the DNA of the Anglican Communion. The original Lambeth Conference in 1867 was called in part to deal with a perceived breach of orthodoxy by Bishop Colenso of Natal. However, as Professor Owen Chadwick points out, there was a contradiction in the very calling of a council of bishops through a mother church ruled by Princes (Article XXI).

> If the [Lambeth] meeting was to be acceptable to some of its more moderate opponents, it seemed to be necessary to say that the meeting was only of a discussion group, and none of its decisions would have any authority. Archbishop Longley of Canterbury would only summon the meeting, and several bishops would only attend it, if its resolutions were declared beforehand to have no binding force. Some of the American bishops who were

determined to take no orders out of England were equally strong that this meeting was "only" for consultation…

Now the chief makers of the first Lambeth Conference had no idea whatever of a meeting that would produce nothing. Selwyn and Robert Gray were fighting for an absolute principle, that the Church of Christ teaches truth and that it has the freedom to determine what is compatible with that truth. Nothing could be less irresponsible than their Athanasian stance. But the difficulty was that in order to have a meeting at all you must concede it to have no authority, and that necessity produced danger for the future.[32]

The problem of Communion identity and coherence was recognized early. The Lambeth Quadrilateral, adopted in 1888, set forth certain identity markers for the purposes of ecumenical relations. Successive Conferences considered proposals for a central tribunal or executive council, but these were not adopted. The problem was taken up again by the 1930 Lambeth Conference, which articulated the classic definition of the Communion:

The Anglican Communion is a fellowship, within the one Holy Catholic and Apostolic Church, of those duly constituted dioceses, provinces or regional Churches in communion with the See of Canterbury, that have the following characteristics:

(a) They uphold and propagate the Catholic and Apostolic faith and order as they are generally set forth in the Book of Common Prayer as authorized in their several Churches;

(b) They are particular or national Churches, and, as such, promote within each of their territories a national expression of Christian faith, life and worship; and

(c) They are bound together not by a central legislative and executive authority but by mutual loyalty sustained through the common counsel of the bishops in conference.

The Committee which produced this definition made clear that "being in communion with the See of Canterbury" did not make the Communion a monarchical structure. In fact, it went the other way in proposing "that the true constitution of the Catholic Church involves the principle of the autonomy of particular Churches based upon a common faith and order" (Resolution 48). But suppose one of the Provinces should fail to uphold the historic faith and order: what then? The Committee opined:

This freedom naturally and necessarily carries with it the risk of divergence to the point even of disruption. In case any such risk should actually arise, it is clear that the Lambeth Conference as such could not take any disciplinary action. Formal action would belong to the several Churches of the Anglican Communion individually; but the advice of the Lambeth Conference, sought before action is taken by the constituent Churches, would carry very great moral weight. And we believe in the Holy Spirit. We trust in His power working in every part of His Church to hold us together.[33]

In one sense, the confidence in God's guidance may have been justified in that the Communion has held together with somewhat muddled evangelical and catholic faith and order – until now. But what Lambeth 1930 feared has now come upon us. Its guidance seems to be: let Lambeth advise and Provinces act by breaking communion. That is what indeed seems to have happened since 2003.[34] A number of churches in the Global South have broken communion with the Episcopal Church on the basis of the latter's false teaching and practice and clear violation of the Lambeth Resolution. Several of these churches have logically taken in tow North American clergy, congregations and dioceses that have themselves departed from the Episcopal Church. The piecemeal way in which this has occurred, though consistent with the advice of Lambeth 1930, seems contrary to good order and has added to the sense of malaise within the Communion and scandal without.

"TO MEND THE NET"
A ROAD NOT TAKEN

In late 2001, Archbishops Drexel Gomez and Maurice Sinclair offered to the Primates' Meeting a proposal called "To Mend the Net."[35] This was an alternative to piecemeal breaking of communion. Had it been taken seriously and implemented, it might have avoided the chaos that ensued in the wake of the Gene Robinson debacle in 2003. This remarkable proposal with excellent supporting essays could have forged a way for Anglicans to face the specter foreseen dimly in 1930 that had come to haunt the Communion. As I see it, "To Mend the Net" answered two key questions in matters of Communion discipline. First, it asked: *what process should be employed* to confront, correct and exclude churches that have transgressed the limits of Anglican orthodoxy? Secondly, it asked: *who should drive the process?*

With regard to the first question, some of us have become inured to empty talk of process; there is, however, a biblical basis for a process of discipline. Jesus himself teaches that when a brother causes offense, he should be approached by the person offended, then by a small group (as in crisis intervention) and finally by the wider church (Matthew 18:15-18). Likewise "To Mend the Net"

141

recognized the virtue of a "strategy of time" in dealing with innovations in the church, as set out, for example, in the "reception process" for women's ordination. But it noted that "the strategy of time must work two ways: not only the avoidance of explosive reaction but also the enablement of timely intervention."[36]

With regard to the second question, "To Mend the Net" recalled a major theme of recent Lambeth Conferences: the *enhanced role of the Primates*. In a Resolution on "Issues concerning the whole Anglican Communion," Lambeth 1978 stated:

> The Conference advises member Churches not to take action regarding issues which are of concern to the whole Anglican Communion without consultation with a Lambeth Conference or with the episcopate through the Primates Committee, and requests the primates to initiate a study of the nature of authority within the Anglican Communion.[37]

A further Resolution in 1988 on the "Anglican Communion: Identity and Authority" continued the direction of the previous Conference in calling on the Primates' Meeting "to exercise an enhanced responsibility in offering guidance on doctrinal, and moral matters"[38]:

> We see an enhanced role for the primates as a key to a growth of interdependence within the Communion. We do not see any inter-Anglican jurisdiction as possible or desirable; an inter-Anglican synodical structure would be virtually unworkable and highly expensive. A collegial role for the primates by contrast could easily be developed, and their collective judgment and advice would carry considerable weight.[39]

Resolution III.6 of Lambeth 1998 reaffirmed once again the call for the Primates to exercise enhanced responsibility in doctrinal, moral and pastoral matters and further asks that the Primates' Meeting under the presidency of the Archbishop of Canterbury, include amongst its responsibilities positive encouragement to mission, intervention in cases of exceptional emergency, which are incapable of internal resolution within Provinces, and giving of guidelines on the limits of Anglican diversity, in submission to the sovereign authority of Holy Scripture and in loyalty to our Anglican tradition and formularies...

Drawing from these Resolutions, "To Mend the Net" was not only seeking a solution to the sexuality crisis but addressing the larger problem of authority and discipline in the Anglican Communion. It was offering a clear vision of conciliar governance; indeed its proposals were aimed to lead the Communion into clarifying the murky relationships among the Instruments of Unity and between the daughter churches and the Mother.

"To Mend the Net" brought together a strategy of time and the enhanced authority of the Primates in a concrete proposal, outlining steps to deal with "cases of exceptional emergency"[40]:

1. *Self-examination* by the Primates individually and corporately to test whether a particular doctrine or practice involves legitimate diversity or a violation of Christian truth.
2. An *educative role* by which the Primates explain their understanding of their role in the disciplinary process and the limits of diversity.
3. *Advanced sharing* of these matters with each other through annual meetings and constant communication.
4. *Preparation of guidelines* for right teaching and practice on any disputed issue, with a communal commitment that any minority group among the Primates will adhere to them.

5. *Godly admonition* to churches or bishops who refuse to observe the guidelines, with the intent of calling them back to the truth.
6. Relegation to *observer status* in international meetings for any members who refuse to respond adequately to the admonition.
7. Authorizing efforts at *continuing evangelization* in the jurisdiction so relegated, presumably outside its official leadership.
8. Formation and recognition of a *new jurisdiction* in the case of "prolonged and evidently permanent rejection of the guidelines," after which the rebellious jurisdiction would be excommunicated.[41]

"To Mend the Net" failed to receive the discussion and evaluation it deserved. This was not accidental. In a sense, it fell victim to the same dilemma that faced those who called for the first Lambeth Conference. Because the Archbishop of Canterbury and the Anglican Communion Office controlled the agenda of the Primates' Meeting held in Kanuga, North Carolina, in March 2001, "To Mend the Net" was never seriously considered by the Primates, being relegated to a fireside chat and then referred to the Inter-Anglican Theological and Doctrinal Commission. This Commission, which was appointed by Canterbury and did not share the urgency that motivated "To Mend the Net," proceeded to smother the proposal in the cradle. In the Commission's final Report, "To Mend the Net" is not even mentioned.[42]

As noted above, "To Mend the Net" attempted more than just dealing with Communion discipline. It also proposed a reform of Communion governance. Lambeth 1930 had argued that the Communion was more like the autocephalous churches of Orthodoxy than like the hierarchical structure of Rome. "To Mend the Net" envisioned a conciliar form of Communion governance by which Primates would work together to promote the mission of the church and to oversee its doctrine and discipline. One anomaly remained: "To Mend the Net" seemed to imagine that the Primates would function as a council of equals with the Archbishop of Canterbury as *primus inter pares*, but a supporting essay grounded the political authority of the Primates to discipline erring members in the power of the Archbishop to "gather" by invitation bishops to the Lambeth Conference and all other meetings of the Instruments.[43] In my opinion, this grounding was a flaw in the proposal, as it leaves a hierarchical mace in the hands of a single individual. As it turned out, the challenge to Canterbury's role came in spite of "To Mend the Net."

THE ROAD TO DAR AND BEYOND

The election and consecration of Bishop Gene Robinson opens a new chapter in our history. Robinson was the in-your-face embodiment of the Episcopal Church's rejection of the authority of Scripture and the Lambeth Conference. From the point of view of a number of African Primates, Robinson's elevation to the episcopate was the final signal after five years that the Episcopal Church was not turning back. They insisted on an emergency Primates' Meeting in London in October 2003 to deal with the crisis decisively, and afterward, one by one, Provincial bodies declared a state of broken or impaired communion with the Episcopal Church.

At the meeting in London, the new Archbishop of Canterbury, Rowan Williams, showing no interest in reviving the proposal for collective discipline in "To Mend the Net," begged for time to come up with another process.[44] In getting his way, he took the initiative away from those Primates who had come to London ready to act together against the Episcopal Church. The Archbishop not only delayed the disciplinary process but redefined it, using his "gathering" authority to appoint a "diverse" Commission to produce what became the Windsor Report. Some of the African Primates thought that this Report was intended to challenge the Episcopal Church on their behalf to repent or walk apart. Fifteen months later they brought that understanding to the Primates' Meeting at Dromantine in Ireland where the Windsor Report was received. As presented by the Lambeth establishment, on the contrary, the Windsor Report was merely the first step in the Windsor process, which led on to the Covenant process and the "indaba" process at Lambeth 2008.[45]

The two understandings of discipline and the roles of Canterbury and the Primates collided at the Primates' Meeting in Dar es Salaam in February 2007. The early rounds of the conflict went to Rowan Williams, who had invited Presiding Bishop Katherine Schori despite a recommendation in the Dromantine Communiqué that Episcopal Church officials refrain from attending Communion events until Lambeth 2008. He then set the agenda of the meeting with only four hours devoted to the Episcopal Church's reaction, and he endorsed a Joint Standing Committee report which claimed that the Episcopal Church had satisfied the conditions of the Windsor Report and the Dromantine Communiqué.

At this point, the Global South Primates interrupted the set agenda and pushed back.[46] The final Communiqué was surprisingly strong, in which the Primates "unanimously" made the following points:[47]

1. They repeated the words of Lambeth 1.10 to the effect that "[the Conference] upholds faithfulness in marriage between a man and a woman in

lifelong union, and believes that abstinence is right for those who are not called to marriage." They went on to warn that "a change in the formal teaching of any one Province would indicate a departure from the standard upheld by the Communion as a whole" (para. 11).

2. They concluded that "The Episcopal Church has departed from the standard of teaching on human sexuality accepted by the Communion in the 1998 Resolution 1.10" (para. 17). The Primates were reaching back through the intervening veils to the doctrinal standard itself.

3. They stated "the response of The Episcopal Church to the requests made at Dromantine has not persuaded this meeting that we are yet in a position to recognise that The Episcopal Church has mended its broken relationships." This statement was in direct contradiction to the judgment brought by Canterbury to the meeting.

4. They placed a series of disciplinary hurdles before the Episcopal Church. The first was the formation of a Pastoral Council for disaffected churches and dioceses, with members appointed by the Primates, Canterbury and the Presiding Bishop, which Council was to report to the Primates. The Primates also called for a cessation of all lawsuits by the Episcopal Church. Finally, they called for a clearer avowal by the Episcopal House of Bishops that they would not consecrate any practicing homosexual or authorize any same-sex blessing rite.

5. Then in a statement reminiscent of "To Mend the Net," step 7, they stated:

The Primates request that the answer of the House of Bishops is conveyed to the Primates by the Presiding Bishop by 30th September 2007.

If the reassurances requested by the House of Bishops cannot in good conscience be given, the relationship between The Episcopal Church and the Anglican Communion as a whole remains damaged at best, and this has consequences for the full participation of the Church in the life of the Communion.

The promulgation of the Dar Communiqué sent shock waves around the Communion. The Episcopal bishops were incensed and quickly moved to scuttle the Pastoral Scheme. Presiding Bishop Schori, soon after returning to New York, reneged on her commitment at Dar.[48] Several weeks later, the Bishop of Florida turned a priest and congregation out of its premises, against the express recommendation of the Panel of Reference and personal plea of Rowan Williams.[49] Clearly, Episcopal leaders had no scruples about exercising their version of ecclesiastical discipline administered through the secular courts.

For a few brief weeks, it appeared that a final separation was imminent. Then Canterbury struck back:

1. by issuing invitations to Lambeth 2008 to all Episcopal bishops except Gene Robinson (May 2007);

2. by accepting an invitation to the House of Bishops meeting in New Orleans (September 2007) and commissioning a report from the Joint Standing Committee that was not part of the Dar "process";[50]

3. by denying by word and deed that September 30 was a real deadline; and

4. by giving the Episcopal Church a weak pass in his Advent 2007 letter, which was all that was necessary to get it over the hurdles posed by the Dar Communiqué.

Most significantly, in the year intervening between Dar and Lambeth 2008, Archbishop Rowan Williams refused to call a follow-up Primates' Meeting, despite the clear expectation in the Communiqué that he would reconvene the Primates to judge the Episcopal Church's response and despite an urgent appeal from the Global South Steering Committee that he do so. Apparently the Archbishop had concluded from the Dar es Salaam Meeting that the Primates' authority had been enhanced too much and that they needed to be relegated to the B-league as an honorary council of advice.[51] The hope of Communion-wide discipline of those who had broken fundamental Christian doctrine had evaporated in a cloud of verbiage and dithering.

"THE ROAD TO LAMBETH" BECOMES THE ROAD TO JERUSALEM

I now back up to my involvement in the story. In March 2006, I received a letter from Archbishop Peter Akinola, as Chairman of the Council of Anglican Provinces of Africa (CAPA), asking me to work with several others to draft a document called "The Road to Lambeth."[52] Archbishop Akinola made clear from the beginning what the thrust of the document should be: an apologia for attending the Lambeth Conference only if the Episcopal Church had been properly disciplined beforehand. So we wrote:

The Anglican Communion is at a crossroad. The idea of a crossroad – a meeting and parting of two ways – is woven into the fabric of Scripture. The people of Israel is confronted with the choice of ways – the way of the

149

Covenant or the way of idolatry – and more often than not choose the latter (Jeremiah 6:16). So too Jesus describes a narrow road that leads to life and a broad avenue to perdition (Matthew 7:13). Hence the church must choose to walk in the light and turn from the darkness of sin and error (1 John 1:6-7).

Ephraim Radner has rightly insisted that the church find its guidance in the narrative of Scripture.[53] This, in fact, is what "The Road to Lambeth" attempted to do: to see the present crisis of the Communion in terms of the prophetic record of God's judgment on the corrupt and idolatrous kingdoms of Israel and Judah. One can find prophets like Isaiah who protested while remaining loyal to the existing establishment. One can also find those like Jeremiah who at a later point in that history concluded that God's judgment had fallen and that the only faithful road led into exile. "The Road to Lambeth" offered a genuine incentive to Canterbury as he prepared for the Primates' Meeting in Dar and the Lambeth Conference to use his "gathering" authority to exercise discipline against those who had stubbornly refused to adhere to Lambeth Resolution 1.10. When he sent out invitations to the Episcopal Church House of Bishops to Lambeth in May 2007, he chose to ignore the warning of "The Road to Lambeth" and instead adopted a strategy to divide and conquer the Global South coalition. The result was a Lambeth Conference lacking more than 250 bishops, mainly from the largest provinces in Africa.

When it became clear in late 2007 that Canterbury was not going to heed the call for Communion discipline, the coalition of provinces behind "The Road to Lambeth" – it had lost some members who chose to go to Lambeth and gained one diocese (Sydney) that had previously stayed on the sideline in the Anglican wars – decided to host an

150

alternative Conference, the Global Anglican Future Conference (GAFCON). So the churches whose voice was heard in "The Road to Lambeth" went into voluntary exile, an exile that took us along "ancient paths" to Jerusalem and the land of Jesus.

GAFCON was, in the view of those who attended, a movement in the Spirit. It was the fulfillment of more than a decade of global relationships that had been growing since the first Anglican Life and Mission Conference as well as in the Global South Encounters.

GAFCON ADDRESSES DOCTRINE AND DISCIPLINE

I was a member of the Theological Resource Group preparing for the Conference and then served on the Statement Committee at the Conference. In that capacity I want to comment briefly on how the "Statement on the Global Anglican Future," including the "Jerusalem Declaration," constitutes a response to the crisis of doctrine and discipline in the Communion. The section on "Global Anglican Contexts" presents a prophetic indictment, stating three facts about the state of the Communion:[54]

> The first fact is the acceptance and promotion within the provinces of the Anglican Communion of a different 'gospel' (cf. Galatians 1:6-8) which is contrary to the apostolic gospel... The second fact is the declaration by provincial bodies in the Global South that they are out of communion with bishops and churches that promote this false gospel... The third fact is the manifest failure of the Communion Instruments to exercise discipline in the face of overt heterodoxy.

Put simply, the acceptance of false doctrine has led to a crisis of discipline, which has been addressed regionally by provinces breaking communion with other provinces but which has failed at the highest level. The Communion fabric has been irreparably torn. It cannot simply be stitched together again. The Statement insists, like the writings of the latter Prophets of Israel, that it is necessary to accept these facts of God's judgment.

Just as the Prophets' oracles do not end in doom, neither does the Statement. It sees emerging out of the crisis a faithful remnant which looks to the future and to the God of the future.[55] And just as the Prophets claimed not to be traitors to Israel but its true heirs, so also the Fellowship of Confessing Anglicans (FCA) states clearly that it holds the title deeds of Anglican identity[56]:

> Our fellowship is not breaking away from the Anglican Communion. We, together with many other faithful Anglicans throughout the world, believe the doctrinal foundation of Anglicanism, which defines our core identity as Anglicans, is expressed in these words: <u>The doctrine of the Church is grounded in the Holy Scriptures and in such teachings of the ancient Fathers and Councils of the Church as are agreeable to the said Scriptures. In particular, such doctrine is to be found in the Thirty-nine Articles of Religion, the Book of Common Prayer and the Ordinal.</u>

The first half of the Jerusalem Declaration traces the way "back to the sources" of Christian identity: in the Gospel message that Jesus is Savior and Lord, in the authority of Scripture, in the Creeds, Councils and Articles of Religion, in the sacraments and threefold order of ministry. These affirmations are in one sense commonplace, but many of us can attest that they are routinely denied, compromised, or ignored in the churches of the West and even neglected in some churches of the Global South. The Jerusalem Declaration is not a reactionary call to do things the same old way; in its second half, it brings those sources to bear on the situation of the

Church in the world today, looking at the mandates for mission, marriage, justice and mercy, and ecumenism, and all in the perspective of Christ's coming Kingdom.

The Fellowship does not claim to have the final word on Christian doctrine. Clause 12 states:

> We celebrate the God-given diversity among us which enriches our global fellowship, and we acknowledge freedom in secondary matters. We pledge to work together to seek the mind of Christ on issues that divide us.

This clause is two-edged. On the one hand, it recognizes and even celebrates the diversity which resulted when Anglican Christianity went out from England to the ends of the earth and other issues brought up by modernity and post-modernity which require careful deliberation. On the other hand, it recognizes existing differences that could divide its members and commits the Fellowship to confer about them. Women's ordination and diaconal and lay presidency at the Eucharist are two such issues where there are diverse opinions and practices among the churches represented at Jerusalem. The ideal of Anglican comprehensiveness is not mistaken simply because it has been abused in the current climate of "diversity." It is possible that one side or one party among the orthodox may "win out" in future deliberations, or it may be that accommodations will be made for diverse traditions. But whatever comes from such discussions, it will be from people who share common Christian commitments and a desire to preserve the unity of the Spirit in the bond of peace.

Having laid the doctrinal foundation, the Jerusalem Declaration now turns in clause 13 to the matter of discipline:

We reject the authority of those churches and leaders who have denied the orthodox faith in word or deed. We pray for them and call on them to repent and return to the Lord.

This statement, I suggest, should be read in the light of "To Mend the Net" as a reassertion of the Anglican position on heresy and excommunication. It is not rushing to judgment. It is basing its judgment, in the case of the Episcopal Church, on more than a decade of intense debate and futile attempts to convince that church and its leaders to turn back. As noted above, most of the FCA primates represent churches that have formally broken communion with the Episcopal Church. What they are saying in this clause is that they will exercise this discernment collectively. This is a step forward from the stance taken by Lambeth 1930, a stance which I believe was overly influenced by the belief that the Communion was helpless to exercise final authority.

The excommunication clause of the Jerusalem Declaration leads directly to the final section of the Statement recommending that the FCA Primates' Council encourage the formation of a "Common Cause" province in North America. At this point, the Statement moves to the eighth and final step of "To Mend the Net," in which the repeated stubbornness of an existing province leads to the formation of a replacement province.[57]

TOWARD CONCILIAR COMMUNION

The "Global Anglican Future Statement" addresses the concerns for doctrine and discipline that have plagued the Anglican Communion for many years and critically of late. The formation of the FCA Primates' Council is equally an important step in restoring the direction of the Communion toward conciliar governance, a direction which had been well under way until it was interrupted by the Archbishop of Canterbury, especially since the Dar es Salaam meeting.

The idea of conciliar authority can be seen as inherent in the first Lambeth Conference, which was attended by 76 bishops, just double the number of Primates today. Once the Conference became established as a ten-year event, the need for a "consultative body" between times became apparent. The 1958 Conference designated the Primates and a few other bishops to constitute this body, but in 1968, the formation of the Anglican Consultative Council changed direction, including representative bishops, clergy and laity from various regions. Ten years later the Primates' Committee (now Meeting) itself was born out of a felt need for the provincial heads to confer.

Recently, Dr. Ephraim Radner gave an eloquent defense of conciliarism as a mode of Communion governance under the title "Wheels Within Wheels: The Promise and Scandal of Anglican Conciliarism." In this essay, he notes:

> With the emergence at the same time, in the 1950's and 1960's, of newly independent younger churches, in Africa and Asia, Anglicanism was poised to present itself in a new form, as a restored conciliarist body, a Communion of churches bound by deep Scriptural roots of Reformation and Catholic concern, and representing, more perhaps than any other church, the shape of the primitive ecclesial ideal.... The younger churches, many engaged in what appeared (and not only romantically) to be a reconnection with the thrill of the Primitive Church's evangelical ardor both Scripturally and evangelistically, were bringing to the staid structures of the Communion's gatherings a sense of divine vitality and power.[58]

This description is roughly accurate, but it should also be noted that the kind of collegiality among Global South primates and provinces has occurred in spite of opposition from the Anglican Communion bureaucracy and has been frequently deterred by the lack of ardor from Canterbury himself. The Letter of the Global South Primates attending Lambeth 2008 makes clear that this collegiality will continue, even if it has been temporarily weakened.[59]

Ephraim Radner has not been a supporter of the FCA movement. I do think, however, his recent paper, "Truthful Language and Orderly Separation," might form a basis for a convergence of the so-called "communion conservatives" and "federal conservatives, " represented today by the "Communion Partners" and the "Common Cause Partners."[60] In this essay, he notes the "assymetrical" responses of revisionists and conservatives to the issues plaguing the Communion. Liberals find change (repentance) "pragmatically impossible," having made commitments to the gay rights movement that cannot be retracted. Conservatives, on the other hand, are open to change, reformation, for the very reason that they look to Scripture and tradition for authority. Even the most intractable of these issues, such as women's ordination and diaconal and lay presidency at the Eucharist, are not beyond the bounds of "ecumenical" deliberation.

The Fellowship of Confessing Anglicans is one such conservative group. One can of course object that the FCA Primates' Council is a self-appointed body. Out of necessity, I would argue. It has not been formed with a sense of superiority or exclusiveness. Its members have said explicitly they are not leaving the Communion and they have stated that they do not consider themselves the only true Anglicans. In particular, they have extended the hand of fellowship to non-members in CAPA and the Global South movement. Contrary to some stereotypes, the FCA is eager to talk with fellow Anglicans.

This eagerness, I believe, applies to two particular issues raised by the 2008 Lambeth Conference. The first is the Anglican Communion Covenant. It is true that the FCA Theological Resource Group gave a negative evaluation of the St. Andrew's Covenant, overly negative in my opinion. This does not mean, however, that the FCA would not accept a Covenant at all. I myself was involved, at arm's length, in the Global South and then the Lambeth covenant drafts. I believe a well-wrought Covenant could provide the constitutional basis for a unified and missionary Communion.[61]

One key to a good Covenant is a clear identity statement, including doctrinal and moral essentials.[62] The Lambeth drafts to date take hesitant steps in this direction in the section on "Our Inheritance of Faith." The Jerusalem Declaration itself would, I think, constitute a far stronger statement, but the two are not that far apart. The second key is a clear and effective disciplinary process such as that proposed in "To Mend the Net." Here the St. Andrews Draft is a failure.[63] Dr. Radner, a member of the Drafting Group, seems to realize the need for a final "differentiation" when he writes:

> We must not fear the kind of clarity and accessible steps of implementation that would allow for such a differentiation [of orthodox and revisionist] if that is indeed the end towards which the present logics turn out to be moving.... A Covenant that makes clear that diversity has its limits and attaches consequences for violation of those limits preserves Communion while holding open the possibility of reconciliation.[64]

I believe such clarity is necessary to convince the FCA provinces to join in. If Lambeth cannot convince the largest provinces in the Communion to sign on, the Covenant process will have been an exercise in futility.

157

The second big issue has to do with the authority of the Archbishop of Canterbury. Does Rowan Williams share the vision of conciliar government? His lecture given in June 2008 and titled "Rome, Constantinople, and Canterbury: Mother Churches?" makes one wonder.[65] The very title recalls the "Branch theory" by which Roman Catholic, Orthodox and Anglican are all validated as apostolic streams as opposed to Protestantism, which is sectarian.[66] While lauding the "communion theology" of Orthodox theologians like Afanasiev and Zizioulas, who emphasize the sufficiency of the local bishop-in-church, Williams says that the pendulum has swung too far and needs to return to a recognition of the dependence of churches on a mother church:

> Hence the relation of local churches to a 'mother church' or a 'primatial church' is not a purely antiquarian matter. From very early in the church's history, certain local churches have been recognised as having had a distinctive *generative* importance... A local church is indeed at one level a community to which is given all the gifts necessary for being Christ's Body in this particular place; but among those gifts is the gift of having received the Gospel from others and being still called to receive it. Relation with the history of mission is part of the church's identity.

In his characteristically interrogative way, Rowan Williams asks if Canterbury is not such a mother church and that the Archbishop of Canterbury is a kind of Ecumenical Patriarch. The only problem is that this idea has never been affirmed in any authoritative Anglican documents. In 1897, the Lambeth Conference regularized the role of archbishop as metropolitan, but it is also made clear that Anglican archbishops do not owe allegiance to Canterbury.[67] The 1930 Lambeth Committee, which reflected high hopes for the ecumenical movement, likened

Communion governance to Orthodoxy, but it did not liken the Archbishop of Canterbury to the Ecumenical Patriarch.[68]

In my view, conciliar governance can coexist with a lead bishop who is *Primus inter pares* – a "focus of unity" in the sense of representing the communion to those outside it – but not with a lead bishop who rules over his brother bishops by fiat or through a manipulative bureaucracy.[69] The "gathering power" of the Archbishop of Canterbury is a holdover of Crown and Empire that must be given up if the Instruments of Anglican Communion – and here I see primarily, Canterbury, Primates and Lambeth Conference – are to function as "wheels within wheels."[70]

Rowan Williams is said to be influenced by his dialectical view of God's action in history. In one sense, the ground is prepared in North America for a resolution. The Episcopal Church and Anglican Church of Canada have knowingly departed from the biblical and catholic consensus on marriage and sexuality – and other classic doctrines if the truth be told. The FCA Primates have, for good reason, broken communion with the Episcopal Church and Anglican Church of Canada. With the formation of the Anglican Church in North America (ACNA), the establishment of an alternative province is, for all intents and purposes, a *fait accompli*. In the current politics of standoff the question arises: how soon this church will be recognized by the "Instruments" of the Communion? Certainly the betting man's wager is that it will take some time, given the political alignments in the Communion, but if Canterbury would make the first move and graciously recognize the ACNA, it would be a huge step toward clarifying true loyalties in the Communion.

I have been critical of the actions of Rowan Williams as Archbishop, which I think derive from his personal theological convictions. Nevertheless, I think he also wishes the peace of the Communion and recognizes that the primary responsibility for disorder rests with the revisionists. As Radner says, the revisionist leaders of the Episcopal Church will simply not change and will not brook opposition. Their willingness to walk apart will become clear as day as soon as they lose their claim on Canterbury's favor.[71] Is it possible that the brazen arrogance and lawlessness of Katherine Schori and her cronies toward Robert Duncan and Jack Iker may open his eyes to the impossibility of reconciliation within the old order of things? Many people in the Communion have been hoping and praying that in the end Rowan Williams will come through for orthodoxy and the greater good of the Communion. We shall see, perhaps at the upcoming Primates' Meeting in February 2009. If not then, give the Episcopal Church a few more years – or months – and it may accomplish the task on its own.

CONCLUSION

In this essay, I have tried to narrate the recent history of the Episcopal Church and the Anglican Communion according to the grid-lines of doctrine and discipline. I maintain that the breakdown of orthodox doctrine in the former over the past half-century caused a crisis of discipline within the latter. The result has been a heretical church and a dysfunctional Communion. The crisis has also revealed a long-standing flaw in the governance of the Communion by an anomalous Mother Church and its Primate, anomalous in its Establishment form, in its late-modern cultural accommodation, and in its residual colonial mindset. This is the Communion that is no more.

The recent conference in Jerusalem concluded: "We believe the Anglican Communion should and will be reformed around the biblical gospel and mandate to go into all the world and present Christ to the nations." The churches that gathered in Jerusalem do not want to go it alone. Like all Anglicans, they hold a high view of the catholicity of Christ's Body, and they believe that God has gifted the Communion with potential to reach out to the many nations. The Prophets of Israel always followed up their oracles of judgment with words of consolation and restoration for God's chosen people. I believe that the history of decline and fall has another chapter coming, one in which the Lord will address our Communion with love and hope for a new beginning.

> "Is not Ephraim my dear son, the child in whom I delight? Though I often speak against him, I still remember him. Therefore my heart yearns for him; I have great compassion for him," declares the LORD. Set up road signs; put up guideposts. Take note of the highway, the road that you take. Return, O Virgin Israel, to your towns. (Jeremiah 31:20-21)

ESSAY 5
LAMBETH DIARY 1998
A WEEK TO REMEMBER

I attended the Lambeth Conference as part of a team from the American Anglican Council. Our goal was to help the orthodox bishops, especially those from the Global South, to understand the issues involved in the sexuality debate and to penetrate the political and media maze erected by the Anglican Communion Office. After much initial haggling, I was given a pink "Media" badge and was allowed into the daily, highly-orchestrated press briefings. I published an online "Lambeth Diary" for each of the three weeks of the Conference. I include here the third week's diary as an eyewitness report of how the climactic vote on what became Resolution I.10 on Human Sexuality proceeded and came to fruition.

This has been an historic session" announced the moderator Archbishop Robin Eames as he announced that Resolution I.10 [or A31] on Human Sexuality had passed by the margin of 526 for, 70 against, and 45 abstaining.

Indeed it was. And the outcome was hardly assured until the day itself, Wednesday, August 5. Despite pronouncements of "a spirit of unity descending" by the *Lambeth Daily*, there had been frantic backroom dealing, which was brought to a halt at the eleventh hour by George Carey, the Archbishop of Canterbury, whose "intervention" led to a landmark Resolution on Human Sexuality.

THE SETTING

While bishops debated some of the other 108 Resolutions, the Rev. Dr. Arnold Klukas gave some of us a tour of the Cathedral. Arnie wrote his doctoral thesis on the architectural symbolism of Canterbury Cathedral, which is a kind of catechism in stone. He pointed out, for instance, the typology of the windows, which juxtaposes Old Testament saints with Jesus Christ and with Thomas Becket, martyr and exemplar of the Christian disciple. Much of the cult of Thomas Becket had to be purged at the Reformation, but the cathedral endures as a sign that we are to live out the life of Christ in our own day following the patterns of faith given in Scripture and in the lives of the saints who looked to Jesus as their pioneer. Such a message seems quite relevant to the challenges facing the Church today.

Canterbury has been comfortably full of secular pilgrims. Every time I am in England I am stunned by how secular a country it is, more like Europe than the U.S., burdened with the legacy of an ideal, the Christian commonwealth, now long defunct. The Church of England, writes Bishop Colin Buchanan, "loves fantasy and unreality, invents rationales that no one can actually believe, conceives that fudge is better than principle on many issues, expands minor issues into major principles, and hates having to grapple with reality." This phrase occurred to me later in the week as Resolution after numbing Resolution trudged its way through the Conference. Can Resolutions breathe life into a somnolent Body? Hardly, no more than they can on New Year's Day.

Yet several of the Resolutions may signal a new day and a new locus of authority for this historic body. The British newspapers have not been reticent about declaring a "shift to the South" (and that's not whistling Dixie!). There is a split in the Communion that is missiological, between those whose faith is young and confident and eloquent and those who are encumbered by a decadent Westernism. The latter is embodied in the ponderous "Virginia Report," recited by episcopal bureaucrats like a mantra, as much as by the bombastic blasphemies of Bishop Spong.

As we walked the stone streets, I remembered that last summer the Rev. Jon Shuler had led a team on an evangelistic campaign here. I recalled that the first archbishop of Canterbury had been a missionary whose goal was reaching the pagan tribes of Britain for Christ. All the Cathedrals and all the Resolutions should not replace this primary focus of the call of Jesus to raise up children to Abraham, to make disciples and witnesses to his Name.

THE EVENTS

The third week is set aside for debate in full session. The plenary sessions began on Tuesday; by Monday the proposed list of Resolutions was out. Moses had 10, Luther 95, John Spong 12, but despite all efforts to reduce the number of Resolutions, there were 108, which guarantees that they will be seldom read by laypeople. Many of them were "agreed," requiring no debate and seem something like "pork barrel" legislation that representatives can take to the folks back home.

FIRST SKIRMISHES IN THE SEXUALITY DEBATE

As at Gettysburg in the Civil War, the Battle of the Sexualities went for three days. The first skirmish happened off-stage on Monday. On Sunday evening when the list of Resolutions appeared, the Resolution from the official "section" on Sexuality appeared in a form no one recognized. It seemed to be a conservative proposal minus the phrase "*in consequence we cannot legitimize or bless, or ordain those involved in, same gender unions.*" Conservatives were furious, claiming that the section chairman Bishop Duncan Buchanan [not to be confused with Colin Buchanan above] had unilaterally gutted it.

The story became more bizarre. Buchanan claimed (rightly) that the section had not had time to complete their Resolution and that he had simply inserted something to "hold a space." On Monday, then, the section set down to work and came up with another Resolution (labelled A 31). This Resolution included the phrase "*cannot advise the legitimizing or blessing same sex unions nor ordaining those involved in same gender unions.*" It also stated that the Conference, "*in view of the teaching of Scripture, upholds faithfulness in marriage between a man and a woman in lifelong union, and believes that abstinence is right for those who are not called to marriage.*"

On Tuesday morning, Bishop Buchanan circulated the A31 Resolution at the daily press conference and announced that *this* was the Resolution that would be debated the next day. As the press grilled him on this Resolution, it became clear that it would be considered a conservative statement. The original "three ways" typology, which included long-term homosexual partnerships as an option, had now been dropped in favor of two ways: marriage and chastity.

The meaning of "chastity" then came up. While most spokesmen interpreted it to mean abstinence, one imaginative bishop from Canada suggested that it simply meant "purity," which is in the eye of the beholder. Sigh! There goes another fine English word. I'd much rather name a daughter Chastity than Abstinence; but then there was also a time I would have considered naming a daughter Gay too.

It was settled, or so it seemed. The section that included Bishops Jim Stanton and Jack Spong at last had a

Resolution. Or did it? The "process" took a final bizarre turn. In the mid-afternoon Tuesday, there suddenly came an announcement that the faceless "Steering Committee" had declared that the earlier printed Resolution and not Buchanan's "A 31" would be the version debated the next day. This smacked so clearly of manipulation that everyone was in an uproar. Conservatives, of course, felt betrayed, but so did liberals from the section.

THE TURNING POINT

"Integrity" [the gay lobby] supporters arrived on Wednesday with smiles on their faces. The sexuality debate seemed doomed to deadlock. The revisionists had two things going for them. First, the printed Resolution was so bland that it could be easily spun as a signal to go ahead with the gay agenda. Secondly, the entire debate had been allotted but two hours and there were six Resolutions to deal with.

Four of these Resolutions came from "regional" caucuses. All these Resolutions were orthodox, and the two from Africa were very strongly worded, calling revisionists to repentance and speaking of the gay agenda as "evangelical suicide." Many of the Third World bishops were saying, "Let's pass them all." This was not likely to happen in a two hour Western-style debate. More likely, none would get a majority. Anticipating this possibility, the revisionists entered an Amendment (not printed and therefore something of a sleeper) that would have referred all the Resolutions to the Primates and the ACC. In effect, the Lambeth Conference, on a major matter of principle, would have abdicated responsibility in favor of a study commission. And we Americans know from experience how that works out – *nada*.

One further sidelight. The debate had originally been scheduled for 2:30 pm Wednesday but was then postponed until 3:30. This rattled conservatives because it was known that up to 90 Church Army bishops were leaving for London at 4 pm to see the Queen Mum, who turned 99 that day. Since most Church Army bishops are conservative, this looked like just one more ploy. As it turned out, the Church Army bishops stayed for the debate.

What happened next is only known in bare outline. Apparently, the Archbishop of Canterbury became aware of the switcheroo made by the Steering Committee. He also began to heed reports that African bishops were determined to pass a clear Resolution or else – and that the "or else" might include a walkout. Up to that point, the Archbishop had not been active in the debate. He has made it clear that he holds to traditional Christian teaching on sexuality and is deeply concerned for the unity of the Anglican Communion. These concerns apparently coalesced in such a way that by the Wednesday afternoon of the debate the Integrity folks were no longer smiling. The Archbishop had apparently insisted that the process should be set up so that the Conference might express its mind. This is what happened.

THE ROUT

The sexuality debate was solemn and orderly. With a few exceptions. One Pakistani bishop went over the top suggesting that Lambeth 2008 would be asked to approve blessing of cat lovers and their pets. A Nigerian bishop afterward tried to lay hands on Richard Kirker, a homosexual advocate, to cure him of his addiction. The media of course picked up on these excesses. But the vast majority of speakers, such as Bishop Eustace Kaminyire of Uganda and Archbishop Donald Mtetemela of Tanzania, were measured and articulate. Bishop John Sentamu was particularly delightful as he extolled "the glories of abstinence." Archbishop Robin Eames conducted the session with clarity and dignity.

Bishop Adebiyi of Nigeria told the delegates that the African church was simply upholding the faith brought to them by missionaries. "The CMS brought Christianity to Western African about 150 years ago," he told the delegates. "And when the CMS came, they came holding the Bible, telling us that what they believe is what has come from the word of God. And, so our forefathers meticulously accepted the Christian faith and religion that was tied to the word of God and the Scriptures. Therefore, we accept the Scripture as the most authentic we should follow."

Delegates upon arrival received a clearly spelled-out "Notice Paper," outlining their choices among Resolutions. In fact, the major shape of the final Resolution had already been crafted by a compromise among evangelical Westerners and the Africans. The printed Resolution was quickly replaced by A 31, which then became the base text for a series of amendments.

The bellwether amendment came from Archbishop Mtetemela, which added the phrase *while rejecting homosexual practice as incompatible with Scripture.* This amendment focused the concerns of the Africans about the whole issue. As they have said repeatedly, homosexuality is not their problem and they do not want to waste time talking about it. But they do care passionately for the authority of Scripture, and they saw the West, and the American Church in particular, as endangering this core principle.

To be honest, I was not sure, before I began to meet them in numbers this past year, whether the Third World bishops had the will to stand up and fight on the sexuality question. Some people feared, totally without warrant as it

169

turns out, that they might be pressured into acquiescence out of financial dependence on the West. Just the opposite is true. They saw the issue threatening the Communion clearly, and they never wavered in their determination to speak to it. The African Resolution, as it turned out, was the best of the lot because it saw the issue in biblical terms as involving sin and repentance.

And they were of one mind. The speakers for Resolution A31 and the amendments to it were multi-cultural, whereas the speakers against were very white and hailed exclusively from the Western provinces. They later accused us American conservatives of buying votes with chicken barbecues. This is a demeaning accusation against the Third Word delegates, many of whom have put their lives on the line for the Gospel. Opponents who said this are not, in my opinion, racists, but they are cultural imperialists. They cannot believe that someone who holds to a straightforward biblical morality is either not "superstitious" (a la animism) or "fundamentalistic" (a la Islamic jihad).

Mtetemela's key amendment passed 390 to 190. After that, conservatives got two more victories. They amended "chastity" to "abstinence" in order to close the linguistic loophole. They also changed the condemnation of "homophobia" to a condemnation of "the irrational fear of homosexuals." I thought this was a particularly nice touch, suggested by the Africans. Finally, Bishop Richard Harries of Oxford spoke eloquently on behalf of the Kuala Lumpur Statement, and reference to it was added.

Those who opposed the amended Resolution never addressed the core principles of Scripture, or God's purposes for male and female. Their main arguments were that the Resolution threatened the unity of the Communion and sent negative signals to gays and lesbians.

They did pass an amendment calling for the Church to listen to the experience of homosexual people (I assume this will include celibate and ex-gay people). When the final Resolution came to a vote, there was remarkable unity – 526 for and only 70 against – to constitute what Archbishop Carey later called the "mind of the Church."

THE AFTERMATH: A PERSONAL ANECDOTE

The aftermath of the historic vote on Lambeth Resolution I.10 requires a separate history and the ramifications of that vote are continuing to the present day. I shall, however, sum up with a personal anecdote.

I watched the debate over Resolution I.10 unfold via a video feed in a large tent on the campus of University of Kent. I was sitting close to the exit of the tent, and when the final vote was taken and the session adjourned, I walked out almost in a daze. Right opposite the tent, there stood several long tables filled with bottles of the local brew called "Bishops Finger Ale." In my euphoria, I grabbed a complimentary bottle and took a swig. Before I knew it, I was being interviewed on camera, not about the Lambeth Resolution, but about the virtues of the Bishops Finger.

As it turns out, "bishops finger" refers to the signposts in Kent, which consist in vertical signage on a narrow white arrow. These were the same signs that Churchill removed after Dunkirk so as to deter the expected Nazi invaders.

Anyway, it occurred to me later that there was some symbolism to the bishops' finger. Bishops are ordained to defend the catholic and apostolic faith, to protect the sheep from false shepherds, and to point the way to heaven. The bishops of the Anglican Communion had done this on August 5, and they had done so at the historic font of Anglicanism, in Canterbury. Indeed the Archbishop of Canterbury himself had facilitated the passage of Lambeth I.10.

Unfortunately, Canterbury was not to stand firm. Two days after the vote, I listened to an interview with George Carey on BBC Radio 4. As one might expect, the interviewer was all sneers about the primitive and homophobic action taken by the Third World bishops. Carey was quick to assure the interviewer that Lambeth I.10 was not the end but the beginning of an ongoing dialogue about sexuality in the Communion. In my view, this was precisely the wrong reading of the Resolution. As I see it, the bishops were saying to those who were promoting the sexuality gospel: "Cease and desist, and conform to the biblical norms of marriage and abstinence." Archbishop Carey's – and his successors' – failure to communicate that message was to have destructive after-effects, which I have documented elsewhere.

ESSAY 6

LAMBETH SPEAKS PLAINLY

LAMBETH RESOLUTION I.10
WITH INTRODUCTION AND COMMENTARY

(2000)

It became clear immediately after Lambeth 1998 that the Episcopal Church as a whole had no intention to conform to the teaching of Resolution I.10. In fact, as it prepared for the 2000 General Convention, the Church's Standing Commission on Liturgy and Music produced a collection of essays clearing the ground for various free-form same-sex liturgies. I helped to edit a counter-collection titled *Mixed Blessings: Why Same-Sex Blessings Will Divide the Church* and contributed an essay of my own expounding the meaning of Resolution I.10.

T he Anglican Communion, in the providence of God, has been thrust into an identity crisis. At its inception the Church of England was guided by the Bible, doctrine (Articles of Religion), worship (Book of Common Prayer), and church order (Establishment). The planting and growth to independence of daughter churches throughout the world stretched but did not break this identity, as the Lambeth Quadrilateral, use of locally adapted Prayer Books, and decennial Lambeth Conferences built on the original foundation.

Anglicanism has had mixed success in coping with the modernist critique of Christianity. Some have questioned the "integrity of Anglicanism," especially in the Western Provinces (U.K. and North America). At the same time, vigorous evangelical Anglican provinces have emerged in the Provinces of "the South," which now greatly outnumber the original churches. The differences between West and South came to a head at the Lambeth Conference of 1998. While the Conference retained much of the civility of the first Lambeth tea party, the issue of homosexuality ignited a kind of Boston Tea Party, with bishops from the South demanding the right to express their understanding of Biblical teaching on the subject.

The resulting Resolution (I.10) is striking for its theological clarity and pastoral charity, or so I argue below. Nevertheless the Resolution has evoked great hostility and non-compliance in the West, of which the Report and Resolution of the Standing Committee on Liturgy and Music is the latest example. One sign of the bite which Lambeth Resolution I.10 has had is the fact that *nowhere in the entire SCLM Report is it ever mentioned.* Furthermore, the end result of the proposed General Convention Resolution will be a two-headed church, with Lambeth-abiding dioceses and Lambeth-rejecting dioceses.

I wrote the following piece shortly after Lambeth 1998 to expound its "plain sense." I hope this exposition will help clarify the reasons that the identity crisis facing the Episcopal Church and the Anglican Communion cannot be avoided.

INTRODUCTION
THE SIGNIFICANCE OF THE VOTE
ON HUMAN SEXUALITY

Everyone knew it. The media knew it. The bishops, liberal and conservative, from the West and from the Third World, knew it. The vote on homosexuality was to be the defining moment of the international Lambeth Conference of Anglican bishops. When the time for the debate on the "human sexuality" resolutions came, a sense of solemnity descended on the full assembly of 700 bishops on the afternoon of August 5, 1998.

Shortly before he raised his hand in favor of Resolution I.10 on Human Sexuality, Archbishop George Carey said he hoped Lambeth 1998 would not be remembered only for sex. Perhaps his wish will be partially fulfilled: the Conference did indeed pass a number of significant resolutions – on mission, on euthanasia, on international debt. But only partially, because homosexuality was the presenting symptom of an identity crisis that had to be dealt with in order for the Anglican Communion to speak with credibility on these other issues and prepare itself to present the Gospel in the next century.

The deeper question facing the Communion was whether Anglicans hold certain truths to be fundamental. To do so is not fundamentalism but the Anglican "middle way" (*via media*): "In essentials, unity; in non-essentials, liberty; in all things, charity." The norm of sex only in marriage is one of those essential truths. An earlier Lambeth Conference, addressing the sexual revolution of Sigmund Freud, had not flinched from stating an unequivocal position:

> Recognizing that to live a pure and chaste life before and after marriage is, for both sexes, the unchangeable Christian standard, attainable and attained through the help of the Holy Spirit by men and women of every age, the Conference desires to proclaim the universal obligation of this standard, and its vital importance as an essential condition of human happiness. (Lambeth 1920, Resolution 66)

If Lambeth 1920 was correct that marriage is the *exclusive and unchangeable* Christian standard, then those who repudiate this standard do not stand in the middle way but are outside the bounds of historic Christian (and Anglican) teaching. The question facing the bishops in 1998 was whether the historic standard was changeable. And if this teaching were changeable, what other unchangeable doctrines could be revised by some region or church of the Communion?

The sexuality issue forced the bishops to ask an even deeper question: by what authority does the Church determine what is essential truth and what is not? The answer given in the past has been clear: *the Bible is our primary authority* in matters of faith and morals. The Anglican Communion can condone or endorse a sexual practice that is forbidden in both Old and New Testaments only by changing its historic foundation.

On August 5, the bishops at Lambeth answered the question by passing a strong, clear statement on human sexuality by a majority of 526 to 70, with 45 abstaining. By this act, they restated the historic teaching of the Christian Church and reaffirmed the foundation of that teaching in the revealed will of God in Holy Scripture.

The Times of London called the resolution a "surprisingly trenchant verdict." The resolution is unusually free of the jargon found in many official church statements that can be "spun" in various directions. Resolution I.10 has been universally understood as a reaffirmation of the Church's traditional teaching. Only those who refuse to read it as a whole can find it "paradoxical," as Presiding Bishop Frank Griswold has characterized it. It invites the kind of conversation that begins with a moral compass: that *God created human nature with the aim that the two sexes should become one flesh in exclusive and lifelong marriage.*

The Lambeth Conference had its defining moment when it passed Resolution I.10, spelling out the biblical, historic, and normative teaching of the Church. Now we in the Episcopal Church face our defining moment, whether to embrace this teaching or to spurn it.

THE TEXT

This Conference:

(a) commends to the Church the subsection report on Human Sexuality;

Resolution I.10 was accompanied by a report from a group ("subsection") of bishops who met during the first two weeks of the Conference. The subsection on human sexuality was the most volatile and publicized group at Lambeth, reflecting the deep divisions on homosexuality that exist between some Western bishops and the Third World bishops (Bishop Spong, for instance, was in this subsection). Hence the subsection report, unlike the Resolution I.10, reads at times like an opinion poll. Nevertheless, when all was said and done, the subsection presented the Conference with the resolution that was finally passed (with clarifying amendments). Significantly, the subsection *did not issue a minority report.*

The subsection report reaffirmed Lambeth 1920's "unchangeable Christian standard" of sexual morality by rejecting a preliminary proposal to see some non-marital relationships, including homosexual partnerships and polygamous marriages, as faithful to God's will. The subsection report commends *only two ways of sexual faithfulness: marriage and chastity.* (Because a few bishops sought to define "chastity" as allowing homosexual relationships, the Conference made the meaning absolutely clear by changing "chastity" to "abstinence" in the final resolution.)

(b) in view of the teaching of Scripture, upholds faithfulness in marriage between a man and a woman in lifelong union, and

believes that abstinence is right for those who are not called to marriage;

Here the bishops state their key moral premise that *homosexuality is to be judged on the basis of God's design for marriage.* By speaking of a "call" to marriage, the resolution raises holy matrimony above its biological and civic purposes to signify the "mystery of Christ and his Church." At the same time, the resolution holds *both marriage and abstinence to be genuine ways of following Jesus.* Because marriage is so honored by God, abstinence gains equal honor as self-denial for the sake of Christ and his kingdom. The call to abstinence may or may not be lifelong, but in a special way it too serves as a sign – of single-minded devotion to the Master.

The moral premise is made *in view of the teaching of Scripture.* The Conference intends to make clear that moral norms are based on biblical authority. *Scripture comes first.* In a separate Resolution (III.1) the Conference "reaffirms the primary authority of the Scriptures, according to their testimony and supported by our own historic formularies." Two of these historic formularies are relevant here: Article XX of the Thirty-Nine Articles declares that "it is not lawful for the Church to ordain anything that is contrary to God's Word written." The Lambeth Quadrilateral, adopted by the Lambeth Conference in 1888 as the basis of Christian unity, holds that the Bible is "the rule and standard of faith."

The resolution is not treating the Bible merely as a rule book. The Bible tells the Great Story of God's salvation in Jesus Christ. But a story without rules is like a house without foundation and beams. God our Father teaches his children, saying "this way and not that way." He does this for our good. With Lambeth 1920, the bishops are saying that the reason we must accept the marital standard is "its vital importance as an essential condition of human happiness."

(c)   recognises that there are among us persons who experience themselves as having a homosexual orientation. Many of these are members of the Church and are seeking the pastoral care, moral direction of the Church, and God's transforming power for the living of their lives and the ordering of relationships. We commit ourselves to listen to the experience of homosexual persons and we wish to assure them that they are loved by God and that all baptised, believing and faithful persons, regardless of sexual orientation, are full members of the Body of Christ;

This phrase carefully *defines homosexuality as a matter of self-image.* It asserts neither that all homosexuals have chosen to be that way nor that they are born that way. By so defining "orientation," the Resolution acknowledges the psychological and social dynamics of homosexuality without thereby accepting them as right or inevitable and unchangeable. Clearly some think of themselves as homosexuals and have built their lives around this understanding. The Church's pastoral ministry must take this reality seriously.

The resolution makes clear that *homosexual inclinations or orientation are not incompatible with membership in the Church.* All Christians without distinction are offspring of God by creation and sons of God by adoption and grace (Acts 17:28; Galatians 4:4-8). The resolution goes on to suggest that "homosexual persons" may be led to the Church out of their experience, as are all others who know their need for God. But because Christians are not to come to the Church "for solace only, and not for strength; for pardon only and not for renewal," the resolution couples the Church's welcome to all with the challenge of spiritual

179

transformation (Romans 12:1-2). A pastoral vision for "homosexual persons" might include reorientation to a heterosexual self-image or the building of chaste friendships with people of the same or opposite sex.

In light of the biblical moral norms, this clause *challenges the Church to help those who think of themselves as homosexual to frame their self-understanding in terms set by the Gospel.* The call to listen to the experience of homosexual persons was added by amendment and accepted by the majority of bishops in the context of the whole resolution. They recognize that homosexual orientation is psychologically complex and socially constructed in such a way that the Church must consider carefully how to bring the health of the Gospel to people so oriented. While pastors are urged to listen patiently to those who think of themselves as homosexual, their call is to bring such persons to understand themselves simply as disciples of Jesus, committed to him and to his standards of holiness.

(d)   while rejecting homosexual practice as incompatible with Scripture, calls on all our people to minister pastorally and sensitively to all irrespective of sexual orientation and to condemn irrational fear of homosexuals, violence within marriage and any trivialization and commercialization of sex;

This clause, like the whole resolution, balances moral principle and pastoral exhortation. Third World bishops insisted on including the words *rejecting homosexual practice as incompatible with Scripture* in order to make clear that pastoral sensitivity must include the call to repentance and discipline. Their amendment, which carried by a vote of 390 to 180, encapsulates the conviction of many bishops that the authority of Scripture undergirds Anglican teaching and identity. These words declare the norm to be absolute and unchangeable and close the door on any "discontinuous" alternatives, such as "same-sex unions."

The bishops are speaking the truth in love in the current context of the "sexual revolution" in the West. They are calling on the Church to be leaven in the midst of a culture that has replaced love of God with various substitutes. It is therefore appropriate that they mention other manifestations of disorder in society such as bigotry, violence, and pornography. Third World bishops proposed and passed an amendment of the original resolution, changing the word "homophobia" to the "irrational fear of homosexuality." Thus the resolution states clearly that hatred and prejudice against homosexuals is not godly, but it rejects the political use of "homophobia" to depict opponents of the gay-rights movement as driven by dark inner fears and hatred.

(e)   cannot advise the legitimising or blessing of same sex unions nor ordaining those involved in same gender unions;

This clause is *a pointed challenge from the Anglican Communion to the Episcopal Church to adhere to the biblical and historic teaching on sexuality.* The word "advise" acknowledges the fact that the Lambeth Conference cannot force member churches to conform, but the resolution was clearly intended to˙ be heeded and responded to. The regional resolution from Central and East Africa was quite blunt at this point: "Those persons who practise homosexuality and live in promiscuity, as well as those Bishops who knowingly ordain them or encourage these practices, act contrary to the Scriptures and the teaching of the Church. We call upon them to repent."

(f)   requests the Primates and the ACC [Anglican Consultative Council] to establish a means of monitoring the work done on the

subject of human sexuality in the Communion and to share statements and resources among us;

The bishops of the Communion are highly critical of the unilateral actions of Episcopal bishops in permitting the ordination of practicing homosexuals and performance of same-sex "blessings." They believe these actions, by rejecting historic Christian teaching, have threatened the unity of the Communion as well as ecumenical relationships with the worldwide Christian fellowship. They intend to give their Western colleagues time to rethink their position, but they expect the leaders of the Episcopal Church to answer to the formulation of Anglican teaching in this resolution. *Ultimately, they are calling for conformity.* Hence the monitoring process by the Primates (i.e., the archbishops) and the Anglican Consultative Council, which are the oversight bodies between Lambeth Conferences.

(g) notes the significance of the Kuala Lumpur Statement on Human Sexuality and the concerns expressed in resolutions IV.26, V.1, V.10, V.23 and V.35 on the authority of Scripture in matters of marriage and sexuality and asks the Primates and the ACC to include them in their monitoring process.

There were five substantive resolutions on the floor at Lambeth in addition to Resolution I.10, all of them from the Third World churches and all of them reaffirming the historic teaching of the Church. Some bishops wanted to pass them all, but by way of compromise they accepted this clause as making clear the harmony among the resolutions. Conversely, *there is no minority resolution that differs from the normative teaching found in all these resolutions.* Thus while individual bishops voted against the resolution, the official position of the Anglican Communion is a clear and unequivocal reaffirmation of the biblical teaching.

ESSAY 7

THE JERUSALEM DECLARATION
A COMMENTARY FOR ANGLICANS IN UGANDA
(2008)

The Jerusalem Declaration has been widely seen by the members of GAFCON and the Global South network to express the beliefs and commitments of the Global Anglican Communion.

Shortly after the Jerusalem conference in 2008, I gathered with colleagues of the Bishop Tucker School of Divinity and Theology at Uganda Christian University and we produced a catechism or commentary on the Jerusalem Declaration. It was intended for clergy and catechists, who might then instruct the people of the church. In order to make it widely available, we translated it into four local languages: Luganda, Rwankole-Rukiga, Lugisu, and Akoli. The Commentary was made available on the University website to be copied and used free of charge. Unfortunately, there was little follow-up, and I do not think it achieved its goal.

It may seem rather localized in its address, i.e., to Ugandans only. However, it seems to me that it would be quite easy for teachers in other settings to make some adaptations and apply it to Anglicans in their region.

T he Anglican Communion is the family of Christian churches historically related to the Church of England. Anglican Christianity came to Uganda in 1875 with the first missionaries sent from the Church Mission

Society in England. After a time of troubles that led to the death of Bishop Hannington and the Uganda Martyrs in 1886, the Church of Uganda (Anglican) began to spread from Buganda to other regions of East Africa. The East African Revival, beginning in 1925 and continuing to this day, relit the flame of Anglican Christianity, so that today nine million Ugandans call themselves Anglican.

Anglican Christianity grew and prospered after the close of the colonial era. In 1965, the first Ugandan archbishop, the Most Rev. Erica Sabiti, was elected, and the Church of Uganda became an independent "Province" of the Anglican Communion. The Anglican Communion now has 38 Provinces on six continents representing 80 million Anglicans. Bishops of the various churches normally attend the Lambeth Conference of Anglican bishops held every ten years in Canterbury, England. However, Lambeth 2008 was different.

Over the past decade the Anglican Communion has been troubled by the actions of churches in North America. Despite a clear statement by the Lambeth Conference in 1998 that the practice of homosexuality is "incompatible with Scripture," the Episcopal Church in the USA elected and consecrated a practicing homosexual as bishop in 2003. The bishops of the churches in the Global South (Africa, Asia and South America) strongly denounced this action, but the Archbishop of Canterbury, the nominal head of the Communion, has been unwilling or unable to stop the practice. For this reason, bishops in Africa, including the House of Bishops of the Church of Uganda, warned him that they would not attend the 2008 Lambeth Conference if the renegade American bishops were invited. When he went ahead and invited them, these bishops organized a separate "Global Anglican Future Conference" in Jerusalem in June 2008. More than one hundred bishops and wives and other representatives from the Church of Uganda attended.

At the closing worship service of the seven-day Conference, Archbishop Henry Orombi read the Conference Statement to the assembled members. The Jerusalem Declaration was part of the Statement, setting forth the basic beliefs of the Conference and the "Fellowship of Confessing Anglicans" that emerged from it. The Jerusalem Declaration was approved with joy by over one thousand delegates and 280 bishops from many countries but chiefly from Africa. We think it says important things about what it means to be a Christian today, what it means to be part of a Global Anglican Communion. We therefore offer this brief commentary for lay people in our churches. May God speak through these words to build up His people!

THE TEXT

In the name of God the Father, God the Son and God the Holy Spirit.

We, the participants in the Global Anglican Future Conference, have met in the land of Jesus' birth. We express our loyalty as disciples to the King of kings, the Lord Jesus. We joyfully embrace His command to proclaim the reality of His kingdom which he first announced in this land. The gospel of the kingdom is the good news of salvation, liberation and transformation for all. In light of the above, we agree to chart a way forward together that promotes and protects the biblical gospel and mission to the world, solemnly declaring the following tenets of orthodoxy which underpin our Anglican identity.

1. We rejoice in the gospel of God through which we have been saved by grace through faith in Jesus Christ by the power of the Holy Spirit. Because God first loved us, we love him and as believers bring forth fruits

of love, ongoing repentance, lively hope and thanksgiving to God in all things.

2. We believe the Holy Scriptures of the Old and New Testaments to be the Word of God written and to contain all things necessary for salvation. The Bible is to be translated, read, preached, taught and obeyed in its plain and canonical sense, respectful of the church's historic and consensual reading.

3. We uphold the four Ecumenical Councils and the three historic Creeds as expressing the rule of faith of the one holy catholic and apostolic Church.

4. We uphold the Thirty-nine Articles as containing the true doctrine of the Church agreeing with God's Word and as authoritative for Anglicans today.

5. We gladly proclaim and submit to the unique and universal Lordship of Jesus Christ, the Son of God, humanity's only Saviour from sin, judgement and hell, who lived the life we could not live and died the death that we deserve. By his atoning death and glorious resurrection, he secured the redemption of all who come to him in repentance and faith.

6. We rejoice in our Anglican sacramental and liturgical heritage as an expression of the gospel, and we uphold the 1662 Book of Common Prayer as a true and authoritative standard of worship and prayer, to be translated and locally adapted for each culture.

7. We recognise that God has called and gifted bishops, priests and deacons in historic succession to equip all the people of God for their ministry in the world. We uphold the classic Anglican Ordinal as an authoritative standard of clerical orders.

8. We acknowledge God's creation of humankind as male and female and the unchangeable standard of Christian marriage between one man and one woman as the proper place for sexual intimacy and the basis of the family. We repent of our failures to maintain this standard and call for a renewed commitment to

lifelong fidelity in marriage and abstinence for those who are not married.

9. We gladly accept the Great Commission of the risen Lord to make disciples of all nations, to seek those who do not know Christ and to baptise, teach and bring new believers to maturity.

10. We are mindful of our responsibility to be good stewards of God's creation, to uphold and advocate justice in society, and to seek relief and empowerment of the poor and needy.

11. We are committed to the unity of all those who know and love Christ and to building authentic ecumenical relationships. We recognise the orders and jurisdiction of those Anglicans who uphold orthodox faith and practice, and we encourage them to join us in this declaration.

12. We celebrate the God-given diversity among us which enriches our global fellowship, and we acknowledge freedom in secondary matters. We pledge to work together to seek the mind of Christ on issues that divide us.

13. We reject the authority of those churches and leaders who have denied the orthodox faith in word or deed. We pray for them and call on them to repent and return to the Lord.

14. We rejoice at the prospect of Jesus' coming again in glory, and while we await this final event of history, we praise him for the way he builds up his church through his Spirit by miraculously changing lives.

COMMENTARY

NAMING OUR GOD

The Jerusalem Declaration begins by naming the God we believe and serve:

In the name of God the Father, God the Son and God the Holy Spirit:

189

Our God is one God in three Persons. The Jewish people – the children of Abraham, Isaac and Jacob – were called by God who declared: "Hear O Israel, the Lord is God, the Lord is One" (Deuteronomy 6:4). To this day, Christians, in continuity with this declaration, hold that there is only one God, Maker of heaven and earth.

This God, Christians say, has made Himself known as the Father, the Son and the Holy Spirit, as the famous hymn puts it, "God in three Persons, blessed Trinity." How has He made Himself known?

He has made himself known as the Son, who saves us. "God so loved the world that He gave His only-begotten Son that whoever believes in Him shall not die but have eternal life." (John 3:16)

The Son has made known the true nature of the Father. "Anyone who has seen me has seen the Father." (John 14:9)

We know the Father and the Son through the Holy Spirit. "We know that we live in Him and He in us, because He has given us of His Spirit." (1 John 4:13)

We know God as Father, Son and Holy Spirit, and we praise Him, saying "Glory to the Father and to the Son and to the Holy Spirit, as it was in the beginning, is now, and ever shall be. Amen."

It is this God who called Anglican Christians together in Jerusalem to worship Him. It is this God who sends all Christians out to witness to Him to the ends of the earth, baptizing in the Name of the Father, and of the Son and of the Holy Spirit (Matthew 28:19).

COMING TO THE LAND OF JESUS

We, the participants in the Global Anglican Future Conference, have met in the land of Jesus' birth.

In June 2008 one thousand Anglican Christians gathered in the Holy Land. We visited Bethlehem, the town where our Lord Jesus Christ was born. We visited the Sea of Galilee, where He called fishermen to follow him, healed the sick and performed miracles. We stood in the Garden of Gethsemane, where He prayed and where he was arrested. We walked the streets of Jerusalem, where He carried the cross. We saw the tomb where He was buried, which was empty on Easter morning and is empty today – because He is risen!

EXPRESSING OUR LOYALTY TO KING JESUS

We express our loyalty as disciples to the King of kings, the Lord Jesus.

Jesus called the first disciples, saying: "Come, follow me, and I shall make you fishers of men" (Mark 1:17). He calls disciples in the same way today. Every Christian, however great or small, rich or poor, is a disciple. Jesus is the Master Teacher, and we are His students. When a person is confirmed, he is asked: "Do you promise to follow Jesus Christ as your Lord and Saviour?" We answer Yes, not only with our lips but with our lives. We joyfully embrace His command to proclaim the reality of His kingdom which he first announced in this land.

Some kings use fear to get their people to obey them. Jesus is a different kind of King. He rules by love, and we obey Him because we love Him and trust His Word. His commands are not heavy because they fill us with joy (Matthew 11:28-29). We are asked to invite others, our family, friends and neighbours, into a new way of life, a kingdom that is different from any other on earth, one that is ruled by love, a love that lasts for ever. Who would not wish to be a messenger of this King and this Kingdom?

The Gospel of the Kingdom is Good News

The gospel of the kingdom is the good news of salvation, liberation and transformation for all.

The *gospel* means Good News (Luke 4:18, 43). Most news in our newspapers or on radio is bad news: news of wars, news of deaths on roads, news of corruption and defilement. Imagine an "all good-news" newspaper or radio channel. The truth is, this world is full of darkness and evil (John 3:19). The truth is that God has sent His Son into this world to save us from evil: that is the good news of salvation. Being saved means being freed from the prison of sin, where the jailors of anger and fear and lust keep us in bondage. Jesus Christ has defeated Satan, who has kept us in chains, and He has led us into the light of day. Having freed us from the world, the flesh and the Devil, He now wants to transform us by His powerful Spirit. Think of the witness of John Newton, the slave trader who wrote the hymn "Amazing Grace": "I once was lost but now I'm found, was blind but now I see." The gospel is the good news that we too can be rescued from Satan, sin, death and hell.

Agreeing to Chart a Way Forward

In light of the above, we agree to chart a way forward together that promotes and protects the biblical gospel and mission to the world, solemnly declaring the following tenets of orthodoxy which underpin our Anglican identity.

The Gospel is the basic message of Christianity. It can be grasped by a peasant digging her field as well as by a prince or a bishop in his palace. In fact, Jesus calls His message "good news for the poor" (Luke 4:18). The Gospel is also "mere Anglicanism." Anglicans are not some special tribe. They are simply Christians who have heard the good news through those who came originally from England and from those local people who heard their word and believed. These basic beliefs are called "tenets of orthodoxy." "Tenets" are things a person holds dear, like family jewels. "Orthodoxy" means "correct belief." The opposite of "orthodoxy" is called "heresy," which means wrong belief. Wrong belief is now being held as true by some of the Anglican leaders and churches, especially in North America and Europe. They have got the gospel story wrong; in fact, they are holding to a different gospel, one that does not save, indeed that sees no need for a Saviour. It is because of the confusion this false gospel has sown in our worldwide church that Anglicans gathered in Jerusalem to find ways to protect and promote true belief or orthodoxy.

The Jerusalem Declaration is a new statement, but it tells the old, old story "of Jesus and His glory, of Jesus and His love."

1. THE GOSPEL

We rejoice in the gospel of God through which we have been saved by grace through faith in Jesus Christ by the power of the Holy Spirit. Because God first loved us, we love him and as believers bring forth fruits of love, ongoing repentance, lively hope and thanksgiving to God in all things.

One day the Evangelist Philip met a man from Ethiopia riding in a chariot and reading the Bible (Acts 8:26-40). The man was reading from the Old Testament Prophet Isaiah about a Man who suffered for others. "Who is the Prophet talking about," the Ethiopian asked, "himself or another?" Then Philip preached the Gospel to him, explaining that the Prophet was speaking of Jesus. As they passed by some water, the Ethiopian asked to be baptized and became the first African convert, "and he went on his way rejoicing." Since that day millions of Africans have rejoiced when they accepted the Lord Jesus Christ as Saviour.

Every man or woman who comes to Christ is "saved by grace through faith" (Ephesians 2:8). What do these words mean? *Grace* is the free gift of God's love. God loved us before the world began. He created us in His image and He sent His Son to die for our sins. By grace, he gives us ears to hear the Gospel through preachers like Philip. And we accept His offer freely by faith, His grace working in us. We have *faith* when we put our whole trust in Jesus Christ. God pours His Holy Spirit into our hearts so that we might be born again and receive eternal life (John 3:4-8).

Anglicans, along with other Protestants (Evangelicals), hold that a person is "justified by faith alone." Think of the thief on the cross, who called on Jesus to remember him (Luke 23:42). Jesus promised that man a place in Paradise without a single good deed. The apostle Paul, who had tried to be perfect according to the Jewish law, gave it all up "in order to gain Christ and be found in him, not having a righteousness of my own that comes from the law, but that which is through faith in Christ – the righteousness that comes from God and is by faith" (Philippians 3:8-9).

Does that mean Christians do not need to do good? Does the Bible not say "faith without works is dead" (James 2:18-26)? Yes, Christians do need to do good. Indeed Jesus challenged His disciples to have a righteousness even greater than their Jewish opponents (Matthew 5:20). But Christian good works are not actions we do to earn God's favour; rather they are actions we do out of thanks for God's salvation. As we are saved by grace through faith, so we are also made holy by faith through the Holy Spirit working in us (2 Thessalonians 2:13; Ephesians 2:10). St.

John describes the relationship between faith and action simply, saying: "we love, because he first loved us" (1 John 4:19).

When we are born again, we are set free from the power of sin and death (Romans 8:2). At the same time, so long as we live in this fallen world in our decaying bodies, we shall continue to fall into sin and need to turn back to the Lord in ongoing repentance. In the Prayer Book, after we confess our sins and receive the Lord's Body and Blood for the forgiveness of sin, then we ask God "so to assist us by Your grace that we may do all those things which You have prepared for us to walk in." As in Jesus' parable, Christians are not to think like the Pharisee who thanked God that he was more righteous than other men, but rather like the publican who prayed, "God, have mercy on me, a sinner" (Luke 18:10-14).

2. The Bible

We believe the Holy Scriptures of the Old and New Testaments to be the Word of God written and to contain all things necessary for salvation. The Bible is to be translated, read, preached, taught and obeyed in its plain and canonical sense, respectful of the church's historic and consensual reading.

When Bishop Alfred Tucker came to Uganda in 1890, he told one of his missionaries, George Pilkington, to spend all his time translating the Bible into Luganda. Shortly before he was killed in a fight with Muslims, Pilkington completed his work, and the Bible passed into the hands of the evangelists such as Apolo Kivebulaya, who took the message of Christ far and wide through East Africa.

The very first words of the Bible are that "In the beginning God *said...* and it was so" (Genesis 1:1-3). John's Gospel explains it this way: "In the beginning was the

Word, and the Word was with God and the Word was God" (John 1:1). God is by His very nature a speaking God, and all creation, everything we know, holds together because of His Word and Wisdom. Wise men have always known that there is a Reason – some Africans call this Reason a Creator God - behind the world we see, what is true and good and beautiful. God's Word is that Reason for all things. What the wise men did not know is that the Word was not far away and impersonal, but very near and Personal because "the Word became flesh and lived among us" (John 1:14). Jesus Christ is the Word of God!

If Jesus is the Word, then what is the Bible? It too is God's Word. "In the past God spoke to our forefathers through the prophets at many times and in various ways, but in these last days he has spoken to us by his Son" (Hebrews 1:1-2). The Old Testament is God's word to the people of Israel, preparing the way of the Lord, who is called Messiah or Christ. The Jews looked for Him in various forms: as prophet, as priest, as king, and Jesus said to them: "You search the scriptures, because you think that in them you have eternal life; and it is they that bear witness to me" (John 5:39). But most of them could not accept the Word made flesh. Those who did accept Him were His witnesses, and their report of Him is found in the New Testament. So both Old and New Testament point to Jesus Christ: the Old looking ahead to Him who was to come, the New testifying of Him who has come.

This record of Jesus as the Word was written down in various ways and times. It includes the 39 books of the Old Testament and the 27 books of the New Testament. Joined together, these 66 books are called the canon (or rule) of Scripture. The Church has received this canon, but it cannot change it or add to it because it is chosen by God –

"God-breathed" – for our benefit (2 Timothy 3:16-17). St. John states the purpose of Scripture clearly: "These things are written so you may believe that Jesus is the Christ, the Son of God, and that by believing you may have life in his name" (John 20:31). The Bible contains all things we need to know for salvation and for living a life pleasing to God. Other books have useful information about all sorts of things, but this book only is the road map to heaven.

Therefore it is important for every Christian to read the Bible, mark down what it says, memorize its verses, and take it in like food for our souls. The first Christians in Uganda were called "readers," but in fact all Christians are to become Bible readers. Those who cannot read learn the Scripture by memory. They are also to be hearers of the Word, because God calls preachers and teachers to proclaim and explain the full meaning of His Word. And they are to be doers of the word, putting the words into action (James 1:22).

Christians throughout history have taken God at His Word in Scripture. Jesus said to Peter and John: "Come, follow me," and they left their nets and followed him. God said to St. Francis, "Build my church," and he began to rebuild the church, first physically, then spiritually. God told Aberi Balya, who became the first African bishop in Uganda: "Take off your shoes, you are on holy ground" (Exodus 3:5), and he walked barefoot for the rest of his life. Christians like these have read Scripture before us and have left their conclusions in writing. We can learn from those who came before, both to guide us to a common mind in the right way of understanding Scripture and to avoid false interpretations that always sprout alongside the good seed of the Word (Mark 4:15-20).

Sadly, today some Anglicans, highly educated ones in fact, have lost confidence in the Bible as God's Word.

Once they have lost this anchor, their views of God and Jesus and salvation drift like a boat on open seas. They miss the message of salvation in Scripture as they hawk new readings unknown to God's church, like vendors selling cheap watches on the roadside. The Jerusalem Declaration is resetting that anchor of our Christian hope on the firm foundation of the Word of God. Not for the first time, God has chosen the humble who read the plain meaning of the Bible and blinded those who are wise in their own eyes and twist the Scripture (1 Corinthians 1:21). Today it seems Africans in particular are called to stand firm for the plain truth of God's Word.

3. CREEDS AND COUNCILS

We uphold the four Ecumenical Councils and the three historic Creeds as expressing the rule of faith of the one holy catholic and apostolic church.

In the Jerusalem Declaration, Anglicans commit themselves to the "old old story" of salvation in Scripture. They also commit themselves to the church of the ages. Jesus Christ is the same, yesterday, today and for ever; so also His church will stand on the Rock and the gates of hell will not threaten it.

Many Anglicans recite the creed every week without asking where it came from and why it is important. Christians are heirs of a long history of those who believe, all the way back to Abraham and Moses and Peter and Paul. The Church itself has a 2000-year history in which it learned lessons about the truth revealed in Scripture. In the first five centuries after Christ (AD), Christians struggled to understand and teach the full nature of the Trinity – one God in three Persons – and of Jesus Christ as fully God and fully Man. Heretics took parts of the New Testament and distorted its witness, just as some modern teachers do today. During these five centuries the bishops of the worldwide church met in council to settle these matters: four times in four different cities (Nicaea 325 AD, Constantinople 381 AD, Ephesus 431 AD, and Chalcedon 451 AD). These Councils are called Ecumenical, a word which means of universal relevance, and they confirmed the apostolic teaching – sometimes called the "rule of faith" – about God in Three Persons and Jesus Christ as the God-Man. Their decisions on this subject define "orthodox" or "catholic" belief, and Anglicans consider themselves orthodox and catholic because they believe these creeds and councils are true. They share this belief with Roman Catholics and with Eastern Orthodox as well as with most Protestants. There were later Councils as well that dealt with other matters of the faith. Some Christians accept them as having binding authority; others do not.

As for the Creeds, the *Apostles' Creed* is the shortest. It outlines briefly the nature of God the Father, Maker of heaven and earth. It recounts the key moments of Jesus' life, His Virgin Birth, His suffering and death under Pontius Pilate, His going down into hell (the place of the dead), His Rising to life and going up into heaven, and His Second Coming in glory. It then turns to God the Holy Spirit in the universal church, which includes the communion of saints across space and time. It concludes with several other key teachings: the forgiveness of sins, the resurrection of the body at the end of this age and life everlasting in the age to come. The *Nicene Creed* includes the teachings of the Apostles' Creed, but adds an explanation of the Trinity, particularly saying that Jesus is fully God, of one being or nature with the Father, and that the Holy Spirit is Lord, proceeding from the Father and the Son. The *Athanasian Creed* is not used as often in church. It expands on the nature of the Trinity and Divine

Manhood of Jesus Christ, and clarifies that right belief is necessary for salvation, and that those who deny orthodox belief cut themselves off from the true church.

4. THE ARTICLES OF RELIGION

We uphold the Thirty-nine Articles as containing the true doctrine of the Church agreeing with God's Word and as authoritative for Anglicans today.

Christians have found it helpful to summarise their faith in short statements. "Jesus Christ is Lord!" and "Come Lord Jesus!" are early statements of faith found in the New Testament (Philippians 2:11; Revelation 22:20). The Creeds are themselves summaries of important teaching at a critical moment in history. Another such time was the Reformation of the 16th century in Europe. At that time, the Protestant churches recovered the centrality of faith in Christ and the authority of Scripture as the Word of God. Among these churches, the Protestant Church of England under Archbishop Thomas Cranmer produced a summary of faith called the Articles of Religion, also known as the Thirty-Nine Articles. The Articles are included in the Book of Common Prayer. For most of Anglican history, these articles have been accepted as the official teaching of the Church. In the twentieth century, however, the Church of England loosened its commitment to the Articles and the American Church has set them aside almost entirely. The Jerusalem Declaration aims to put them back in their proper place as our authority in matters of doctrine.

Let's take a quick overview of the Articles of Religion:

Articles 1-5 affirm the teaching of the Creeds on the nature of God as Father, Son and Holy Spirit and the full Deity and Manhood of Jesus Christ.

200

Articles 6-8 are very important because they establish the sole authority of the Bible as God's Word: "Scripture contains all things necessary for salvation," which means that no other beliefs can be required than those clearly taught in the Bible. Even the Creeds are true because they are biblical. The Articles go on to list the 66 books of the Bible and state that "the Old Testament is not contrary to the New, for in both the Old and New Testament, everlasting life is offered to mankind by Christ."

Articles 9-18 state the way of salvation found in the Gospel. Because of our inborn sinfulness, we cannot please God by our own free will. We are saved by God's grace and Christ's death for our sins, not by any works we do before or after baptism but only by faith in Him, "for Holy Scripture sets out for us only the Name of Jesus Christ by which we can be saved."

Articles 19-22 speak of the Church. The Church does have authority to order its life in its particular cultural setting, but because Scripture is supreme, "it is not lawful for the church to ordain anything contrary to God's Word written." Church councils and traditions, however old, are not infallible and are subject to the Bible. The Roman Catholic teaching on purgatory as a place to work off one's sins is contrary to the gospel offer of everlasting life to all who believe.

Articles 23-34 cover the ministry and sacraments. Ministers in God's church are to be called to preach and minister the sacraments. The two Sacraments of Baptism and Holy Communion are to be understood as "sure witnesses and effective signs of God's good will to us." Other rites like confirmation, marriage, ordination, private confession and anointing with oil are good but not sacraments, since Christ ordained only those two.

Articles 36-39 speak to political duties. One duty is to honour those in authority; another is to be a good steward of private property; the final duty is to limit oath-taking to formal legal occasions, with no loose taking of the Lord's Name in vain.

The Thirty-Nine Articles were written almost 500 years ago for the Church in England. Some issues they address do not apply to modern society or other cultures. Some issues, like homosexuality and abortion, were not even mentioned because their condemnation seemed self-evident from the Scriptures. Even after all these years, the Articles give global Anglicans clear lights to steer by.

5. THE LORDSHIP OF CHRIST

We gladly proclaim and submit to the unique and universal Lordship of Jesus Christ, the Son of God, humanity's only Saviour from sin, judgment and hell, who lived the life we could not live and died the death that we deserve. By his atoning death and glorious resurrection, he secured the redemption of all who come to him in repentance and faith.

Jesus said: "All authority in heaven and earth is mine (Matthew 28:16). He is Lord over all things, and he is Lord over our lives. Jesus said: "I am the Way, the Truth and the Life. No one comes to the Father except through me" (John 14:6). He is the only Saviour, He is the Lamb of God, who takes away the sins of the world. He is the Rider on the White Horse, who has conquered Satan, the ancient dragon and his forces of darkness (Revelation19:11-20).

Jesus lived the life we could not live because we are children of Adam, bearing Adam's burden of sin and curse of death (Romans 5:12-21). Though equal to God, Jesus humbled Himself to become man, being born as a servant (Philippians 2:5-11). Though without sin, he became sin for us, enduring the curse of the Cross for our sake (2 Corinthians 5:21; Galatians 3:13).

Here is what St. Paul says of Jesus' atoning death: "God presented him as a sacrifice of atonement, through faith in his blood. He did this to demonstrate his justice, because in his forbearance he had left the sins committed beforehand unpunished – he did it to demonstrate his justice at the present time, so as to be just and the one who justifies those who have faith in Jesus" (Romans 3:25-26). Receiving His righteousness by faith, we sing, "O, the Blood of Jesus, it cleanses white as snow."

6. THE PRAYER BOOK

We rejoice in our Anglican sacramental and liturgical heritage as an expression of the gospel, and we uphold the 1662 Book of Common Prayer as a true and authoritative standard of worship and prayer, to be translated and locally adapted for each culture.

Anglicans through the years have given praise and thanks to God for the sacrifice of His Son in the words of the Book of Common Prayer:

All glory be to thee, Almighty God, our heavenly Father, for that thou, of thy tender mercy didst give thy only Son Jesus Christ to suffer death upon the Cross for our redemption; who made there (by his one oblation of himself once offered) a full, perfect, and sufficient sacrifice, oblation and satisfaction for the sins of the world.

These ancient words – *redemption*, or buying back; *oblation*, or full offering; *satisfaction*, meeting the demands of justice – all point to the once-for-all act of *atonement*, another ancient word meaning reconciliation of enemies (Romans 5:10-11). These words of course come to most

Africans and others not in their original English but in translation. This is good and right, because Archbishop Thomas Cranmer when he wrote them intended them to be "understood by the people." Before that time, the only language of worship was Latin, known only to scholars. After that time, the Bible and the Prayer Book were in the vernacular so that the ordinary person could join in.

One scholar has talked about "mission as translation." The first missionaries learned the local languages and saw translation as a first priority, but they also saw value in keeping the substance, the liturgy of the Prayer Book and Hymnals. "Liturgy" is a word meaning the "work of the people." Liturgy forms the way people think and pray. So we say "praying shapes believing." Anglicans have been blessed by beautiful and powerful prayers like the "Collect for Purity," the "General Thanksgiving" and the "Prayer of Humble Access." These have continuing power to shape our lives as Christians. At the same time, influences from the modern and global environment should also enrich worship. The Kenyan liturgy, for instance, adds distinctive African features and choruses like "Jabulane, Africa" ["Sing for Joy, O Africa"] and "Lubanga na te" ["God is with us"] which should take their place along more traditional hymns like "Stand Up, Stand Up for Jesus."

The Jerusalem Declaration claims that the classic Book of Common Prayer remains the standard for other revisions and adaptations, and that such revisions and adaptations should be encouraged so that Anglican worship can reach and strengthen people who come from very un-English backgrounds.

7. THE ORDAINED MINISTRY

We recognise that God has called and gifted bishops, priests and deacons in historic succession to equip all the people of God for their ministry in the world. We uphold the classic Anglican Ordinal as an authoritative standard of clerical orders.

God has always chosen political leaders for His people from Abraham to Moses to Joshua to David. God has chosen prophets to speak truth to His people, from Elijah to Isaiah to Daniel. He has also chosen priests to teach and lead His people in worship from Levi to Aaron to Zadok. In Jesus Christ, all these roles of prophet, priest and king combine, as He is all in all. Jesus himself chose twelve apostles and gave them authority to preach the gospel and heal the sick (Luke 9:2). After His resurrection, He renewed the commission of the apostles to be His witnesses to the ends of the earth.

St. Paul describes a variety of leadership roles: "In the church God has appointed first of all apostles, second prophets, third teachers, then workers of miracles, also those having gifts of healing, those able to help others, those with gifts of administration, and those speaking in different kinds of tongues" (1 Corinthians 12:28). Some of these gifts are charismatic, depending on specific and even temporary gifts of the Holy Spirit. In another place Paul describes a more regular order of ministry: "His gifts were that some should be apostles, some prophets, some evangelists, some pastors and teachers" (Ephesians 4:11). The purpose of these ministers working together was "to equip the saints for the work of ministry, for building up the body of Christ" (verse 12). It is very important to note that a clergyman is not intended to do all the work of the church. Rather he is like a coach, training the laypeople to reach their neighbours for Christ.

At yet a later stage, fixed leadership arises in the church in the offices of deacon, presbyter (priest) and bishop. Deacons were church social workers, distributing goods to the poor and visiting the sick, and they also preached and evangelized as they worked. Priests and Bishops seem to have overlapping roles overseeing the congregations and house churches. About one hundred years later, the bishop was recognized as the sole head of a particular diocese, while a number of priests served under him.

This historic succession of the threefold pattern of ministry has been maintained in the Anglican churches down to the present. The Book of Common Prayer contains an "Ordinal" with services for the Ordination of a Deacon and a Priest and the Consecration of a Bishop. The word "ordination" means that a person is called by God into a spiritual office not of his own making. All those ordained are "ministers" in the sense that they are called to serve God's people, just as Jesus served His disciples. The priest is above all a pastor and teacher, and he receives a symbolic Bible and is commissioned to "preach the Word of God." Bishops are also priests but they are consecrated to lead a diocese; archbishops are bishops who are appointed to lead a group of dioceses called a Province.

The Jerusalem Declaration is reaffirming the historic pattern of ministry. However, for the church to flourish, it must raise up able and gifted clergy to lead the flock. The Christian ministry is not a paved highway to worldly success, but it comes with a rich promise from our Lord when he says: "no one who has left home or brothers or sisters or mother or father or children or fields for me and the gospel will fail to receive a hundred times as much in this present age (homes, brothers, sisters, mothers, children and fields – and with them, persecutions) and in the age to come, eternal life" (Mark 10:29-30).

8. SEXUALITY AND MARRIAGE

We acknowledge God's creation of humankind as male and female and the unchangeable standard of Christian marriage between one man and one woman as the proper place for sexual intimacy and the basis of the family. We repent of our failures to maintain this standard and call for a renewed commitment to lifelong fidelity in marriage and abstinence for those who are not married.

"God made man in His own image...male and female He made them" (Gen 1:27). "Therefore a man shall leave his father and mother and be joined to his wife, and they shall become one flesh" (Gen 2:24).

These two sentences contain one of the deepest truths of human nature. "It's a boy!" we cry, or "It's a girl!" when a child comes into the world. The pastor stands up and says: "I announce that John, the son of... plans to wed Mary, the daughter of..." How much our lives are shaped around this plain truth of God making us for each other. The Lord Jesus Himself recognized the love and joy of marriage when he attended a wedding feast at Cana and gave the couple much fresh wine to enjoy the event (John 2:1-10). He referred back to God's purpose when He taught that marriage is life-long and intended for one man and one woman (Mark 10:6-8).

The Prayer Book says that God ordained marriage for the mutual love of partners, for the procreation of children and for the avoidance of sexual immorality. Each of these purposes is necessary for the happiness of the human family and well-being of society. Children in particular are a blessing from the Lord (Psalm 127:3-5) and it is the duty of parents to protect and nurture them. As they are "knit together from the moment of conception in the mother's womb" (Psalm 139:13), children must be protected from violence. Therefore the Church must speak out against the practice of abortion, abuse and defilement.

The "unchangeable standard of Christian marriage" is both natural and unnatural, easy and hard to maintain. It is obvious that males and females are born in equal numbers so that one man, one women makes sense. At the same time, some males in their greed for sex and power take for themselves more than one woman. This is polygamy and it has been practiced through most of history and in many cultures. It is common, but it is not the Christian way. Why? First of all, God's standard looks to stability for children and society, whereas polygamy involves jealousy and rivalry and hatred. God's standard looks to the equal status of man and woman, father and mother; polygamy involves men dominating women.

Finally, God's standard seeks to put love first, seeks to see in human love something of the exclusive relationship of love that God has with His people, that Christ has for His Church. St. Paul puts it this way: "Now as the church submits to Christ, so also wives should submit to their husbands in everything. Husbands, love your wives, just as Christ loved the church and gave himself up for her" (Ephesians 5:24-25). This kind of mutual submitting of wife to husband and husband to wife cannot happen in multiple relationships. It can only happen when two people commit all they have to each other and do so with the help of God.

Marriage is God's way for most people, but it is not the only way. Young people live for many years before they wed and old people often survive for years as widows. A few people spend their whole lives single, whether by choice or by circumstance. God has a plan for them as well. Jesus speaks of "eunuchs" for the Kingdom of God, that is, people who have sacrificed sexual relations in order to serve a higher good, the Kingdom of God (Matthew 19:12). Many of the great saints, many of the missionaries did not marry in order to carry out their work. All of these single people are called by God to abstinence, putting away physical fulfillment of desire. Married couples in their own way practice purity by keeping faithful to each other and putting aside any temptations to adultery.

For many Africans, homosexuality is a taboo subject. Christians need to give reasons for their convictions. To understand homosexuality, we must see it in the context of God's good purposes in marriage and the perversion of those purposes by human lust. Scripture says that homosexuality, along with idolatry, is a sign of man's fallen desires (Romans 1:24-27). It is important for Christians to uphold God's standard and resist those, in the church or outside it, who promote homosexuality. It is also important for Christians to condemn the sin and love the sinners (John 8:11). Many homosexuals come from broken families or schools where sexual defilement is common. They need patient love to find help and healing, and they must find it from caring Christians.

Good marriages make a good society, but a corrupt society will corrupt marriage as well. In Western society the tolerance of divorce and remarriage, which is a kind of polygamy, has undermined the church's authority in society. Likewise in Africa, many prominent Christians have "customary" wives on the side, and this has weakened the church's voice. The Jerusalem Declaration calls the Church, North and South, to repent and return to God's standard of "one man, one woman, two sexes, one flesh."

9. THE CHURCH'S MISSION

We gladly accept the Great Commission of the risen Lord to make disciples of all nations, to seek those who do not know Christ and to baptise, teach and bring new believers to maturity.

Jesus gave two Great Commandments, "Love God and love your neighbour" (Mark 12:30-31), and one Great Commission, where he says:

"All authority in heaven and on earth has been given to me. Therefore go and make disciples of all nations, baptizing them in the name of the Father and of the Son and of the Holy Spirit, and teaching them to obey everything I have commanded you. And surely I am with you always, to the very end of the age." (Matthew 28:18-20)

The Great Commission is a call to "mission," which involves first of all evangelising those who do not know Christ and bringing them to baptism and full conversion and maturity. It was God's great plan in choosing one nation, the children of Abraham, that in his offspring all the nations would be blessed (Genesis 12: 3). Israel was to be a light to the nations (Isaiah 49:6). Israel's destiny was fulfilled by Jesus Christ, who came to save not only the Jewish people but every nation, tribe, people and language (Revelation 7:4-9).

The Great Commission is given to the apostles and through them to the whole church. Some members literally go out to foreign lands, which is how they came to Africa. Other members pray for the mission work. Others give financially to support the work. Some missionaries witness to Christ through works of love in areas such as medicine and health, education, disaster relief and economic development.

Whereas most mission work in the 19th century was done by Europeans, sometimes in a patronizing way, in the late 20th and 21st century, mission is seen more in terms of partnership among equals. Many Christians from nations that had been evangelized are now sending their own missionaries to other lands. Sometimes these missionaries have easier access to the local people than a Westerner would have. Effective missionary work requires cross-cultural knowledge and sensitivity, learning local languages and accepting local customs that are not directly against God's Word.

About 3 billion people, more than half the world's population, have never heard the Gospel for themselves. Since our God seeks to be worshipped by every nation, tribe, people and language (Revelation 7:9), Christians have a privilege and duty to pray and work to reach these peoples. We thank God that today the gospel is spreading rapidly in parts of Africa and in China.

10. SOCIAL RESPONSIBILITY

We are mindful of our responsibility to be good stewards of God's creation, to uphold and advocate justice in society, and to seek relief and empowerment of the poor and needy.

When God created Adam, he placed him in the Garden of Eden to "tend and keep it" (Genesis 2:15). Mankind is neither to be a tyrant over the earth nor a slave to it. After the Fall, work becomes burdensome as the man struggles to make the earth productive. The woman too labors in pain to bring forth children, and the good housewife works from early morning to evening at home (Proverbs 31:10-31). Hard work is also rewarding, and the harvest of success is the reward of much planning and effort. In a global society, work has become increasingly compartmentalized with each "professional" focusing on a particular task. Often these jobs involve more mental work than physical, but the same attitude of diligence is required (Proverbs 10:4). Care for the environment is an aspect of stewardship. It includes large issues like global warming and small matters of keeping a compound clean and attractive.

God has also instituted government to punish crime and maintain justice (Romans 13:1-7). Each person is a subject or citizen and is obligated to obey the law of the land and to pay taxes to "Caesar" (Mark 12:17). The governor is himself subject to the government of laws and a constitution and finally to God Himself. In a democratic society, citizens take some responsibility for the conduct of government, especially through elections. They must therefore keep informed through the news media. The Church is not directly involved in politics, but it does lay down basic moral rules that have political implications. For instance, the Church maintains that God gives life and takes it away. Therefore the practice of abortion is not only taking a human life but grasping authority that belongs to God alone.

The Bible and the Lord Jesus show a special concern for the poor (Leviticus 25; Matthew 19:21). Giving alms is a requirement of the Jewish law and of Jesus as well. In response to this concern, the early church appointed deacons to see that no member went hungry. The church has founded hospitals and orphanages for the wider society as well. In many countries, governments have taken over many of the social services, but it remains true that church leaders are often the most effective in social work because they know the poor and have their trust. They are also called to hold governments accountable, to uphold human dignity and rights and to oppose corruption and exploitation.

Charity to the poor is a virtue, but empowerment is equally important. A Chinese proverb says: "Give a man a fish and you feed him for a day; teach a man to fish and you feed him for a lifetime." Empowerment looks to equip poor people to support themselves. We believe that God has given everyone certain abilities and the will to survive and do well. Christians in the helping professions should not try to keep others dependent on them but rather challenge them to become independent. There are many ways today that poor people can raise themselves. One is through education. Another is through micro-enterprise projects. Capacity-building is a political matter as well. Governments must fight corruption and make laws that make it possible for their people to use their God-given property and talents. Once again, the church may initiate its own projects as well as holding government accountable.

11. SEEKING CHRISTIAN UNITY

We are committed to the unity of all those who know and love Christ and to building authentic ecumenical relationships. We recognise the orders and jurisdiction of those Anglicans who uphold orthodox faith and practice, and we encourage them to join us in this declaration.

Unity among Christians is at the heart of the gospel. On the night before He died, our Lord Jesus Christ offered to His Father this prayer concerning His Church: "My prayer is not for [these disciples] alone. I pray also for those who will believe in me through their message, that all of them may be one, Father, just as you are in me and I am in you" (John 17:20-21). It is said of the first gathering of the church: "All the believers were together and had everything in common" (Acts 2:44). Of course, as the church grew and the gospel passed from nation to nation, Christians were separated by time and space and by culture. Nevertheless, they sensed they were part of one holy catholic and apostolic church.

From the very beginning Satan has been at work sowing divisions between believers. In particular, Christians often have shown partiality based on class or race or tribe, and this division has reached tragic proportions in genocides in supposedly Christian countries. The official church has also been divided by Catholic and Protestant, or by Anglican and Pentecostal. Following our Lord's wish, Church leaders are called to break down artificial barriers and seek to build ecumenical relationships with other Church leaders. Catholics and Protestants, for instance, have much more in common with each other than with secularists or Muslims.

Even among Anglicans, there have been very sad divisions. Some of these are based on matters of truth, and these cannot simply be ignored. Some believing Anglicans in North America have been forced to leave their church buildings, and clergy have been removed from office because they will not accept the practice of homosexuality in the Church. The Jerusalem Declaration offers them the hand of fellowship across the ocean and across official church lines.

12. FREEDOM IN SECONDARY MATTERS

We celebrate the God-given diversity among us which enriches our global fellowship, and we acknowledge freedom in secondary matters. We pledge to work together to seek the mind of Christ on issues that divide us.

St. Paul describes the Church as a Body, with many parts working together. "Now there are varieties of gifts, but the same Spirit; and there are varieties of service, but the same Lord; and there are varieties of working, but it is the same God who inspires them all in every one (1 Corinthians 12:4-6). Every parish church needs all the people working together, not just the clergy, not just the Mothers' Union, but all of them.

In the worldwide church, there is also a wide variety of cultures, but we are to speak together to the glory of God. On the day of Pentecost, they exclaimed:

> "How is it that we hear, each of us in his own native language? Parthians and Medes and Elamites and

214

residents of Mesopotamia, Judea and Cappadocia, Pontus and Asia, Phrygia and Pamphylia, Egypt and the parts of Libya belonging to Cyrene, and visitors from Rome, both Jews and proselytes, Cretans and Arabians, we hear them telling in our own tongues the mighty works of God." (Acts 2:8-11)

As of now, the Anglican Communion has 38 provinces on all habitable continents of the world, representing all races, hundreds of languages, and vast differences of wealth. In addition to these cultural differences, the Communion represents a variety of spiritual traditions. Some Anglicans learned their faith from the Evangelical missionaries, who emphasized preaching and Bible reading and who taught that alcohol is sinful. Other Anglicans come from a more "catholic" tradition, which emphasizes frequent Communion, calling the pastor "Father" and remembering saints' days. Yet others are more pentecostal, with worship choruses, speaking in tongues, and prophecies. Some Anglicans ordain women as priests and others think it is unbiblical. Some Anglicans think Jesus is truly present in the Communion bread and wine; others believe Jesus is spiritually present in the Communion but not in the physical elements themselves.

These are some of the important but secondary differences among those who agree on the essential truths of the faith outlined in the Creeds and the Articles of Religion. The Jerusalem Declaration represents a variety of Anglicans, and we are committed to listening patiently to each other on these secondary matters.

13. REJECTING FALSE TEACHERS

We reject the authority of those churches and leaders who have denied the orthodox faith in word or deed. We pray for them and call on them to repent and return to the Lord.

"How good and pleasant it is when brothers live together in unity" (Psalm 133:1). Unfortunately, sometimes they do not. Worse still, sometimes it appears that they are false brothers and false shepherds that lead Christ's flock astray. In that case the good shepherd must take action.

Jesus lays down the following rule for confronting a brother or sister who has sinned against you.

> "If your brother sins against you, go and show him his fault, just between the two of you. If he listens to you, you have won your brother over. But if he will not listen, take one or two others along, so that 'every matter may be established by the testimony of two or three witnesses.' If he refuses to listen to them, tell it to the church; and if he refuses to listen even to the church, treat him as you would a pagan or a tax collector. I tell you the truth, whatever you bind on earth will be bound in heaven, and whatever you loose on earth will be loosed in heaven." (Matthew 18:15-18)

This rule applies not only to individuals but to churches and church leaders as well. Indeed it has happened in our beloved Anglican Communion. Ten years ago, the Lambeth Conference of Anglican bishops voted 526 to 70 that homosexual practice is "incompatible with Scripture" and "cannot be advised." The leaders of the official Anglican churches in North America deliberately refused to follow this Resolution, and in 2003 they made a man bishop who had divorced his wife and was living with another man (now this couple claim to be married). After repeated warnings, the churches of the Global South took the last step of breaking communion with the Episcopal Church in North America.

To break communion means that you will no longer break bread together in the Holy Communion. It means that the Anglican Communion is like a garment that has been ripped at the seams. In breaking communion with the official Episcopal Church, the churches in the Global South recognized that there were many faithful Anglicans stranded there. In fact, these people have been persecuted through lawsuits and clergy have lost their positions and their property. It is in that context that the Jerusalem Declaration states that we shall not recognize the authority of a heretical church. It is for that reason that the Primates' Council of the Fellowship of Confessing Anglicans called for a new Province in North America to be recognized. It is sad that such action was necessary, since we bear the common name Christian and Anglican, but not to act would be worse, as it would compromise our witness in the wider world. We should pray that they would turn to God, but until they do, we have to follow our Lord's advice and have nothing to do with them.

14. JESUS' COMING IN GLORY

We rejoice at the prospect of Jesus' coming again in glory, and while we await this final event of history, we praise him for the way he builds up his church through his Spirit by miraculously changing lives.

In the Nicene Creed we say: "He will come again in glory to judge the living and the dead." We expect that as Jesus came in Bethlehem at Christmas, so He will come again to bring time and history to an end. He himself promised this when He said: "you will see the Son of man seated at the right hand of Power, and coming with the clouds of heaven" (Mark 14:62). When Jesus ascended bodily into heaven, two angels told the disciples: "Men of Galilee, why stand you gazing up into heaven? This same Jesus, who is taken up from you into heaven, shall come in the same manner as you have seen him go into heaven" (Acts 1:11).

How are we to live in the meantime, between the first and second coming of Jesus? The Book of Acts goes on to show how. The apostles were filled with the Holy Spirit on the Day of Pentecost and became witnesses of Jesus to the ends of the earth. They prayed for and expected God to work miracles in their midst (Mark 16:17). That is why the world is full of Christians today and why we need to reach others with the message of hope. Jesus told His followers on the night He was betrayed that they would do "greater things" because He was going to the Father and would send the Holy Spirit to be with them (John 14:12). Jesus' earthly ministry lasted only three years and covered a very small territory. In sending the Holy Spirit through the church, Jesus' gospel has spread to millions of people over the entire globe and two thousand years of history whose lives have been transformed by faith in Him.

When will it all end? "No one knows about that day or hour," Jesus said, "not even the angels in heaven, nor the Son, but only the Father" (Mark 13:32). Christians should be expectant, like a mother preparing to give birth. St. Paul gives us good mid-wife advice:

> Now, brothers, about times and dates we do not need to write to you, for you know very well that the day of the Lord will come like a thief in the night. While people are saying, "Peace and safety," destruction will come on them suddenly, as labor pains on a pregnant woman, and they will not escape. But you, brothers, are not in darkness so that this day should surprise you like a thief. You are all sons of the light and sons of the day. We do not belong to the night or to the darkness. So then, let us not be like others, who are asleep, but let us be alert and self-controlled. For those who sleep, sleep at night, and those who get drunk, get drunk at night. But since we belong to the day, let us be self-controlled, putting on faith and love as a breastplate, and the hope of salvation as a helmet.

218

For God did not appoint us to suffer wrath but to receive salvation through our Lord Jesus Christ. He died for us so that, whether we are awake or asleep, we may live together with him. Therefore encourage one another and build each other up, just as in fact you are doing. (1 Thessalonians 5:1-11)

The birth-pangs of the new creation may not be easy. The Book of Revelation portrays a time when Satan – the ancient Serpent – makes war on those who obey God's commandments and hold firm to their testimony to Jesus (Revelation 12:17). Again, the history of the church is written in the blood of the martyrs, those who like the page-boys in Uganda, would rather die than renounce their true King Jesus. The past century has seen more martyrs than all the others put together, saints whose faith is known only to God. The Book of Revelation also lets us see the end of the story, the outcome of the last battle: "[His enemies] will make war on the Lamb, and the Lamb will conquer them, for He is Lord of lords and King of kings, and those with him are called and chosen and faithful" (Revelation 17:14).

So also we say with all the church, "Amen! Come, Lord Jesus."

Section Three

Is There a Global Anglican Future?

The Road Ahead 2008-2018

The Global Anglican Future Conference claimed to be "not a moment in time, but a movement in the Spirit." Such a claim of course must be tested by reality. Writing now at ten years distance, I would argue that the claim has been vindicated by ongoing developments in the Anglican Communion but that the reform and renewal of the Anglican Communion is far from a finished project.

The first two essays here are based on my sense that there are several major ecclesiological challenges facing the Global South that are rooted in the past which extend into the future. The *first* one is a matter of *governance*: *how will the movement govern itself?* The second has to do with *unity* and in particular *how will the parallel streams of the Global South network and GAFCON come together as an effective "instrument" of Anglican unity?*

It is my hope that proceeding from Cairo in 2016 to Jerusalem in 2018 there will be a strengthened alliance, not only built on the common ties of the Global South but on the common confession of the biblical and classic Anglican faith and on a common ecclesial bond, whether that is called a covenant or some other basis.

Is there a future for a Global Anglican Communion? I think it is obvious that I hope that there is. But to speak of the future is to speak of the contingency of God's ordering of history, of *eschatology*, the mysterious judgments of God, before which even the biblical prophets stand silent (1 Peter 1:10-12). The final clause of the Jerusalem Declaration explicitly looks to the future:

> 14. We rejoice at the prospect of Jesus' coming again in glory, and while we await this final event of history, we praise him for the way he builds up his church through his Spirit by miraculously changing lives.

The doctrine of "last things" is hardly new to Christian teaching. It is present in the Bible and in the Creeds and Confessions, and we even have a season of the church year dedicated to it – Advent. The challenge to the church has been and is still how to understand the "signs of the times" and how to respond to them.

The last two essays in this final section are expositions of two eschatological books of the New Testament: the Book of Revelation and the Epistle of Jude. While I am addressing two different audiences – Nigerian Christians facing Islamic persecution and seminarians preparing for ministry in post-Christian America – I argue that both groups are contending not with flesh and blood but with spiritual forces of evil in the heavenly places (Ephesians 6:10).

I suppose some may consider me "fundamentalistic" in my way of reading the signs of the times. So be it, but I do call to my defense one of the finest current Anglican theologians, Professor Oliver O'Donovan, commenting on modern and postmodern pretensions:

> We are tempted to think, perhaps, that the concept of Antichrist, capable of such shifting and contrasting

applications from age to age, is useless for serious theological analysis, but it is not so. There is no one Antichrist; but in any period of history Antichrist may take shape as one thing, challenging the claims of God's Kingdom with its own.... When believers find themselves confronted with an order that, implicitly or explicitly, offers itself as the sufficient and necessary condition of human welfare, they will recognise the beast. When a political structure makes this claim, we call it 'totalitarian'. More subtle and more pernicious is the same claim made by a society, or by a civilisation, in a series of self-interpreting doctrines which define metaphysical parameters of thought and action (even innocently disavowing metaphysical intentions). (*The Desire of the Nations*, pages 273-274).

I am not a prophet nor a prophet's son, but I do believe that every Christian has a responsibility to search and inquire about the darkness of the present age in the light of the Advent of the true Light that enlightens every man, our Lord and Savior Jesus Christ:

Concerning this salvation, the prophets who prophesied about the grace that was to be yours searched and inquired carefully, inquiring what person or time the Spirit of Christ in them was indicating when he predicted the sufferings of Christ and the subsequent glories. It was revealed to them that they were serving not themselves but you, in the things that have now been announced to you through those who preached the good news to you by the Holy Spirit sent from heaven, things into which angels long to look. (1 Peter 1:10-12)

ESSAY 8

SEA CHANGE IN THE ANGLICAN COMMUNION

GAFCON AND COMMUNION GOVERNANCE, WITH AN AFTERWORD FROM THE NAIROBI CONFERENCE

(2013)

This essay retraces the narrative of Essay 4 but with a different focus, on types of governance or polity within the Anglican Communion. It begins with the indictment made in the Jerusalem Statement that the four "Instruments of Unity" – the Archbishop of Canterbury, Lambeth Conference, Primates' Meeting and Anglican Consultative Council – had been tested and found wanting in the crisis set off by Lambeth 1998. The question is: where do we go from there?

I argue that the apparent "separation of powers" among these Instruments was chimerical and that in fact power was centralized under the "Lambeth bureaucracy," which was staffed and financed to a large extent by revisionists from the USA and UK. Not surprisingly, the goal of the various directives, commissions, and processes set up by Lambeth had one final aim: giving the Episcopal Church and the Anglican Church of Canada a pass, even at the risk of schism within those churches and losing major churches of the Global South.

The Global Anglican Future Conference established a theological and political alternative to Lambeth, with a set of "fundamental declarations" (the Jerusalem Declaration) and a representative council, the Gafcon Primates' Council. This was an essential first step in reconstituting the Anglican Communion. The Gafcon Primates have adopted conciliar practices among themselves. There is, however, further work to be done. For instance, there is a need for subsidiary bodies under the Primates. I believe this need will be addressed at GAFCON 2018.

Gafcon as a polity remains fragile. Any new endeavor risks failure due to different personalities, communication problems across cultures, and shortage of funds. In the case of Gafcon, one must factor in the active opposition of the New York-London establishment to weaken and divide the Global South. I am convinced that if this new entity does not succeed, it will not mean a return to the status quo ante but rather the dissolution of Anglicanism into disparate regional churches only loosely related to one another and with no coherent Gospel to proclaim.

I wrote this essay in preparation for the 2013 Global Anglican Future Conference in Nairobi. After the Conference, I reflected on its achievements. I want to clarify one statement in this essay. When I speak of governance constituted by the model of conciliar authority of bishops, I do not mean to leave out clergy and lay participation in a plenary assembly. Bishops are charged particularly with upholding doctrine and discipline and hence must at times meet separately, but the life of the church lies in its daily worship, ministry, and mission. The presence of clergy and laity at the GAFCON assemblies is therefore a sign of the fullness of Christ's body, equipped so that when each part is working properly the body grows and builds itself up in love (Ephesians 4:16).

There has been a sea change in the Anglican Communion over the past two decades. The vestments may be the same, the assorted "reverend" titles untouched, the official Communion website still showing smiling Global South Anglican faces. The reality is far different. The foundation of Anglican identity has been shaken, and with the Psalmist, many rightly wonder: "if the foundations are destroyed, what can the righteous do?" (Psalm 11:3).

The presenting cause of this sea change, as is widely known, is the acceptance and promotion of homosexuality and the redefinition of marriage. For 350 years, Anglican weddings in England and abroad have begun with these words:

> Dearly beloved, we are gathered together here in the sight of God, and in the face of this congregation, to join together this Man and this Woman in holy Matrimony; which is an honourable estate, instituted of God in the time of man's innocency, signifying unto us the mystical union that is betwixt Christ and his Church...

When this doctrine of Holy Matrimony was challenged in the 1990s by gay-rights advocates in two Provinces (The Episcopal Church USA and the Anglican Church of Canada), the Lambeth Conference of bishops answered decisively that

> This Conference, in view of the teaching of Scripture, upholds faithfulness in marriage between a man and a woman in lifelong union, and believes that abstinence is right for those who are not called to marriage. (Resolution I.10)

The Lambeth Resolution led to a decade of strife within the Communion as the North Americans flatly rejected its norm and now are on the brink of providing official same-sex marriage rites. In the UK, same-sex marriage has now been signed into law by the Queen, and the Prime Minister vows to export it to the Commonwealth partners. While the Church of England has not approved same-sex marriage, the Archbishop of Canterbury argues that same-sex civil unions are a neglected moral obligation: "It is clearly essential that stable and faithful same sex relationships should, where those involved want it, be recognised and supported with as much dignity and the same legal effect as marriage" (Speech in House of Lords, 3 June 2013).

But isn't sex outside marriage "incompatible with Scripture" (1998 Lambeth Resolution I.10; cf. Resolutions III.1 and III.5)? Indeed the larger question underlying the sexuality debate entails the authority of the Bible. To which question Presiding Bishop Katherine Jefferts Schori echoes Humpty Dumpty's upside-down "hermeneutic": "when I use the Word, it means just what I choose it to mean – neither more nor less." Or so it seems. Here is how Bishop Schori interprets St. Paul's exorcism of a slave girl, oppressed by demonic and human masters (Acts 16:16-18):

> Paul can't abide something he won't see as beautiful or holy, so he tries to destroy it. It gets him thrown in prison. That's pretty much where he's put himself by his own refusal to recognize that she, too, shares in God's nature, just as much as he does – maybe more so!

Permit me, as a biblical scholar to protest: the fact that an apostolic leader can twist the text of Scripture and rebuke St. Paul as she does is emblematic of the false Gospel rampant in her church, and the fact that she remains unrebuked and in good standing with her elders in the Communion is emblematic of the utter dysfunction of that body. In what sense can one call it a "Communion" when such denial of the faith passes for normal?

COMMUNION GOVERNANCE

This essay is not about hermeneutics or sexuality but about "ecclesiastical polity," how the Church constitutes and organizes its common life. But the two topics are linked; indeed the sea change in Biblical interpretation and morality has caused a sea change in Communion governance as well.

In classical political theory, there are only so many models of polity: *rule by one, rule by the few,* and *rule by the many.* Aristotle commended a *mixed polity* as the most feasible of regimes, but a mixed regime is not the same as a mixed-up regime; it must have a coherent rationale, as in the instance of constitutional republics.

Classical theorists were doubtful about how far genuine polity could extend beyond a particular city or nation, into what we now call international relations. The Church, however, is by its mission charter a worldwide institution, stretching to the ends of the earth, and the Anglican Communion, with churches "locally adapted" to their regions, reflects that global character better than many other church bodies.

I will argue that there are three basic models of Communion governance: *a loose association of purely autonomous Provinces,* a *communion of churches led by bishops in council,* and an *executive bureaucracy.*

FIRST MODEL: PURE AUTONOMY

One could argue that pure autonomy is the starting point of Anglican polity, going back to Henry VIII detaching the national church from the Roman See. "Provincial" autonomy, usually based on national boundaries, is a bedrock principle of the Anglican Communion. It was not always so. When the English began founding overseas colonies, the Church of England maintained control from afar. This policy weakened the Anglican Church in the American colonies and led to the formation of independent Methodist and Episcopal churches there. Other colonial churches remained formally tethered to the Mother Church, which eventually awarded them missionary bishops and provincial synods.

The calling of the first Lambeth Conference in 1867 was precipitated by a theological and political crisis in South Africa – the so-called Colenso affair. The meeting of 76 bishops established two precedents: that "provinces" would be organized on a one-per-region basis as recognized by the Archbishop of Canterbury; and that the "conference" of bishops would have no legal authority within England or other jurisdictions. Both these precedents continue to this day. Although there are a few anomalous overlapping jurisdictions, the 38 listed provinces are the only "official" churches of the Communion. And while there have been proposals for structuring the Communion more formally – e.g., in 1930, more of which below – these proposals have been stillborn.

Once a geographical province is recognized, are there any limits on its autonomy in terms of doctrine, discipline and worship? The answer is, theoretically, yes. The American Prayer Book (1789) states that liturgical alterations are acceptable "provided the substance of the Faith be kept entire." The first Lambeth Conference took a similar stance: while allowing for liturgical adaptation, it stated that "it is necessary that [provinces] receive and maintain without alteration the standards of the faith and doctrine as now in use in that [the Mother] Church" (Resolution 8).

The 1930 Report on the Anglican Communion poses the nightmare scenario of a formally autonomous church exercising its freedom and departing the faith:

> This freedom naturally and necessarily carries with it the risk of divergence to the point even of disruption. In case any such risk should actually arise, it is clear that the Lambeth Conference as such could not take any

disciplinary action. Formal action would belong to the several Churches of the Anglican Communion individually; but the advice of the Lambeth Conference, sought before action is taken by the constituent Churches, would carry very great moral weight. And we believe in the Holy Spirit. We trust in His power working in every part of His Church to hold us together.

The conclusion from 1930 is that the Anglican Communion per se has no authority to deal with heresy and schism and leaves any action to each autonomous province. Nevertheless, the "moral weight" of Christian unity did indeed work as hoped for – until recently.

The Episcopal Church USA and Anglican Church of Canada are the nightmare come true. Repeatedly boasting of their provincial autonomy, the North Americans obstructed the will of the larger Communion with little more than insincere expressions of "regret" and porous "moratoria" which expire whenever the next bishop or diocese decides to take "prophetic" action, e.g. in adding "transgender rights" to marriage and ordination.

Given their functional autonomy, one might ask why these churches care to remain in the Communion. The truth is, their radical agenda is transnational and they believe they can eventually infiltrate the official structures and divide and conquer the poorer churches of the Communion. If the Communion bodies were somehow to fight back and exercise discipline in such a way that these churches had to choose between conforming to its standards and "walking apart," they would separate and take some of their client churches with them.

While the crisis of the last decade has in some ways united churches of the Global South, they too are tempted to throw up their hands in frustration and operate autonomously. They have their own independent constitutions and have been growing without significant help from the West. They do not have funds, unless lured from the Western coffers, to travel worldwide to international meetings. The radical agenda has been, at least until recently, foreign to their culture, and they face greater challenges from Islam and Pentecostalism. "No more meetings," some say, "let's just mind the church here at home." Ironically, this attitude opens the door for TEC and ACoC to enter the Global South, bribing weaker members with "development aid."

The sea change in theology has weakened the ties that bind Anglicans around the world and raised the question whether "Communion" is not an empty label. There is nothing inherently wrong with autonomous governance of a church so long as it preserves the faith intact. Many Protestant and free-church bodies operate this way. Such autonomy does, however, fall short of the ideal of a worldwide Communion expressed in Ellerton's famous hymn:

> As o'er each continent and island
> The dawn leads on another day,
> The voice of prayer is never silent,
> Nor dies the strain of praise away.

SECOND MODEL:
THE CONCILIAR AUTHORITY OF BISHOPS

The model of ecclesiastical polity that I think best reflects the role of the historic episcopate in Anglicanism is *rule by bishops in council.* "Conciliarity" can mean a variety of things. It does not mean the absolute authority of bishops, either independently or collegially. Bishops are responsible to the whole church through their diocesan synods of clergy and laity, and Primates are responsible to their provincial synods. Nevertheless, the historic tradition of the church has always granted bishops a special role in matters of doctrine and discipline. In terms of ecclesiology, the idea of the church being guided by bishops begins with the Council of Jerusalem in Acts 15 and proceeds to the ecumenical councils of the undivided church.

The Great Schism in 1054 and the rise of papalism in the late Middle Ages introduced an alternative form of church order among Roman Catholics, although recollections of conciliar governance surfaced briefly at the Council of Constance (1414-1418). The Reformers, including Thomas Cranmer, held out some hope for a Protestant general council, but dominance of the autonomous state church model in Europe prevented its implementation.

The advent of the Anglican Communion in the mid-19th century necessitated a rethinking of authority in Anglicanism. Several promoters of the first Lambeth Conference hoped to convene a council of bishops that would deal with specific concerns for doctrine and discipline raised by Bishop Colenso's attack on biblical authority. While Archbishop Longley certainly accepted that bishops were the proper invitees, he steered the meeting clear of being considered a council by declaring it a "conference" only, with no authority over the autonomous churches, especially the Church of England. Hence as Paul Valliere notes, "the Lambeth Conference is a living monument to Anglican ambivalence about conciliarism. The gatherings at Lambeth look like episcopal councils, yet they are not. In fact, they were purposely designed not to be councils."

There were periodic attempts by Anglicans to identify the Anglican Communion as conciliar in character, the most important of those coming at the Lambeth

Conference in 1930. Lambeth 1930 is best known for its adoption of the definition of the Communion as "a fellowship, within the One Holy Catholic and Apostolic Church, of those duly constituted Dioceses, Provinces or Regional Churches in communion with the See of Canterbury" (Resolution 49). The Resolution was accompanied by a Report on The Anglican Communion, which was commended but not formally adopted by the Conference.

The Report attempts to describe the essence of Anglican Communion governance thus:

a. The Anglican Communion sees itself as part of the wider catholic, apostolic and missionary church, which has arisen out of the historical accidents of the divisions within Christendom but which is ecumenical in its hope of final reunion.

b. The Communion's identity as "Anglican" is an accident of its derivation from the British Isles, but the flourishing young churches of the Communion have now become autonomous. (This statement, in my view, demystifies the idea of churches being "in communion with the See of Canterbury." It is the historical connection, the "jurisdiction of honor," that binds the churches of the Communion together with Canterbury.)

c. Of the two available paradigms – Rome and Orthodoxy – the Communion is likened to the latter, which is seen to be the more ancient, as "the first four centuries were bound together by no administrative bond."

d. Conciliarity is not inconsistent with regional autonomy in matters of governance, because the churches are bound together spiritually by a common faith and practice.

So what differentiates conciliarism as a form of polity from a confederation of purely autonomous Provinces? The answer, it seems to me, is that conciliar governance involves *common consent to an agreed upon deposit of faith and worship and mutual submission of elders in the Spirit.* The common faith of the church involves a "concordant" reading of Scripture – "the rule of faith" – epitomized in the ecumenical creeds and historic confessions. The ecumenical Creeds carry the weight of the ages and the authority of the undivided church; the confessions reflect the more particular reading of that deposit within a particular historic tradition.

In the case of the Anglican Communion, the common deposit of faith is summarized in the Lambeth Quadrilateral (looking outward to other traditions) and the Thirty-Nine Articles and Book of Common Prayer (looking inward to those in our own tradition). The 1662 Prayer Book and the Articles carry the weight of having stood the test of time in an historical tradition. Occasions arise, however, where the church must address new issues either with a one-off injunction like the Lambeth Resolution I.10 of 1998 on Human Sexuality or with a new statement of faith, like the Jerusalem Declaration of GAFCON 2008. And all are to be continually tested for their conformity to the Scripture (Acts 17:11).

The proper instruments of conciliar governance in Anglicanism have been the Lambeth Conference of bishops and the Primates' "Meeting." The role of the former body is well-established. Despite the ambiguities of its start, the Lambeth Conference has functioned as a moral and spiritual authority for a century and a half. It is the very rejection of that authority following 1998 that has thrown the Communion into disarray. The Primates' Meeting had a shaky beginning, but a series of Lambeth resolutions from 1978 to 1998 speak of the "enhanced role" of the Primates in Communion governance. According to the Virginia Report (§6.32 [1995]) and the Windsor Report (§65 [2005]), the Primates have an *inherent authority* grounded in the role of bishops as successors of the apostles. This authority is not merely a matter of institutional power but of the truth of the apostolic gospel transmitted through the Scripture and the offices of the Church.

In my opinion, the conciliar model has the strongest claim among others as the foundation for Anglican Communion governance in a post-colonial era and has roots in the development of the Anglican Communion. However, a different model has grown up in the past few years, one that undermines true conciliarity.

THIRD MODEL: THE LAMBETH BUREAUCRACY

The third model, the executive bureaucracy, is the most common secular regime today, from totalitarian versions in the former Soviet Union and China to soft-power versions in Europe and North America. In an executive bureaucracy, it is often difficult to discern who exercises the greater power, the chief executive or the bureaucrats. In fact, when running well, the executive and the bureaucracy operate hand in glove.

In the case of the Anglican Communion, I use the phrase "Lambeth bureaucracy" because it combines two elements: the historical (and colonial) role of the Archbishop of Canterbury as first bishop among equals, with the American project of building a centralized bureaucracy. The key component of the bureaucracy is the Anglican Communion Office (ACO) and its chief administrator, the Secretary General. The wheels of the bureaucracy are greased with money, coming primarily from the United States and the UK.

Like any of its secular counterparts, the Lambeth bureaucracy pretends to be a broadly representative servant ministry. It is not. One striking feature of the ACO is the overwhelmingly lily-white complexion of its staff, which is probably less a matter of overt racism than a reflection of the old-boy network that requires purebred bureaucrats to come from the Anglo-American stable. Many contemporary bureaucracies employ methods of manipulation to maintain power and achieve their ends. In the case of the Lambeth bureaucracy, the official method is called "indaba."

Despite its African etymology with an aura of communal wisdom, indaba is in practice a means to *manipulate* opinion and results. The preparation of agenda, the writing of reports, the control of media all require careful oversight by "professionals," who happen also to be committed to the bureaucratic status quo. One may wonder whether the primacy of the Archbishop of Canterbury might be a check against the Communion Office. Theoretically yes perhaps, but actually not. Even the Bishop of Rome, whose primacy is theologically grounded, has difficulty overcoming the Vatican bureaucracy. The Archbishop of Canterbury is as enmeshed in the Lambeth bureaucracy as he is in the British Establishment, which explains the recent change of Archbishops resulting in no change in policies at the top.

Can executive bureaucracy be an authentic form of Communion governance? Certainly: the Pope and Vatican have functioned successfully for half a millennium. But the Vatican, unlike Lambeth, makes no pretense that its worldwide churches are autonomous or that there is no central authority in its ecclesiastical governance. Equally important, the Roman bureaucracy has resisted letting the forces of revisionism spin out of control. The current Lambeth bureaucracy, by contrast, has been protecting its liberal constituencies over the past decade and has done so at a high cost: alienation of a huge bloc of churches. Finally, for all the mystery of insider politics, Rome has found a way to elect pontiffs who are non-Italian and represent genuinely global concerns, whereas the Lambeth bureaucracy is still legally, politically, and ideologically tied to England and the secular West. It is significant that in 2012, the Primate chosen to represent the wider Anglican Communion on the Crown Nominations Commission, the body that nominated the current Archbishop of Canterbury, was Dr Barry Morgan, Primate of The Church in Wales, whose theological views are greatly at odds with the Global South churches.

THE EBB AND FLOW OF COMMUNION POWER 1998-2008

Lambeth Resolution I.10 represented not only a theological watershed in Anglican history but a political one as well. The Lambeth Conference of bishops by a wide majority had expressed itself on a central matter of Christian faith and morality. The two churches most directly affected exercised their autonomy to reject that authority. Indeed, in 2003, the Episcopal Church authorized and its Primate presided at the consecration of a practicing homosexual bishop, V. Gene Robinson. For the first time in its history – at least since its formation in 1867 – the Communion faced a critical question: could it discipline a member church that openly violated Communion and biblical norms?

The burden of this question fell on the Primates, who met in 2000, 2002, 2003, 2005 and 2007 to respond to the reaction, inaction and provocative action of The Episcopal Church. The Lambeth bureaucracy ran interference for TEC, turning aside a concrete proposal for discipline ("To Mend the Net") and setting up a "Windsor Process" that delayed action by the Primates for four years. Meeting in Dar es Salaam in 2007, the Primates, led by Abp. Peter Akinola, finally issued a communiqué with concrete conditions and an ultimate sanction of exclusion from Communion bodies. Although he was a signatory to the communiqué, the Archbishop of Canterbury reneged on applying the key sanctions. In particular, he proceeded to invite all the TEC bishops (except Gene Robinson) to attend Lambeth 2008 as full members – and this in spite of warnings from Global South churches that they would boycott the meeting if he did so.

The die was cast. The Lambeth bureaucracy proceeded to smother the Lambeth Conference – minus 280 bishops – with meaningless indaba interspersed by primatial addresses from Canterbury. The Archbishop made clear that the Primates had overstepped their authority and would subsequently be confined to the plantation of friendly conversation. On the other side, the Primates and bishops of seven Provinces attended the 2008 Global Anglican Future Conference (GAFCON) in Jerusalem and have since attended Communion functions sporadically.

The tide of conciliar governance had flowed to the full at Lambeth 1998. By 2008, one could hear its long, withdrawing roar from the shores of Albion, soon to break anew on the coasts of the Levant and Africa.

GAFCON AND THE FUTURE OF
THE ANGLICAN COMMUNION

It is my contention that in the past fifteen years, a sea change has come to the Anglican Communion, which has moved from conflict to crisis to dissolution. The Anglican Communion of Ellerton's hymn is no more. Yeats's vision is closer to reality: "things fall apart, the centre cannot hold." The tide of postmodern skepticism has undermined the seawall of Anglican collegiality and deference to tradition and has flooded some of the most prestigious churches, even as a new tide of the Spirit has been rising in the Global South. The "Instruments of Unity" have failed to guard the faith and unity of the Church, and in many cases have collaborated in promoting a false gospel. It is not possible to go back. Hence, the importance of the GAFCON movement.

GAFCON 2008 was remarkable in many ways. Organized on short notice and a modest budget, it drew more than 1,000 bishops, clergy and laity from 35 countries to the birthplace of the Church, Jerusalem. The Conference included inter-cultural fellowship, various topical seminars, lively worship, and pilgrimages to the holy places of Jesus and the apostles.

GAFCON 2008 was not merely a conference. Whereas the 2008 Lambeth Conference carefully avoided any decision-making, GAFCON acted "synodally," to borrow a term from Bishop Michael Nazir-Ali, and produced a succinct Statement, which did the following:

- It judged that the Anglican Communion was threatened by a departure from the truth of the Gospel and that the existing "Instruments" had proved unable or unwilling to deal with this crisis.

- It claimed not to depart from the Anglican Communion but "to reform, heal and revitalise the Anglican Communion and expand its mission to the world."

- It grounded its authority on the primary authority of Scripture, the creeds and councils of the ancient church, the Reformation Articles of Religion, and a contemporary statement of faith, the Jerusalem Declaration.

- It formed a GAFCON Primates' Council and invited the Anglican Church in North America (ACNA) to seek official recognition and membership on the Council.

- It formed a network, known as the Global Fellowship of Confessing Anglicans.

The GAFCON Statement and Jerusalem Declaration were developed under the supervision of the seven Primates present and in collaboration with bishops, scholars and other church leaders present. It was joyfully affirmed in a plenary session of 1200 participants on the last day of the Conference.

The Global Fellowship of Confessing Anglicans (GFCA) is still a fledgling body, and the Lambeth establishment has studiously ignored its existence. Nevertheless, its Primates' Council has met semi-annually for the past five years. In 2010, the Council recognized the Anglican Church in North America as a legitimate member of the Communion and welcomed its Archbishop, Robert Duncan, as a full member of the Council. Some additional Global South leaders have attended GFCA functions as observers, and many have legitimated the orders of clergy from ACNA who had been defrocked (the present writer included) and thrown out of their churches. GFCA has also authorized the ordination of four deacons (in Kenya) to serve the "Anglican Mission in England."

The burden of my argument is that the GFCA holds the key – and the only key – to a genuinely conciliar form of

Communion governance and the only possible alternative to the Lambeth bureaucracy. The upcoming GAFCON 2013 meeting in Nairobi will be the occasion whereby the movement goes forward, or possibly stalls.

In my view, the next crucial step to take is for GFCA churches to differentiate themselves from the Lambeth "Instruments" and re-form an Anglican polity along these lines:

1. *GFCA understands itself not as departing from the Anglican Communion but rather reconstituting Anglican polity on a theological, missional, and post-colonial basis.* God has given and empowered a vision of the global Anglican future in the rise of evangelical, Spirit-led Christianity among Anglicans in the Global South over the past half-century. The GAFCON movement is a response to that vision and is a truly global fellowship.

2. *GFCA proclaims that true Anglican identity is based on the "faith once for all delivered to the saints."* This faith is grounded in the Scriptures, preserved in the Church's creeds, formularies and liturgies, and adapted locally in the various contexts of mission. GFCA has offered the Jerusalem Statement and Declaration as a statement of the faith relevant to the future development of the Anglican Communion and normative for its members.

3. *GFCA churches and bishops will build internal solidarity and loyalty to the GAFCON movement and the Jerusalem Declaration.* One practical step will be for a majority of bishops and other key representatives from each member Province to meet at GAFCON

242

2013. In particular, a bishops' assembly should begin to see itself as a deliberative body.

4. *GFCA member churches will look to its Primates' Council as the ecclesiastical authority in matters of doctrine, discipline, and worship* – even if some Primates continue to attend the Lambeth Primates' Meeting.

5. *GFCA will establish networks and most likely a representative body of members of different ranks and ages to meet its collective mission.* Much of the collaborative work will be accomplished through networks addressing specific needs, such as education (at all levels), evangelism, development, and public policy.

6. *GFCA Primates' Council will identify a presiding primate, as it has been doing, on the basis of seniority and giftedness, rather than being rooted in a particular see.* It will commit adequate funds and manpower to an effective secretariat to carry forward the work of the Fellowship.

7. *GFCA will continue to accord the Archbishop of Canterbury a "primacy of honour" and work with him, where possible, for the renewal of the Christian faith in England and its daughter churches.* GFCA will seek to build authentic ecumenical relations inside and outside the Anglican fold, including the existing Anglican "Instruments" and non-GFCA provinces. While the Archbishop has not to date publicly recognized the fact that a second polity has emerged under the aegis of the Communion, it would be a bold and welcome step out of the institutional boat if he did.

This agenda expresses my personal aspiration for the polity of the Global Fellowship of Confessing Anglicans. Rome was not built in a day, and no doubt a reformed and renewed Communion will emerge over time, under the mercy of God, from the prayers and wisdom of many others. The upcoming GAFCON 2013 Conference will set many different matters before its membership. It is my conviction that reconstituting the Communion, which was begun dramatically at the first Conference in 2008, will be a piece of its ongoing work, fulfilling its high calling to be "not just a moment in time, but a movement in the Spirit."

AFTERWORD

DID GAFCON 2013 FULFILL MY HOPES?

The Conference is now over. It ended, as do many conferences, on a spiritual high, with the Holy Communion in the august Anglican Cathedral in Nairobi, followed by the reading and acclamation of the Nairobi Communiqué, the many thanks to the organizers and Kenyan hosts, farewells to friends from many countries, and flight home.

I do not intend to report on all my encounters at the Conference nor my privilege in leading a "mini-conference" on the subject of "The Ministry of the Holy Spirit in the Life of the Church." Rather I shall focus on those outcomes of GAFCON 2013 that relate directly to Communion governance and the hopes expressed in my essay.

My first observation is that the Conference was conducted with a sense of authority. We were greeted by the Archbishop of Kenya, who is also the Chairman of the

Primates' Council. The Archbishop is soft-spoken and kindly, but he has also shown his mettle in standing up for the GAFCON movement on many occasions. The Primates met each lunch-time for fellowship and counsel. The Statement Committee, on which I served, was chaired by a bishop and included an archbishop who participated fully in the stresses of writing and revising. The 331 bishops in attendance processed in festive regalia at the opening Eucharist. Later they met *in camera* and discussed current matters. One of their resolutions is cited in the Nairobi Communiqué:

> (Commitment 4) "to affirm and endorse the position of the Primates' Council in providing oversight in cases where provinces and dioceses compromise biblical faith, including the affirmation of a duly discerned call to ministry. This may involve ordination and consecration if the situation requires."

The Nairobi meeting qualifies, in my opinion, as a *conciliar gathering of bishops*. Of course, they were not the only participants. Other delegates included clergy and laity chosen by each Province to represent it. This was not a "come one, come all" gathering. Each delegate was required to affirm the Jerusalem Declaration and Statement as a condition of participation. Hence the make-up of GAFCON 2013 involved *common consent to an agreed upon deposit of faith and worship and mutual submission of elders in the Spirit*.

The reception of the Archbishop of Canterbury bespeaks the authority of GFCA. He came, at his own request, to meet with the GAFCON Primates and later expressed the desire to show solidarity with the victims of the terror attack in Nairobi. He did meet with the Primates informally prior to the Conference. He sent video greetings to conference participants, which were received with polite applause. He offered to pray for the meeting, and the meeting returned that wish and prayed for him on the final day of the Conference. He gave no public indication on either of these occasions that he recognized GFCA as a political entity. Indeed, his reference to his visits to "the 37 provinces" of the Communion presumably refers to the list in London and excludes the Anglican Church in North America, which is recognized as a full member of the GFCA Primates' Council. Throughout the Conference, respect was paid to Canterbury, but there was no sense that the actions taken in Nairobi required his advice and consent.

The crucial ecclesiological principle is stated in the introduction of the Nairobi Communiqué:

> In our gathering, we reaffirmed our view that we are a global fellowship of confessing Anglicans, engaged in a movement of the Holy Spirit which is both personal and ecclesial.... We believe we have acted as an important and effective instrument of Communion during a period in which other instruments of Communion have failed both to uphold gospel priorities in the Church, and to heal the divisions among us.

First, the Communiqué reaffirms the understanding from 2008 that GAFCON is "not a moment in time but a movement of the Spirit." This phrase is not flight of rhetoric but a claim that GFCA is among other things a God-ordained "ecclesial" entity. Secondly, the Conference identifies itself as an "instrument of Communion" called into being because of the failure of other Instruments of Communion. I suppose some will take this claim as an open rebuke of the existing organs of the Lambeth bureaucracy. It is that, and my essays on Communion governance stand as testimony as to why such a rebuke is justified. But it is more than that: it is a positive declaration

246

that the GFCA plans to be a vehicle of God's grace to reform and revitalize the Anglican Communion.

Some may ask by what right the GFCA appoints itself an instrument. In an early draft, the Statement Committee proposed saying that "we are *conscious* that we have become an instrument of Communion." I think that wording is revealing, even if the final form moves consciousness into conviction. What I mean is that the GAFCON movement did not start out intentionally to overturn existing authorities but rather over a period of fifteen years came to realize that no other option was workable and that God had indeed formed new bonds of affection among its members during the times of trial.

So is the GFCA laying the groundwork for a separate Communion? Absolutely not! At the first GAFCON virtually all the delegates were adamant that they were not leaving the Anglican Communion, because "we *are* the Anglican Communion!" Some may think this is verbal trickery. It is not. There is nothing sacrosanct about the so-called Instruments of Communion. To be sure, the role of the Archbishop of Canterbury and the Lambeth Conference carry the weight of almost 150 years' continuance. However, for good or ill, Archbishop Longley refused to grant the first Lambeth Conference ecclesial authority as a council, and by so doing he built in a weakness that has been a major reason for the recent crisis. During the past decade, whenever the Primates proposed more authoritative action – e.g., the "To Mend the Net" proposal or the Dar es Salaam Communiqué – Canterbury squelched the attempt.

How will the GFCA model being an instrument of Communion? I think many features are already clear. First of all, it will be "confessional," i.e., the essentials of the Christian faith in the Anglican tradition will be at the heart

247

of its identity. Secondly, it will be evangelistic and committed to mission. Thirdly, its leadership will come from the Global South, and it will call on special talents from the West. Finally, it will have a form of mixed polity, similar to that of the two Conferences in 2008 and 2013. Finally, the GFCA's "Commitment" is "to meet again at the next GAFCON" (Commitment 9). This is not a threat but a promise that the movement has a future, indeed that it represents the Global Anglican future.

There is much work ahead to turn aspiration into an enduring reality. The GFCA has been more successful at planning conferences than at designing the interim bodies and networks to give life to the movement. The flow of support from Africa to the West and back again has taken new shape as many North American churches have been forced to rebuild their structures from the ground up. The Communiqué faces this problem in the section titled "Strengthening the GFCA." I think there are good reasons to think that our leadership is up to the task of building a necessary central infrastructure to serve the movement while retaining its conciliar form of government.

Did GAFCON 2013 fulfill my hopes? Eminently so!

Of course, the question is not whether I am satisfied but whether God has been at work. The bishop's consecration service of the American Prayer Book contains the following collect:

> O God of unchangeable power and eternal light: Look favorably on your whole Church, that wonderful and sacred mystery; by the effectual working of your providence, carry out in tranquillity the plan of salvation; let the whole world see and know that things which were cast down are being raised up, and things which had grown old are being made new, and that all things are being brought to their perfection by him through whom

all things were made, your Son Jesus Christ our Lord; who lives and reigns with you, in the unity of the Holy Spirit, one God, for ever and ever. *Amen.*

I have always been suspicious of this collect, as it was frequently intoned by various "apostolic pioneers" and doctrinal innovators. Now I have come to think that this collect, prayed in the right way, may well express the hopes and confidence of the GAFCON movement. Perhaps indeed "God has chosen what is low and despised in the world, even things that are not, to bring to nothing things that are" (1 Corinthians 1:28).

ESSAY 9

THE GLOBAL ANGLICAN COMMUNION COVENANT

LOOKING BACK, LOOKING AHEAD

(2016)

One of the claims to historic and evangelistic significance of the Anglican Communion is its worldwide coverage. The 38, now 39, Provinces are spread from continent to continent and island-to-island, with Anglicans officially numbering 85 million members. The large majority of these Anglicans live outside the developed West, especially once one deeply discounts the 26 million nominal Anglicans in England.

The realignment of Anglicans between Global North and Global South has been led through two main networks: the Global South or South-to-South Network and the GAFCON movement. The former network claims 26 provinces (16 were present at the Cairo conference in 2016), while GAFCON claims nine provinces (plus five "branches"). These networks are overlapping since all GAFCON churches are also in the Global South Network; however, GAFCON concentrates the power of the largest provinces – Nigeria, Uganda, Kenya, Rwanda and sometimes Sudan – with a strong governance structure.

In October 2016, I attended the Sixth Global South Conference in Cairo and addressed the Primates gathered there. I made two main points in this address. The first point is that the official Provinces in North America have departed irreversibly from the faith once for all delivered to the saints and that the Church of England is trending in the same direction and is in no position to defend the faith. My second point is that in God's providence, two movements of orthodox Anglicanism have been raised up from the Global South and that these two movements need urgently to lay aside any differences and come together in a stronger alliance, under what I called the "Global Anglican Communion Covenant."

The Primates did not respond directly to my proposal for a joint Covenant. In the Conference Communiqué, however, they did make the following statement on "Unity in the Body":

"22. Our fidelity to this Anglican heritage also prompts us to repent of our failings in keeping the unity of the Spirit through the bond of peace in God's household. We recognise that division and dislocation amongst orthodox Anglicans have arisen during the disputes on human sexuality. We repent of our failings to share with one another more sacrificially across ethnic, national and economic divides in the Global South. We confess that our disunity makes us less able to be an effective sign of God's kingdom in the world:

"a) We affirm and cherish the witness of the Global Anglican Future Conference (GAFCON), and other Anglican Churches and networks that God has raised up in guarding the integrity of the gospel.

"b) We recall, the commitment of the Global South Primates' Steering Committee Communiqué in March 2008 to pursue unity amongst the doctrinally orthodox. We will not allow different convictions and strategies on relating to the Communion over specific issues to disrupt the common vision, unity and trust we share. Therefore, we need to be attentive to what God is speaking to our Churches in the GAFCON Jerusalem Statement and Declaration of 2008, the Nairobi Communiqué of 2013, and look forward to working together with them in guarding and propagating the good deposit of faith that we have received.

"c) This conference rejoices with the 2015 decision of the Global South Primates to welcome the Anglican Church in North America (ACNA) as a partner Province. Additionally, we will continue to extend our support and fellowship to orthodox Anglican dioceses and parishes in those Provinces which have departed from the biblical and historic teaching on human sexuality and marriage.

"d) We need to respect different integrities for those Churches that accept the ordination of women and those who do not. Mutual respect should be given to different streams of Anglo-Catholic, Evangelical and Charismatic Anglicans."

I want to recognize a number of friends and colleagues from the Global South whom I have met over the past years, especially in the decade when I served in Uganda. But I also note that there are many new faces, new bishops and Primates who have taken office recently. Of course, turnover is of the nature of human life, but it also means that sometimes we – the Church – have to relearn or review its teaching, its tradition, its history.

So perhaps I am coming to you as a *watchman*, not a prophet like Jeremiah or Ezekiel, but as one who has viewed and participated in unfolding events, over 30 years in the Episcopal Church and 20 years in the Anglican Communion. So please indulge me as I make a brief survey of *where we have come from* and *where I think we need to go*, of looking back and looking ahead.

A Critical Year – 1998

Let's begin with the Lambeth Conference of 1998 – I believe this was in fact *the last real Lambeth Conference. Several major results* emerged from Lambeth 1998.

The most controversial result was Lambeth Resolution I.10 on Human Sexuality. I am sure you have read it. Here are the *normative* words:

> This Conference, in view of the teaching of Scripture, upholds faithfulness in marriage between a man and a woman in lifelong union, and believes that abstinence is right for those who are not called to marriage; ...rejecting homosexual practice as incompatible with Scripture, [it] cannot advise the legitimising or blessing of same sex unions nor ordaining those involved in same gender unions.

I say these are the *normative* words because they lay out the *moral principle* of God's creating man in his image male and female and the *biblical basis* for seeing homosexual practice and same-sex marriage as sinful and directly contrary to God's will. I'll be looking at the implications of this principle later.

There was a *second result* that undergirds the Resolution on Sexuality and that concerns *the authority of the Holy Scriptures*. There were several resolutions, all from the Global South, affirming the central authority of the Bible for faith and life. Here are two:

> [This Conference] reaffirms the primary authority of the Scriptures, according to their testimony and supported by our own historic formularies; (Resolution III.1)

> [This Conference] affirms that our creator God, transcendent as well as immanent, communicates with us authoritatively through the Holy Scriptures of the Old and New Testaments; and ... that these Holy Scriptures contain 'all things necessary to salvation' and are for us the 'rule and ultimate standard' of faith and practice. (Resolution III.5)

A *third result* was the commitment to *enhance the authority of the Primates' Meeting*: [This Conference] reaffirms

Resolution 18.2(a) of Lambeth 1988 which "urges that encouragement be given to a developing collegial role for the Primates' Meeting under the presidency of the Archbishop of Canterbury, so that the Primates' Meeting is able to exercise an enhanced responsibility in offering guidance on doctrinal, moral and pastoral matters; (Resolution III.6)

There is an inter-locking character to these Resolutions. The Bishops recognized that the issue of homosexuality presented a looming challenge to the historic faith of the Church and would be ultimately divisive of its unity and witness. Therefore the Conference:

- spelled out a clear statement of doctrine;

- grounded that doctrine on the primary authority of Scripture; and

- provided a means to discipline the churches of the Communion should members repudiate its teaching and practice, the means being the council of the Primates executed through the Archbishop of Canterbury.

One *final result* needs to be noted: all of these resolutions *originated from the Global South*, and indeed the Global South bishops threatened to depart the Conference unless these matters were addressed.

THE AFTERMATH OF LAMBETH 1998

The decisions of the 1998 Lambeth Conference were approved by large majorities of bishops present but led to years of tension, strife and diversion from the Church's missionary call, right down to the present day, because the leaders of the Episcopal Church (USA) immediately and expressly rejected them and sealed this rejection in 2003 by consecrating an openly homosexual as a bishop, V. Gene

Robinson. In short, *one member church repudiated by word and deed a doctrinal and moral teaching of Scripture confirmed by fellow bishops around the world.*

Let me stop here and say a word about why the issues of human sexuality are so important. Matters of sexual orientation and practice are not a *secondary* or *indifferent issue* like making the sign of the cross in the liturgy. What is at stake is the fundamental doctrine of human nature – Christian anthropology – of man in the image of God, male and female.

You probably know by now that the Episcopal Church has ordained openly homosexual priests and bishops and has approved same-sex marriage. Bishop Robinson, for instance, while living openly with his partner for many years, married the man once same sex-marriage was legalized in the United States. The marriage didn't last, and Bishop Robinson now is divorced, for the second time (he divorced his wife in 1986). Nevertheless Bishop Robinson remains a bishop in good standing in the Episcopal Church.

It has recently come to light that the Church of England knowingly appointed a homosexual bishop who lives in a celibate relationship with a man. The Anglican Church of Canada just this past week elected a homosexual bishop who is partnered in a non-celibate relationship and whose relationship will presumably be blessed in Holy Matrimony before long, since the Canadian church has now approved same-sex marriage.

In all these matters, the Church is following the culture, what is called the LGBT movement: that stands for Lesbian, Gay, Bisexual, Transgender. This movement advocates not just homosexuality but complete fluidity of one's so-called "gender identity." Let's look at the "T," "transgender." Transgender individuals are those who define their sexual identity in opposition to their genetic or birth sex. Often they seek to adapt their bodies accordingly by hormone treatment or surgery.

Now let me say that there are a rare few people who are born with a genetic defect: they are called "intersex." There are others who have a psychological confusion called "gender dysphoria." It is the Church's call to minister to these people pastorally and sympathetically. What the Church cannot do, however, is to declare that transgender persons are normal and to be emulated. But this is exactly what many Western societies are doing, and in some cases the Church is following right along. One Episcopal priest, formerly a female who now claims to be a male, has preached recently at the Washington National Cathedral. A priest of the Church of England, ordained as a male, has now "transitioned," as they call it, to being a woman. This is apparently now a local option in the Church there. As Western societies actively proselytize young people, even children, to change their sexual identity, such examples will multiply in these churches.

The acceptance of transgender persons in the Episcopal Church is a matter of church law. Here is the relevant canon on ministry of the Episcopal Church.

CANON 1: Of the Ministry of All Baptized Persons

Section 2. No person shall be denied access to the discernment process for any ministry, lay or ordained, in this Church because of race, color, ethnic origin, national origin, sex, *marital status, sexual orientation, gender identity and expression,* disabilities or age, except as otherwise provided by these Canons. [emphasis added]

In this canon, "marital status" means that divorced persons have an absolute right to ordination; further, "sexual orientation" clearly includes homosexual practice; and "gender identity and expression" explicitly includes transgendered persons. Acceptance of these practices is not only *permitted*, but it is *required*. Any priest or bishop who denies one of these individuals access to ordination on one of these grounds may be brought up for trial and deposed.

I apologize for going on at some length here, but I suspect that many of you from the Global South find all this incredible. Would that it were! But beyond that, it illustrates my claim that the North American churches have departed the fundamental teaching of Scripture and the apostolic faith concerning God's good creation of man and woman. Further, once the churches accept the first step on homosexuality, all manner of other deviations follow. *You cannot pull one central thread out of the Church's doctrine without the whole garment fraying and ultimately falling apart.* That is what has happened in Western churches today. To use the language of the Windsor Report: the fabric of the Communion has been torn, and as Jesus said, a torn garment cannot be sewed together (Mark 2:21).

I have now spoken about the unravelling of the *church's doctrine*; this leads to the question of *church discipline*. Various dioceses and provinces have disciplinary canons which deal with the situation where a priest or bishop violates church teaching or practice. But when it comes to the Anglican Communion, there is no such provision for discipline of false teaching or practice. It had been assumed, fairly successfully for more than a century, that Anglicans held all important things in common. After 1998, the Communion was tested and this assumption was found wanting.

Lambeth 1998 did anticipate the problem with its call for the enhanced authority of the Primates' Meeting. The problem was that carrying out the decisions of the Primates' Meeting was left in the hands of the Archbishop of Canterbury and the Anglican Communion Office in London. This was problematic because the Archbishops were under pressure from gay activists in their own church and culture, and the Communion Office was funded by the very churches whose misconduct was being addressed.

Hence, the Primates' decisions were not executed faithfully. A telling example of this situation occurred in 2002. Two Global South Primates, Archbishop Drexel Gomez of the West Indies and Archbishop Maurice Sinclair of the Southern Cone (South America) brought an excellent proposal to the Primates' Meeting in 2002. The proposal was called "To Mend the Net" and included an 8-step process of discernment in the case where a church had violated Communion norms (for a biblical parallel, see Matthew 18:15-18). At the end of the process, if the church involved refused correction, the Primates through the Archbishop of Canterbury could relegate the church to observer status and ultimately authorize the formation of a replacement jurisdiction.

"To Mend the Net" assumes that the Primates are the rightful adjudicators of communion discipline, but it did defer to Canterbury to execute their decisions, even to place the proposal on the agenda. Unfortunately, the outgoing Archbishop, George Carey, missed an historic opportunity and kept "To Mend the Net" off the main agenda of the Meeting. It was referred to committee and never heard of again.

After the consecration of Gene Robinson in 2003, the Primates again gathered urgently and passed resolutions to rein in the Episcopal Church. Once again the North Americans spurned the resolutions, and Rowan Williams, the new Archbishop of Canterbury, diverted the Primates' resolutions into the so-called Windsor process. The Windsor process was ineffective, but it did produce one fruitful idea: the idea of an *Anglican Communion Covenant.*

TWO MOVEMENTS
THE SOUTH-TO-SOUTH ENCOUNTER

1998 was a critical year in the life of the Communion. So was the year 2006. This year, ten years ago, was important because in 2006 *two movements* from the Global South took action to address the crisis caused in the Anglican West.

One movement was the *South-to-South* or *Global South Anglican network*, whose regular "Anglican encounters" from 1994 to the present have brought together delegations from the far-flung provinces of the Communion. The Second Trumpet statement from Kuala Lumpur in 1997 was a firm proclamation of the authority of Scripture and of biblical sexuality, themes that emerged the following year at Lambeth. The Third Trumpet from the Red Sea urged implementation of the Windsor Report, and in particular the Global South Primates took up the idea of an Anglican Communion Covenant.

On 30th May 2006, the Global South Steering Committee produced a draft of a "Proposed Anglican Covenant," which included the following sections:

- Our Intention
- Our Identity and Purpose
- Our Confession
- Our Common Worship
- Our Ordering of Ministers
- Our Communion
- Our Anglican History
- Our Comprehension of Different Traditions
- Our Instruments of Unity
- Our Government and Ecclesiastical Law
- Our Communion Law
- Our Declaration

This draft was placed on the agenda of the Global South Primates' Meeting in Kigali in September 2006. In the meantime, the Archbishop of Canterbury announced the formation of a Communion-wide "Covenant Drafting Committee," to be headed by Archbishops Drexel Gomez and John Chew (Williams did not announce the other members until after Kigali). The Global South Primates accepted Canterbury's offer and said:

> We believe that an Anglican Covenant will demonstrate to the world that it is possible to be a truly global communion where differences are not affirmed at the expense of faith and truth but within the framework of a common confession of faith and mutual accountability.

Some of us who had observed Western tactics feared that Canterbury was seeking to head off an independent Global South initiative and co-opt it. And so it turned out. To be sure, the first draft Covenant, the so-called Nassau Draft, retains a great deal of material from the Global South original. Here are its sections:

- Preamble
- The Life We Share: Common Catholicity, Apostolicity and Confession of Faith
- Our Commitment to the Confession of Faith
- The Life We Share with Others: Our Anglican Vocation
- Our Unity and Common Life
- Unity of the Communion
- Our Declaration

The Nassau Draft is hardly a finished product, and unfortunately, as criticism flooded in from Western churches, subsequent drafts – the St. Andrews Draft and the Ridley Cambridge Draft – became weaker and weaker. Nevertheless, the Ridley draft did retain a provision by which an erring church could be disciplined. In 2009 at ACC-14 in Kingston, Jamaica, most Global South churches were prepared to approve the draft, when at the final moment, Rowan Williams, under pressure from the Episcopal delegation, unilaterally withdrew the key disciplinary provision, took it back to England and neutered it.

The Anglican Communion Covenant never recovered. It has been approved without reservation by nine Provinces but not by the Church of England, the Episcopal Church, the Church of Australia or by the largest Provinces in the Global South.

The Province of South East Asia added a lengthy "preamble" to its letter of accession:

a) that those who accede to the Anglican Communion Covenant will unequivocally abide by Lambeth 1998 Resolution 1.10 in its spirit and intent;

b) that those Provinces and Dioceses whose actions violate Lambeth Resolution 1.10 ... are expected to rescind their actions, and bring their public doctrine and practice in line with Lambeth 1.10, before acceding to the Anglican Communion Covenant; and

c) that Churches that accede to the Anglican Communion Covenant should bear authentic witness to the orthodox faith by an unequivocal commitment to the standards of moral and ethical holiness as set by Biblical norms in all aspects of their communal life.

d) that the Primates Meeting, being responsible for Faith and Order, should be the body to oversee the Anglican Communion Covenant in its implementation.

This preamble clearly upholds the doctrine and discipline of Lambeth 1998 and is an important statement guiding the Global South as it moves forward. These principles should be incorporated in any new draft going forward.

A Canterbury-crafted Anglican Communion Covenant has failed, as did the Windsor process, not surprisingly, as the entire enterprise was designed to avoid any real discipline of the Episcopal Church and Anglican Church of Canada.

TWO MOVEMENTS
THE GLOBAL ANGLICAN FUTURE CONFERENCE

This brings me to the second *Global South* movement that dates back to 2006: the Global Anglican Future Conference, or GAFCON. In early 2006, Archbishop Peter Akinola, the Chairman of CAPA, directed a group of three – Archbishop Nicholas Okoh, Bishop Zac Niringiye, and myself (I was living in Uganda at the time) – to draft a document called "The Road to Lambeth." The Road to Lambeth was commended by CAPA to the Global South Primates in Kigali. Here is the key section:

> The current situation is a twofold crisis for the Anglican Communion: a crisis of doctrine and a crisis of leadership, in which the failure of the "Instruments" of the Communion to exercise discipline has called into question the viability of the Anglican Communion as a united Christian body under a common foundation of faith, as is supposed by the Lambeth Quadrilateral. Due to this breakdown of discipline, we are not sure that we can in good conscience continue to spend our time, our money and our prayers on behalf of a body that proclaims two Gospels, the Gospel of Christ and the Gospel of Sexuality. We must therefore receive assurances from the Primates and the Archbishop of Canterbury that this crisis will be resolved *before* a Lambeth Conference is convened.

The Global South Primates at Kigali commended "The Road to Lambeth" for further study, and it was sent to the Archbishop of Canterbury prior to the 2007 Primates'

Meeting in Dar es Salaam. *Just as Lambeth 1998 was the last real Lambeth Conference, so also Dar es Salaam was the last real Primates' Meeting.* At Dar es Salaam the Primates laid down specific directions for the discipline of the Episcopal Church and stated that unless it repented, its bishops should not be invited to the 2008 Lambeth Conference. Archbishop Rowan Williams reneged on the Resolutions of Dar es Salaam, and hence there was no discipline of the Episcopal Church, *because none was intended by Canterbury.* The 2008 Global Anglican Future Conference in Jerusalem was the result.

GAFCON accomplished a number of things. First, it brought together an assembly of more than 1,000 Anglican bishops, clergy and laypeople from North and South (and Down Under) for a time of teaching, worship, and veneration of the Church's holy places. A second GAFCON conference was held in Nairobi in 2013. Second, it established a strong doctrinal foundation by adopting the classic definition of Anglican identity found in Canon A5 of the Church of England:

> The doctrine of the Church is grounded in the Holy Scriptures and in such teachings of the ancient Fathers and Councils of the Church as are agreeable to the said Scriptures. In particular, such doctrine is to be found in the Thirty-nine Articles of Religion, the Book of Common Prayer and the Ordinal.

It fleshed out that general statement in the Jerusalem Declaration. The Jerusalem Declaration has two main parts. The *first part* affirms the historic Anglican commitment to the catholic and apostolic faith:

1. The primacy of the Gospel received by grace through faith.

2. The authority of Scripture as the Word of God written.

3. The historic Creeds and Councils.

4. The Thirty-nine Articles of Religion as authoritative for Anglicans today.

5. The Lordship and atoning death of Jesus Christ for our redemption.

6. The sacramental heritage of 1662 Book of Common Prayer as a norm for worship and prayer.

7. The threefold order of bishops, priests and deacons and the Ordinal.

The *second part* addresses a range of biblical mandates that are relevant to contemporary society and issues:

8. The creation of man in God's image male and female and the primacy of Christian marriage.

9. The Great Commission of Christ to make disciples of all nations.

10. The call to stewardship of the earth and empowerment of the poor.

11. The call to Christian unity and ecumenism.

12-13. The need for diversity in secondary matters but rejection of those who deny the orthodox faith.

14. The expectation of the Return of Jesus Christ and the ongoing work of the Spirit.

Many people, even some who are not in GAFCON, have praised the Jerusalem Declaration, and it was considered for inclusion in a collection of creeds and confessions. Third, GAFCON addressed in a concrete way the

Episcopal Church's attacks on faithful North American Anglicans, who have been expelled from their churches and their clergy defrocked (count me and others here present in this number). It did so by forming a Primates' Council, which subsequently recognized the newly established Anglican Church in North America and seated Archbishop Duncan as a fellow Primate. (The Global South network, I might add, has also recognized the ACNA and its delegation is present here today.)

The final achievement of GAFCON is that *it began to operate in a conciliar fashion* with a Primates' Council that represented its constituent churches. The Primates' Council speaks authoritatively for the member Provinces. Its Chairman is genuinely "first among equals," and the office has passed so far to three archbishops in succession.

The two movements from the Global South that emerged in 2006 have always overlapped in membership and have a shared vision of a reformed and revitalized Anglican Communion. They need each other, as the Bible says: "Two are better than one, because they have a good reward for their toil" (Ecclesiastes 4:9). It is time to come and work together for the sake of our beloved Communion.

WHERE WE STAND TODAY

Let me sum up. These two movements from the Global South have reconfigured the Anglican Communion as we know it. Each movement has had its achievements:

The South-to-South movement:

- Has gathered representative delegations of laity and clergy, men and women, from the various churches to consult on various matters. One might fairly call them a true "Anglican Consultative Council."

- Has proposed an Anglican Covenant as a way of reforming the Communion to be an instrument of orthodoxy and mission.

The GAFCON movement:

- Has offered a strong Statement of biblical Anglican faith, the Jerusalem Declaration.

- Has sponsored vital spiritual assemblies for Anglicans around the world.

- Has set up a governing structure for its member churches.

These achievements are real but incomplete. They await further development under the direction of the Holy Spirit.

I believe the time is ripe for the next step: to come together behind a *Global Anglican Communion Covenant (and Structure)*. Let me carefully define these terms:

Global – The Covenant will represent the global character of the Anglican churches that are the heirs of the missionary movements from the Church of England. While the covenant will include churches in the global North (and Down Under) as equal members, its impetus will come from the Global South churches.

Anglican Communion – The Covenant will represent the Anglican Communion. Delegates to GAFCON 2008 were asked two questions upon arrival in Jerusalem: "what do you expect from this Conference?" and "do you plan to leave the Anglican Communion?" The overwhelming answers were: "yes, we expect GAFCON to take decisive action"; and "no, we are not leaving the Anglican Communion; we *are* the Anglican Communion."

Covenant – Covenant is a good biblical term bringing together the notions of divine sovereignty and binding commitment, which should be the heart and soul of a fellowship, a *koinonia*, of churches. Given the history I have traced above, some have concluded that "covenant" is a tainted word and prefer something else like "Governing Agreement." Let us not quibble over names.

Structure – Covenants govern. A covenant is the skeleton, the framework of a living "polity," whether of nations or churches. Structures are defined by the covenant and members then carry out the work of the body. A living Global Anglican Communion Covenant will require a governing structure and instruments to carry out the coordinated work of the Communion.

THE WAY FORWARD

What are the necessary steps toward producing a Global Anglican Communion Covenant? Drafting an effective and long-lasting covenant will be an arduous matter and will require further consultation and further drafts. However, let me suggest the following steps:

1. Bring together the leadership of the Global South and GAFCON movements to work on the Covenant.

2. Return to the Nassau Draft of the Covenant as the base text, which is largely the product of the Global South.

3. Integrate into the Nassau Draft the positive fruits of the Global South movements, such as Lambeth Resolution I.10, "To Mend the Net" proposals from Abps. Gomez and Sinclair, Canon A5 and the Jerusalem Declaration from GAFCON, and the "Preamble" from the Province of South East Asia.

4. Highlight the Great Commission and mission priorities of the Church, including evangelism,

church planting, education and economic development.

5. Develop further the conciliar mode of governance that undergirds the idea of the enhanced role of the Primates.

6. Develop appropriate governing structures, including existing ones, to supersede the current Instruments of Unity.

Because the final step will certainly be contested by many in the West, let me explain it further. To begin with, let's dispel the notion that the Instruments of Unity have been carved in stone from ancient times.

- The idea of four coordinated "Instruments of Unity" goes back only 20 years (the Virginia Report) and has no legal standing.

- Two of the Instruments – the Anglican Consultative Council (1968) and the Primates' Meeting (1978) – are of recent vintage with overlapping roles.

- The past twenty years have demonstrated that the Instruments are incapable of leading the Communion or disciplining its erring members.

The convening of bishops at Lambeth by Archbishop Longley goes back to 1866. The Lambeth Conference emerged as an expression of British colonialism, necessary at the time, but now an outdated paradigm. Even at its birth, Archbishop Longley intentionally defined the bishops' meeting as a "conference" rather than a council lest its authority interfere with his role in the Established Church. This tension between the formal authority of the Archbishop of Canterbury in the Church of England and his informal role as head of the Anglican Communion is baked into the relationship, and his commitments to the former inevitably overshadow his role in the latter.

Right now the Church of England is wrestling with how it is to function as a faithful Christian body in a largely secular, even anti-Christian society. It certainly looks like Archbishop Welby and other senior church leaders (represented in the Pilling Report and "Shared Conversations") think they can find a middle way of compromise by refusing same-sex marriage and providing blessings of active homosexual couples. This compromise is theologically incoherent, has nothing in common with the Anglican *via media*, and will not keep the peace with sexual radicals inside and outside the church. We should certainly pray for the Church of England and its leaders, but we should also recognize that they are in no position to lead the wider Communion at this time.

The churches of the Global South are proud of their heritage and grateful for the legacy of the Gospel brought from England. The realignment of the Communion will involve losses as well as gains. The current Instruments will undoubtedly exist alongside the new structures of the Global Anglican Communion Covenant; however, membership in the Covenant will entail a primary loyalty to it and fellow members. The titular role of Canterbury on the world stage will undoubtedly continue, and one wonders whether he might serve as patron much as the Queen is the titular head of the Church of England.

But let me be blunt: *the days of the colonial Anglican Communion are past and will not return.* The question is whether the children of the mother church, having come of age, will find a way to live into the mission that was their inheritance. Failure to do so, I fear, will lead to a fracturing and dissolution of Anglicanism, as was the case of Israel in the days of the Judges when "everyone did what was right in his own eyes" (Judges 21:25).

RADICAL REPENTANCE AND WALKING TOGETHER

Now we come to the final element of the Global Anglican Communion Covenant: *the Declaration of commitment to one another.* Churches must commit themselves to the common goals and structure of the Covenant if it is to become something more than a "friendly society." This will require a delicate balance between the *autonomy* of Provinces and churches, each with its own Constitution and canons, and the *interdependence* of covenanting churches, agreeing to decide important matters of doctrine and discipline consensually. Delicate as the balance may be, it is possible to find that balance by the mercy of God.

What I am proposing today is nothing less than a sea change in the way the Anglican Communion has lived over the past 150 years. Change of any sort is difficult, but I am convinced that if we are prepared to "repent and believe the Gospel" (Mark 1:15), God will be faithful to lead us. Jesus promises to build the church on a firm foundation against the gates of hell. I am bold to think that He will empower us if we are faithful in this present time of crisis.

This is not the first such time of crisis for God's people. A great judgment befell the nation of Israel in the 6th century BC. The prophet Jeremiah appealed to the leaders with these words: "Thus says the LORD: 'Stand by the roads, and look, and ask for the ancient paths, where the good way is; and walk in it, and find rest for your souls.'" Unfortunately, the prophet continues: "But they said, 'We will not walk in it'" (Jeremiah 6:16). I believe a similar crisis arose for the historic Anglican Communion in 1998. It was a crisis of a radically false Gospel in one of its churches that

271

went undisciplined. Like the leaders of Israel, the authorities in Lambeth refused to lead, and the fabric of the Communion has been irreparably torn.

Today a similar crisis faces the Global South churches and those allied to them. Will we walk together? Will we work together? Will we lay aside some of the ways we may have offended each other in the past decade? Will we resist the pressures that will come from outside: the lure of status or money cloaked in terms of invitations to high-level meetings and offers of poverty relief and economic development projects? Surely creating a new Global Anglican Communion Covenant will be met with misunderstanding from some of our own people, and some Global South churches will not choose to participate, even as other Global North churches join in.

God only knows the outcome of such a venture. I do think, however, that we can take heart from the example of the Apostles in the Book of Acts, chapter 15, when the early church was confronted with a crisis of identity: whether and how to include the Gentiles in its midst. Let me note that the crisis arose from the mother church in Jerusalem where some Jewish Christians taught that Gentiles must be circumcised and observe the entire Jewish law. The apostles

- *listened to the testimony of Paul* about God's working in the Gentile mission;

- *searched the Scripture* for God's prophetic word concerning the Gentiles;

- *opened the door to the mission*, led by James, the brother of Jesus and Archbishop of Jerusalem, asking only that they observe basic moral rules of sexual purity and eating of meat;

- *acknowledged the presence of the Holy Spirit* guiding their decision: hence "it seemed good to the Holy Spirit and us"; and

- *confirmed their decision* in writing, *gathered the church* with rejoicing and *experienced a further outpouring of the Spirit.*

My brothers and sisters, one of the strong convictions at the Jerusalem meeting in 2008 was that it was *"not just a moment in time, but a movement in the Spirit."* I believe the time is ripe for Anglicans today, led by the Global South, to repent of our failures, to commit ourselves to work together, and to trust that the Lord will guide and govern us going forward by his Holy Spirit.

O Almighty God,
who hast built thy Church upon the foundation of
the apostles and prophets,
Jesus Christ himself being the head cornerstone:
grant us so to be joined together in unity of spirit by their doctrine,
that we may be made an holy temple acceptable unto thee;
through Jesus Christ thy Son our Lord,
who liveth and reigneth with thee, in the unity of the Holy Spirit,
one God, now and for ever.

ESSAY 10

CROSSING THE RUBICON

LAMBETH RESOLUTION I.10, THE CHURCH OF ENGLAND, AND THE ANGLICAN COMMUNION,

WITH AN APPENDIX ON THE 2017 CANTERBURY PRIMATES' MEETING

(2016)

One of the most difficult and potentially tragic situations facing the GAFCON and Global South movements is the status of the Church of England in the Anglican Communion. The idea that the Mother Church herself might depart from the "faith of our fathers" is horrible to contemplate. But the Bible gives multiple warnings of Israel's unfaithfulness (Hosea 2:2), and the Anglican Articles (XIX) declare that "as the churches of Jerusalem, Antioch and Alexandria have erred, so also the church of Rome has erred, not only in their practice and forms of worship but also in matters of faith." Any church may fall into error and heresy, unless its leaders guard the deposit of faith entrusted to it (1 Timothy 6:20).

On several occasions, I have quoted the Lambeth Bishops' statement in 1920 that "to live a pure and chaste life before and after marriage is, for both sexes, the unchangeable Christian standard." This is the same standard articulated by the 1998 Lambeth Conference, which "upholds faithfulness in marriage between a man and a woman in lifelong union, and believes that abstinence is right for those who are not called to marriage." If truth be told, none of the recent Archbishops of Canterbury has upheld *ex animo* this standard as unchangeable. George Carey began to undermine the authority of Lambeth I.10 immediately after it was passed. Rowan Williams stated on many occasions that the Resolution stated the *current* position of the church – but certainly not unchangeable.

So where does the current Archbishop of Canterbury stand? So far as I know, Justin Welby has never publicly stated that he upholds the authority and teaching of Lambeth I.10, which is why I found the recent letter of Mr. William Nye significant.

My internet essay, posted on 28 November 2016, is an exercise in "fisking" a letter posted on the Church of England website by Mr. William Nye, the Secretary General of the Archbishops' Council in November 2016. Mr. Nye's piece is a response to an essay posted by Canon (now Bishop) Andy Lines on behalf of GAFCON UK, which was a detailed exposé of the various ways in which the Church of England has violated the spirit and letter of Lambeth Resolution I.10.

I found Mr. Nye's reply significant because:

- he clearly speaks for both Archbishops of Canterbury and York;
- he does not contradict any of the facts cited in the GAFCON UK indictment; and
- he clearly wishes to reinterpret Resolution I.10 in a way that is contrary to the history of its enactment and the plain sense of its text.

I called the essay "Crossing the Rubicon" because in this letter the Archbishops of the Church of England made explicit what the GAFCON UK essay had detailed: that they no longer consider Lambeth I.10 as having any authority for the Church of England. If Canterbury and York have erred, they have erred together and taken the Church of England with them.

And not just the Church of England. They hope to take the rest of the Communion over the Rubicon with them. With this threat in mind, I wrote a follow-up piece titled "Ferrying the Primates Across the Rubicon: Lambeth Resolution I.10 and the 2017 Primates'

Meeting." I am including it here as an Appendix.

The two relevant documents for this fisking can be found at:

- http://www.gafconuk.org/news/church-england and-lambeth-i10

- http://www.lawandreligionuk.com/2016/11/22/secretary-general-responds-to-gafcon-uk-on-lambeth-i-10/

E arlier this year I was speaking with an English friend concerned about the direction of the Church of England. "Where do we draw the line?" he asked. "That's easy," I replied: "It's called Lambeth Resolution I.10."

The 1998 Resolution I.10 on Human Sexuality has been and remains the Rubicon for the Anglican Communion. Those who step over that line will have divorced themselves from biblical Christianity, from historic Anglicanism, and from the vast majority of Anglicans worldwide. Several provinces of the Communion have already taken that step. It appears that the Mother Church is about to follow.

I was present at the 1998 Lambeth Conference where the Resolution was passed, and I published an analysis of its text and significance (Essay 6). The Resolution was approved overwhelmingly by the bishops of the Communion, including then Archbishop of Canterbury George Carey, but it was rejected immediately thereafter by the majority of bishops in the Episcopal Church USA. The rejection has led to nearly two decades of strife within the Communion that continues to this day.

Throughout his tenure Archbishop Rowan Williams upheld Lambeth I.10, however tentatively. It was also affirmed in the Windsor Report. The current Archbishop of Canterbury, to my knowledge, has not done so, which may explain the most recent statement from the Archbishops' Council.

The letter of Mr. William Nye published on 22 November 2016 seems to be preparing the ground for retreat by attacking a recent GAFCON UK briefing paper and arguing that Lambeth Resolution I.10 is not authoritative or legally binding on the Church of England. Mr. Nye is Secretary General of the Archbishops' Council and so must be taken as articulating the view of the Archbishops of Canterbury and York.

Mr. Nye begins the attack by stating:

> Resolution 1:10 is one of over 90 Resolutions approved by the Lambeth Conference in 1998. It expressed the will of that Conference. Like all Lambeth Conference resolutions, it is not legally binding on all provinces of the Communion, including the Church of England, though it commends an essential and persuasive view of the attitude of the Communion.

Let's break this paragraph down into a number of points (in italics) and respond to each:

Resolution I.10 was one of many resolutions in 1998. This is true but misleading. Everyone at the Conference in 1998 knew this Resolution was centrally important and hotly contested, and many were surprised at its clarity, so much so that *The Times* of London called it a "surprisingly trenchant verdict."

It expressed the will of that Conference. This verbal sleight of hand turns the Resolution into an historical relic. Indeed, all Lambeth Resolutions are now relics. There is a 130-year history of Lambeth Resolutions, speaking to matters of doctrine, of church order, and of relevant social issues, including those pertaining to marriage and family life. These Resolutions, read together, form a fairly harmonious tradition. Resolution I.10 fits clearly within this tradition. The tradition came to an end after 1998, as the 2008 Lambeth Conference replaced resolutions, which they said had become too controversial, with Indaba (table talk).

Resolution I.10 is not legally binding but commends an essential and persuasive view of an attitude of the Communion. Mr. Nye is factually correct: Lambeth Resolutions have no legal or canonical force but only the force of persuasion. This arrangement was baked into the Anglican cake from the first Conference in 1867, as noted by Professor Owen Chadwick, who states in his introduction to the collected Resolutions:

> If the [Lambeth] meeting was to be acceptable to some of its more moderate opponents, it seemed to be necessary to say that the meeting was only of a discussion group, and none of its decisions would have any authority. Archbishop Longley of Canterbury would only summon the meeting, and several bishops would only attend it, if its resolutions were declared beforehand to have no binding force. Some of the American bishops who were determined to take no orders out of England were equally strong that this meeting was 'only' for consultation.

And indeed 130 years later, the American bishops took home the same attitude and renounced Resolution I.10 and proceeded to ordain a practicing homosexual as bishop in 2003.

Is there a difference between an authoritative teaching and a "persuasive view of an attitude"? Put another way: is there anything that Anglicans hold so dear that some of its members might break fellowship with others over it? Mr. Nye turns to this question in the next two paragraphs:

> Resolution 1:10 sets out teaching on marriage, as being between a man and a woman, and teaching on abstinence outside marriage. It sets out teaching on homosexual

practice. It commits the Conference to listening to the experience of homosexual persons, assures them they are loved by God, and condemns irrational fear of homosexuals. It says nothing about discipline within provinces of the Anglican Communion; the Lambeth Conference has no jurisdiction to do so.

The Resolution is an important document in the history of the Anglican Communion. It is not the only important resolution, from that Conference or others. It does not have the force of Scripture, nor is it part of the deposit of faith. The key elements for the Communion are those within the Chicago Lambeth Quadrilateral.

Again, we'll take his argument (in italics) point by point.

Lambeth I.10 sets out "teaching" about heterosexual, monogamous marriage, abstinence, and about homosexual practice. Curiously, he does not let on that this teaching *affirms* the alternatives of marriage and abstinence but *cannot advise* homosexual practice.

Lambeth I.10 also speaks of pastoral care and moral guidance for "those who experience themselves as having a homosexual orientation ["homosexual persons" - Mr. Nye]." This portion of the Resolution has a normative *pastoral* force, but it is set in a theological framework that "homosexual practice [i]s incompatible with Scripture." Taken as a whole, the Resolution calls the church, both in England and throughout the Communion, to minister to all those who experience sexual and marital brokenness and violence. It does not, however, provide a foundation for approving same-sex civil partnerships or same-sex marriage.

Lambeth I.10 does not have the force of Scripture... This statement contradicts the bishops' claim to speak "in view of the teaching of Scripture" and to teach that homosexual practice is "incompatible with Scripture." Bishops at the time were so adamant on this point that they insisted on referencing other resolutions (IV.26, V.1, V.10, V.23 and V.35) on the authority of Scripture in matters of marriage and sexuality.

...nor is it part of the deposit of faith. By the "deposit of faith," I presume Mr. Nye means the Creeds. The Creeds themselves appealed to Scripture and were never intended to cover every area of Christian orthodoxy, especially what Article VII calls the "Commandments which are called Moral." Neither the church Fathers nor the Reformers were challenged by the modern issues of human sexuality, which is why the Lambeth bishops felt called to address it.

The key elements for the Communion are those within the Chicago Lambeth Quadrilateral. The Lambeth Quadrilateral is an important set of four guidelines defining the church in terms of Scripture, Creeds, sacraments and the historic episcopate. However, there is no basis to elevate it over Lambeth Resolutions, as it was itself a Resolution of the 1888 Conference. Furthermore, in its first article the Quadrilateral refers to "the Holy Scripture of the Old and New Testaments ... as the rule and ultimate standard of faith," which is the very standard to which Lambeth I.10 appeals.

It says nothing about discipline within provinces of the Anglican Communion; the Lambeth Conference has no jurisdiction to do so. Before going further, we need to step aside and define discipline. The Reformers saw discipline as an essential mark of the church:

> The true church is an universal congregation or fellowship of God's faithful and elect people, built on the foundation of the Apostles and Prophets, Jesus Christ himself being the head corner-stone. And it hath always three notes or marks: Pure and sound doctrine; The sacraments ministered according to Christ's holy institution; And the right use of ecclesiastical discipline. (*Homily for Whitsunday*)

281

One most often thinks of discipline in terms of Prayer Book rubrics, canon laws, and other church regulations within a particular diocese or province. In the last resort, discipline can lead to exclusion or excommunication of a person from the church.

Churches also exercise corporate discipline and excommunication, as is the case among Roman Catholic, Orthodox, and Protestant churches. The Reformers did not address the question of inner-Anglican discipline because in their day the Church of England had no colonies, not to mention provinces with separate constitutions and canons. Centuries later the 1930 Lambeth Committee on the Anglican Communion took up the question of a possible breach of intra-communion discipline among autonomous churches:

> This freedom naturally and necessarily carries with it the risk of divergence to the point even of disruption. In case any such risk should actually arise, it is clear that the Lambeth Conference as such could not take any disciplinary action. Formal action would belong to the several Churches of the Anglican Communion individually; but the advice of the Lambeth Conference, sought before action is taken by the constituent Churches, would carry very great moral weight. And we believe in the Holy Spirit. We trust in His power working in every part of His Church to hold us together.

This precise risk of divergence arose after Lambeth 1998 when the Episcopal Church consecrated Gene Robinson in 2003 as Bishop of New Hampshire. The churches did meet in a series of Primates' meetings and made clear the incompatibility of Robinson's consecration with Lambeth Resolution I.10; however, the failure of the Archbishop of Canterbury to carry out the disciplinary measures of the Primates led ultimately to the formation of the GAFCON movement, which has made Lambeth I.10 a touchstone of identity.

Mr. Nye's position about the absence of formal discipline is legally correct but spiritually dangerous in that it appears to be clearing the way for the Church of England to work around Lambeth Resolution I.10. Mr. Nye goes on to cite a number of other actions and documents of the Church of England, which I leave to my English colleagues to handle. It certainly seems as if the end-point of these actions and the so-called "Listening Process" is the approval and blessing of same-sex civil partnerships.

If this indeed is where the Church of England is heading, it is, in my opinion, crossing the Rubicon, or if I may adapt a North American metaphor, barreling over Niagara Falls.

I say this for three reasons. First, blessing homosexual practice in any form is contrary to Scripture and the Christian church's continuous moral tradition, as expressed in Lambeth Resolution I.10.

Secondly, the Church of England will be unable to hold the line at same-sex civil partnerships. The Episcopal Church USA and Anglican Church of Canada are bellwethers in this regard; both having begun with same-sex partnerships have moved on to mandate same-sex marriage. The UK Government will push this process along, as is seen in the number of legal same-sex marriages of clergy in the Church of England, as pointed out in the GAFCON briefing paper.

Thirdly, approval of same-sex civil partnerships will render irreparable what the Windsor Report called the tear in the fabric of the Communion. At the recent meeting in Cairo in October 2016, delegates representing twenty-five provinces and millions of Anglicans, restated the teaching of Lambeth I.10 in a Communiqué:

In this respect, the Church cannot condone same-sex unions as a form of behaviour acceptable to God. To do so would be tampering with the foundation of our faith once for all laid down by the apostles and the prophets, with Christ Jesus himself as the chief cornerstone (Ephesians 2: 20-22; 1 Corinthians 3:10-11; Jude 3).

They go on to warn against the kind of false *modus vivendi* which they foresee coming in England:

Any pastoral provision by a church for a same-sex couple (such as a liturgy or a service to bless their sexual union) that obviates the need for repentance and a commitment to pursue a change of conduct enabled by the power of the Holy Spirit, would contravene the orthodox and historic teaching of the Anglican Communion on marriage and sexuality.

In a separate statement, the Primates of these churches address the great loss that will be incurred if the Mother Church violates her own birthright:

The Church of England (COE) has a unique role in the life of the Communion, which means that decisions it makes on fundamental matters impact the Communion more deeply than those made elsewhere. This is because both of its historical role and the particular role of Archbishop of Canterbury as first among equals amongst the Primates. We are deeply concerned that there appears to be a potential move towards the acceptance of blessing of same-sex union by COE. This would have serious implications for us should it occur.

I do not know how the Global South churches could be clearer. They do not want to break communion with the Church of England, as they have done with the Episcopal Church and Anglican Church of Canada. But they fear she is going the same way as the North Americans.

Let me end on a personal note of warning. I was

baptized in the Episcopal Church fifty years ago this month, as a university student – I guess that makes me a born-again Anglican. I have been ordained for forty-five years. I have lived in the United States, England, and Uganda and have been inspired by the witness of Thomas Cranmer, George Herbert, C.S. Lewis, John Stott, the Uganda martyrs, and Janani Luwum among others.

I am convinced that the loss of the Church of England would be an incalculable blow to her heirs around the world.

The Mother Church seems poised at the edge of the Rubicon, represented by Lambeth Resolution I.10. For the sake of our Lord and his church, do not cross over.

APPENDIX

FERRYING THE PRIMATES ACROSS THE RUBICON

LAMBETH RESOLUTION 1:10 AND THE 2017 CANTERBURY PRIMATES' MEETING

Nearly one year ago I wrote an essay titled "Crossing the Rubicon: Lambeth Resolution I.10, the Church of England, and the Anglican Communion," which began this way:

> Earlier this year I was speaking with an English friend concerned about the direction of the Church of England. "Where do we draw the line?" he asked. "That's easy," I replied: "It's called Lambeth Resolution I.10."

I then analyzed ("fisked") a letter by Mr. William Nye, the Secretary General of the Archbishops' Council, who had clearly been authorized to speak for the Archbishops of Canterbury and York. In this letter Mr. Nye attempts to relativize the 1998 Lambeth Resolution I.10 on Human Sexuality as speaking *for that Conference only*, hence having no ongoing normative authority.

In the light of the Communiqué from the October 2017 Primates' Meeting, I would go a step further and say that in the view of the Lambeth Establishment, Resolution I.10 was a huge mistake and aberration, the effects of which will be undone at Lambeth 2020.

Let me briefly state why the 1998 Lambeth Conference and its key Resolution constitute an historic "Rubicon" moment for Anglicanism:

- The Resolution addressed the major theological issue of our time: God's creation of mankind in his image, male and female, and the "unchangeable standard" of "faithfulness in marriage between a man and a woman in lifelong union" and of "abstinence as right for those who are not called to marriage."

- The Resolution, backed up by several others affirming the authority of the Bible, claims that this standard of marriage and abstinence is held "in view of the teaching of Scripture" and therefore that "homosexual practice is incompatible with Scripture" and "cannot be advised." The Church, in the words of the Articles, has no authority to "ordain any thing that is contrary to God's Word written."

- The Resolution was formulated by and approved overwhelmingly by bishops from the Global South, in opposition to the Conference organizers and those in the West who were promoting the homosexual agenda, now called "LGBTQ."

- The Resolution, in line with other Resolutions since 1978, assumed an enhanced role of the Primates, who would see that it was carried out for the entire Communion. This assumption was tested in a series of Primates' Meetings from 2000 through 2007, culminating in a specific call from the 2007 meeting in Dar es Salaam for repentance by the Episcopal Church, with exclusion from Lambeth 2008 as a consequence of refusal. When the Archbishop of Canterbury chose not to carry out this Resolution, a large number of Global South bishops convened the Global Anglican Future Conference in Jerusalem in 2008.

- Finally, Resolution I.10 *was a Resolution* of the church's moral and spiritual authority, in continuity with those of Lambeth Conferences that preceded it. Since that time, resolutions have been replaced by "indaba," reducing Lambeth to an extended tea party with agenda and conclusions controlled by conference facilitators. By contrast, the Jerusalem Conference in 2008 produced a concise theological statement – the Jerusalem Declaration – and emergency legislation establishing a Primates' Council and inviting formation and membership of the Anglican Church in North America.

The 2017 Lambeth Primates' Communiqué makes no mention of Lambeth I.10 and indeed seeks to undo all of its effects. It expresses "sadness" that the Scottish Episcopal Church, like the Episcopal Church USA before it, has proceeded to bless same-sex marriages in the church in the Name of the Triune God. The "consequences" of this action are a 3-year suspension from representation or voting in certain councils.

What, I might ask, follows when these consequences expire? I think the answer is quite obvious: *by 2020 same-sex marriage will have been accommodated as a moral option within the Anglican Communion.* The Communiqué goes on to say: "We welcomed the news that the Church of England has embarked on a major study of human sexuality in its cultural, scientific, scriptural and theological aspects and anticipated considering the results of this work at a future meeting." Is there any doubt that the new study will discover that the unchangeable standard of marriage and abstinence is, well, changeable after all? Is there any doubt the "cultural and scientific" aspects of postmodernity will open a way around the clear teaching of Scripture?

The 2017 Primates' Meeting was, contrary to appearances, a disenfranchising of the Global South and a dis-enhancing of the Primates' authority. The agenda and Communiqué were clearly prepared in advance, and the indaba process prevented any real dissent. The false tears for the absence of three major Provinces were accompanied by the back-hand of fellowship to the Anglican Church in North America: "you are not Anglican, but we love you as Christian brothers anyway." Read carefully, the 2017 statement is the utter reversal of the Primates' Communiqué ten years ago.

As I see it, the 2017 Primates' Meeting was an attempt, using the prestige of Canterbury and funds from New York, to undo Lambeth I.10 and the Global South movement that resulted from it.

The Archbishops of Canterbury (and York) have crossed the Rubicon and taken the Church of England with them. Now they are seeking to ferry the Global South with them as well.

So how many Global South Primates are actually in this boat – a relevant question since there are no signatories to the Communiqué? And if certain Primates are on board with Canterbury, then how many bishops and churches of their Provinces are willing to go along for the ride?

This is a Joshua 24:15 moment: whom will you serve? We remember the costly answer of our forefathers in the faith: "Here I stand; I can do no other."

ESSAY 11

THY KINGDOM COME

THE CURRENT WORLD CRISIS AND THE CHURCH

(2014)

The German martyr-theologian Dietrich Bonhoeffer, while imprisoned in a Nazi death camp, foresaw the coming post-Christian age and commented:

> Two things alone have still the power to avert the final plunge into the void. One is the miracle of new awakening of faith, and the other is that force the Bible calls the "restrainer" (II Thessalonians 2:7), that is to say the force of order, equipped with great physical strength, which effectively blocks the way of those who are about to plunge into the abyss. (*Ethics*, page 44)

Nearly seventy-five years on, his prophecy stands. Interestingly, it was the Church of Nigeria that took most seriously the call of the 1988 Lambeth Conference for a Decade of Evangelism, and that has led to its numerical dominance among Anglican churches. At the same time, Nigeria as a nation has been threatened by political Islam and many of its churches devastated and its people killed by Muslim zealots.

In 2011, I was invited to bring an address to the "Divine Commonwealth Conference" in Abuja, Nigeria. Archbishop Nicholas Okoh asked me to address the question of eschatology for Anglicans in his country, especially in light of the popular "health and wealth gospel" proclaimed by many Pentecostals in Nigeria. My address in Abuja – from the amazing rotating dais! – was titled "Relating End-Time Prophecy to Contemporary Issues" and was an exposition of the two letters to the Thessalonians.

In 2014, I was invited back to address the General

Synod of the Anglican Church of Nigeria, meeting in Enugu, on the topic of the kingdom of God and the persecuted church. This was the same year that Boko Haram had abducted Christian schoolgirls and carried out several suicide bombings in the city of Kano and the northern Borno state. While this essay touches on some of the same themes and texts of my earlier address, my exposition here is from the Book of Revelation and its prophetic relevance to the state of the church in a hostile world.

L et me begin by saying how honoured I am and humbled to be invited to address you today on the subject of the kingdom of God and the persecuted church. I say humbled because I am not an expert on the persecuted church like Dr. Paul Marshall, Baroness Caroline Cox, and Bishop Michael Nazir-Ali [see brief bibliography at end]. Neither have I experienced the kind of persecution that you have endured every day but which we in the West only see flashing on our TV or computer screens from time to time.

What I do bring you, as a fellow theologian of the GAFCON movement, is a biblical teaching on the Kingdom of God and in the light of that teaching an interpretation of the current world crisis and the church.

AN ANGLICAN APPROACH TO SCRIPTURE

It is hard to think of a more central subject than the Kingdom of God. After all, Jesus came "preaching the Kingdom of God" (Mark 1:15), and He taught His church to pray first of all "Thy Kingdom come, on earth as in heaven." For this reason, the first Global Anglican Future Conference in 2008 prefaced its Jerusalem Declaration thus:

We, the participants in the Global Anglican Future Conference, have met in the land of Jesus' birth. We express our loyalty as disciples to the King of kings, the Lord Jesus. We joyfully embrace his command to proclaim the reality of his kingdom which he first announced in this land. The gospel of the kingdom is the good news of salvation, liberation and transformation for all.

How then are we to understand the Kingdom of God as applied to our context today? The key to the kingdom will be found in the King's book, the Holy Scripture. The same Jerusalem Declaration gives us, I think, some guidance on our approach:

We believe the Holy Scriptures of the Old and New Testaments to be the Word of God written and to contain all things necessary for salvation. The Bible is to be translated, read, preached, taught and obeyed in its plain and canonical sense, respectful of the church's historic and consensual reading.

Let me comment for a moment on the "plain and canonical sense" of Scripture. The "plain sense" is not always so plain and obvious as many people think. I liken it to a three-stranded cord that cannot be broken, which includes a *doctrinal or truth strand*, because God's Word is truth, a *literary strand* because the Bible is literature, and a *salvation-historical strand*, because the Bible testifies to the action of God in the history of Israel, Jesus Christ and the Church. The meaning of any particular book also needs to be read "canonically," noting its place in the entire Bible. This is what St. Paul calls "rightly dividing the word of truth" (2 Timothy 2:15) and what our Anglican collect calls "marking" one text by another ("read, mark, learn and inwardly digest").

The Kingdom of God

So with this brief introduction to biblical interpretation, let me pick up the theme of the Kingdom of God as it relates to the current crisis facing the Church. The theme of God's Kingdom is the focus of a major section of the Old Testament. In particular the Prophets address the Word of the Lord to the kingdom of Israel, God's covenant people, before, during and after the Exile to Babylon. These Prophets have one overarching message: that God has judged the nation and its kings because of their persistent idolatry and has determined to destroy it by means of a great pagan empire, the "rod of his anger" (Isaiah 10:5). They go on to say that God will in turn judge and destroy the pagan empire by means of another empire and then another. God's people will go into exile for a seventy-year period (I believe the seventy-year period is both literal, from roughly 586 to 515 BC, and symbolic of what we might call "this age"). Finally, they announce the restoration and reconstitution of God's Kingdom on the basis of a new Covenant in a new Era in which God will Himself visit His people and they will respond to Him, not with hearts of flesh but with the Spirit.

It is this Kingdom which Jesus announces after His baptism. It is also this Kingdom to which Jesus comes as Messiah, anointed by the Spirit. Jesus' proclamation of the Kingdom is Good News – and it is *new* news because, contrary to the Jewish expectation of a political conqueror, Jesus comes as the Suffering Servant, who offers His life as a ransom for many. The reconciliation of man to God must be accomplished through the Cross, the grave and the resurrection, and the apostles take the tidings of these great events to the world in the power of the Spirit.

Christ's Kingdom is "now and not yet." It is *now* in the sense that the Gospel confronts each person with the call of discipleship. "Follow me... and they left their nets immediately and followed him" (Mark 1:18). It is *not yet* in that believers continue to live in this world and to struggle with temptation from within and tribulation from without (John 16:33). The same Jesus who proclaims that the Kingdom is at hand confesses before Pilate: "My kingdom is not of this world" (John 18:36). St. Paul proclaimed the *now* of the dawning of the new age of history in which "through the church the manifold wisdom of God might now be made known to the rulers and authorities in the heavenly places" (Ephesians 3:10). At the same time, he explained the *not yet*, saying "our citizenship is in heaven, and from it we await a Savior, the Lord Jesus Christ" (Philippians 3:20).

THE RETURN OF CHRIST

So, with the coming of King Jesus, the Church finds its citizenship secure, but during this age believers find themselves "strangers in a strange land," not unlike the Jews in exile. And as in Babylon God comforted His people by prophetic words and visions of hope, so also God comforts the Church by promising Christ's imminent return.

In my address to the Divine Commonwealth conference in 2011, I suggested that in the two Letters to the Thessalonians, St. Paul lays out his basic doctrine of Christ's Second Coming:

> We do not want you to be uninformed, brothers, about those who are asleep, that you may not grieve as others do who have no hope. For since we believe that Jesus died and rose again, even so, through Jesus, God will bring with him those who have fallen asleep. For this we declare to you by a word from the Lord, that we who are alive, who are left until the coming of the Lord, will not precede those who have fallen asleep. For the Lord himself will

descend from heaven with a cry of command, with the voice of an archangel, and with the sound of the trumpet of God. And the dead in Christ will rise first. Then we who are alive, who are left, will be caught up together with them in the clouds to meet the Lord in the air, and so we will always be with the Lord. Therefore encourage one another with these words. (1 Thess 4:13-18)

I noted in my address that some Christians apparently misunderstood this teaching as meaning that the end-time had already arrived and that they could take a holiday from daily work. Paul therefore went on to expand and clarify his teaching:

Let no one deceive you in any way. For that day will not come, unless the rebellion comes first, and the man of lawlessness is revealed, the son of destruction, who opposes and exalts himself against every so-called god or object of worship, so that he takes his seat in the temple of God, proclaiming himself to be God. Do you not remember that when I was still with you I told you these things? And you know what is restraining him now so that he may be revealed in his time. For the mystery of lawlessness is already at work. Only the Restrainer will continue until he is out of the way. And then the lawless one will be revealed, whom the Lord Jesus will kill with the breath of his mouth and bring to nothing by the appearance of his coming. The coming of the lawless one is by the activity of Satan with all power and false signs and wonders, and with all wicked deception for those who are perishing, because they refused to love the truth and so be saved. Therefore God sends them a strong delusion, so that they may believe what is false... (2 Thess 2:4-11)

Let me summarize this apostolic teaching:

• Jesus Christ is coming again surely and certainly.

• No one can predict the exact time of His return, but there will be certain events that will serve as warning signs.

- One such sign will be the emergence of the Man of Lawlessness who, inspired by Satan, will lead the world in delusion, destruction and death.

- This satanic figure will certainly be opposed by a "Restrainer," who has been traditionally associated with the force of government.

THE REVELATION TO JOHN

Presumably St. Paul's teaching comforted his congregation in Thessalonica, who were probably attacked by Jews from the local synagogue and defended by local Roman authorities. Decades later, the Church found itself under a much wider threat from the Romans when they refused to offer sacrifice to the Emperor as divine. The time was right for the revival of prophecy. One towering prophet emerged: John the Divine, the author of the Book of Revelation. His prophecy provides the capstone of the New Testament and the grand finale of creation and salvation history.

Once again, let me interject a comment about interpreting this New Testament prophecy in its plain sense, with its intertwined strands of art, history and truth, The Apocalypse, as it is called, is a work of spiritual imagination, with symbols upon symbols, mostly originating in the Old Testament but now reworked in a brilliant and dynamic burst of sight and sound. It offers a heaven's eye view of salvation history in a spiral of events that are rooted in contemporary history – the city and empire of Rome being prominent – but extending forward to a future yet unseen, such as the New Jerusalem "descending from God." For all its complexity, the book claims to be the absolute truth about the end of all things, concluding: "These words are trustworthy and true. And the Lord, the God of the spirits of the prophets, has sent his angel to show his servants what must soon take place" (Rev 22:18-21).

THE UNHOLY TRINITY

The Revelation to John comes from the Triune God, "from him who is and who was and who is to come, and from the seven spirits who are before his throne, and from Jesus Christ the faithful witness, the firstborn of the dead, and the ruler of kings on earth" (Rev 1:4). The vision of chapters 4 and 5 makes clear the supreme cosmic rule of the One who sits on the throne and with Him the Lamb that was slain (Rev 5:13).

There is, however, an alternative kingdom, revealed in John's dramatic vision in chapter 12 of war in heaven. A woman, representing the people of God, is attacked by a great red dragon seeking to devour her child – in vain: "She gave birth to a male child, one who is to rule all the nations with a rod of iron, but her child was caught up to God and to his throne, and the woman fled into the wilderness..." (Rev 12:5-6). The child is Jesus the Messiah, whose reign is inaugurated when He is seated at the right hand of the Father. Jesus' enthronement leads to war in heaven and the dragon, now identified as "that ancient Serpent, the devil and Satan, the deceiver of the whole world," is defeated by Michael and his host and cast down to earth. The dragon, desperate because he knows his time is short, "became furious with the woman and went off to make war on the rest of her offspring, on those who keep the commandments of God and hold to the testimony of Jesus" (Rev 12:17). Here is a paradox. The victory of Christ and His angels in heaven leads to the dragon's persecution of the church on earth.

The dragon, it turns out, is the head of an unholy trinity. We meet the other two members of this evil threesome in chapter 13. The first is the beast from the sea: "And I saw a beast rising out of the sea, with ten horns and seven heads, with ten diadems on its horns and blasphemous names on its heads" (Rev 13:1). This beast is the fulfillment of the horrible blasphemous fourth empire of the book of Daniel. It is not a particular city or nation but a universal world order devoted to evil. The embodiment of worldly power, this beast demands absolute worship. Like Daniel's friends at the fiery furnace, the saints refuse to bow down to the beast, only this time there is no deliverance: "It was allowed to make war on the saints and to conquer them" (Rev 13:7).

The war against the church is not only a matter of brute power but spiritual deception, as represented by a second beast, the false prophet: "Then I saw another beast rising out of the earth. It had two horns like a lamb and it spoke like a dragon. It exercises all the authority of the first beast in its presence, and makes the earth and its inhabitants worship the first beast" (Rev 13:11-12). The second beast is the propaganda arm of the first. Like Pharaoh's magicians or the Sirens of Greek myth, this beast performs tricks to deceive the peoples of the earth and then enslaves them with the mark of the beast.

THE SAINTS' CONQUEST

There is a second paradox. It appears that the unholy trinity is victorious, dominating the peoples of the earth and killing the saints. But just the opposite is true, John says: the church conquers the anti-Christ by her suffering witness (*martyria*):

"Now the salvation and the power and the kingdom of our God and the authority of his Christ have come, for the accuser of our brothers has been thrown down, who accuses them day and night before our God. And they have conquered him by the blood of the Lamb and by the

299

word of their testimony, for they loved not their lives even unto death." (Rev 12:10-11)

The vision of the beasts is followed immediately in chapter 14 with a vision of "the Lamb, and with him 144,000 who had his name and his Father's name written on their foreheads." The martyrs are safe and sound with Jesus in heaven. The number 144,000 symbolizes the fact that Jesus will not lose one sheep that is His own.

At the same time, this may not be the end of the story. John says that the 144,000 have been redeemed as "first-fruits for God and the Lamb" and he goes on to describe an angel proclaiming an eternal gospel "to those who dwell on earth, to every nation and tribe and language and people" (Rev 14:6). Perhaps these others represent the harvest of the nations, an idea confirmed in chapter 7 where John sees two groups of the redeemed, 144,000 of the tribes of Israel and then "a great multitude that no one could number, from every nation, from all tribes and peoples and languages."

The point is this: the martyrs not only save themselves, but their blood is the seedbed of the church, as Tertullian later put it. John's expansive, missionary vision was in fact fulfilled in the next centuries: the more the Romans persecuted the church, the more it grew. That pattern has held true in subsequent ages, right down to the present.

THE CURRENT CONTEXT: WORLDVIEW WAR

I turn now to the question of how to understand the biblical prophecy in the current situation of the church in the world. The overriding theme of John's Apocalypse is warfare, and I am convinced that theme applies to us today: *the church today is in a worldview war* similar in some ways to that which it faced in John's day. Let me make four basic assertions about this war.

It is total war. It is being engaged in the political realm, in the economic realm, in the social realm, and in the spiritual realm. In other words, it is a war against the Kingdom of God. The Psalmist says: "The kings of the earth set themselves, and the rulers take counsel together, against the LORD and against his Messiah, saying, 'Let us burst their bonds apart and cast away their cords from us'" (Psalm 2:2-3). Today the "kings of the earth" include not only the politicians but the cultural elite, whether they are university professors and journalists and certain bishops in the West or imams in the Islamic world. In either case, their enemy is Jesus Christ and His gracious rule.

It is a two-front war, something like the United States fighting in Europe and the Pacific in World War II. One front is a battle with militant secularism, which has been undermining Western Christianity for several centuries. The second front involves militant Islam, which in some ways has been at war with Christianity even longer but which has gained renewed force over the past few decades.

The war is not simply between the church and outsiders but it is being waged within the church. In the letters to the seven churches in Revelation 2-3, we see the exalted Lord addressing a variety of church situations, including the church in Smyrna, who are faithful under persecution, and the church in Thyatira, who "tolerate that woman Jezebel, who calls herself a prophetess and is teaching and seducing my servants to practice sexual immorality and to eat food sacrificed to idols" (Rev 2:8-11,18-29). The recent history of the Episcopal Church USA, which I served for 37 years, involves a pattern of cultural conformity to the liberal elites and toleration of heresy to the point that only heresy will now be tolerated.

The war cannot be avoided. It cannot be explained away by clever evasions. One of the sillier – and dangerous – notions of the U.S. President has been to deny the "war on terror" by simply rebranding it "kinetic military action" and to declare victory in that war by simply withdrawing forces, when it is clear the other side has not laid down its arms. It is equally naïve – and dangerous – when the Archbishop of Canterbury tries to split the difference on God's purpose for human sexuality by trying to uphold marriage while condoning same-sex civil partnerships.

SATAN IS FOR REAL

The New Testament is perfectly clear on one matter: *Satan is for real.* In fact, one might say he is more real now that Jesus has come. Some scholars, noting the relative lack of references to Satan in the Old Testament, wrongly conclude that a personal devil simply pops out of a first-century Jewish apocalyptic box. But they miss the point, which John brings out. Satan is the "ancient serpent, the deceiver of the whole world." He is ancient in that he led the rebellion in heaven, which is captured in biblical references to Leviathan (Psalm 74:14) and to "Day Star son of Dawn" (Isa 14:12). But he is also the wily Deceiver who prefers to hide behind the principalities and powers of this age and the elemental forces of the world, and to work his destruction through his offspring, sin and death.

John makes the point that the coming of Jesus actually "outs" Satan, as it were. The temptation in the wilderness makes clear the stark choice for Jesus and for us: "Bow down worship me!" or "Be gone, Satan" (Matt 4:9-10). Indeed, Satan does depart from Jesus, knowing his time is short, but in that short time between Christ's Exaltation into heaven and the present, he intensifies his attacks on Christ's offspring on earth.

Secularists have had great trouble in understanding what they call "radical evil" as represented, for instance, in the Holocaust, the systematic destruction of six million Jews by the Nazis. Some secularists believe human nature is basically good, but even those who see human nature as weak and flawed are baffled by the darkness in the human heart that leads to such brutality (an odd word, by the way, as brute animals do not act like this). And in a way, they are right to be troubled. God made man in His image to be good, and Adam and Eve were deceived into sin, not the author of it. Only a supernatural worldview can see that "we do not wrestle against flesh and blood, but against the rulers, against the authorities, against the cosmic powers over this present darkness, against the spiritual forces of evil in the heavenly places" (Eph 6:12).

The battle between the church and Satan is a matter of truth. The devil, Scripture says, "is a liar and the father of lies," whereas "God is light, and in him there is no darkness at all" (John 8:44; 1 John 1:5). The Kingdom of God is not primarily a political regime founded on a myth or an ideology but rather a spiritual community founded on a true Word, the Logos embodied in Jesus Christ the Son of God. Jesus, according to the Book of Revelation, is described in this way: "In his right hand he held seven stars, from his mouth came a sharp two-edged sword, and his face was like the sun shining in full strength" (Rev 1:16). The seven stars represent the mystery of the cosmos – how does the world in all its complexity and beauty hang together – what St. Paul calls "the mystery hidden for ages and generations but now revealed to his saints" (Col 1:26). The church, possessing the sharp two-edged sword of God's Word, is in a unique position to discern God's judgments on Satan and his works and to expose them to a needy world.

FALSE PROPHECY

Both fronts of the worldview war are based on false prophecy. In the case of Islam, the case is clear-cut. Either Mohammed is God's prophet or he is not. In the case of secularism it is not so obvious. Secularists pride themselves on their sophistication and science, and, to be sure, they often possess profound knowledge on various subsidiary matters. However, at the heart of this knowledge is a moral and spiritual vacuum, and this vacuum is the work of Satan.

The Holy Spirit is the Spirit of life; Satan is not only a liar but a murderer (John 8:44). False prophecy can be known for its hatred of human life. Again, I need say little about the recent actions of Boko Haram and ISIS. As Jesus says, "the hour is coming when whoever kills you will think he is offering service to God" (John 16:2). Horrible though the actions of jihadists are, how are they worse than the legalization of abortion in the West, with its advocates proudly promoting a woman's "right to choose" to abort a child in the womb, right down to the day of delivery?

In 1994, Mother Teresa of Calcutta was invited to make remarks at the National Prayer Breakfast in Washington DC. President Bill Clinton and his wife were present, both of whom, though nominal Christians, are pro-abortion zealots. Anyway, in their presence, Mother Teresa stated that the problem of war in the world is a problem of the human heart: "if we accept that the mother can kill even her own child, how can we tell other people not to kill one another?" Mother Teresa was a prophet "speaking truth to power." She continued: "Jesus said, 'If you receive a little child, you receive me.' So every abortion is the denial of receiving Jesus."

How is it possible that such an obvious truth that life and human personhood begin at conception – a truth made clearer by medical science – can be obscured and rejected by the "brightest and best" in the West? The false prophet, according to John, imposes the "mark of the beast" on everyone, whether great or small, rich or poor (Rev 13:16). False prophecy, a godless worldview, creates a culture, a culture of ignorance and fear, in which ordinary people will swim like fish in a polluted pond, unless they know the truth. And those who know and testify to the truth will risk their lives or their livelihoods to do so. Try to be a Christian shopkeeper or schoolmaster in the Middle East or in Europe today and you will find out what this means.

I turn now to a second contemporary example having to do with marriage. Marriage is the fundamental expression of God's love in creating man in His own image, male and female. It is the source of human flourishing, of passing on life from one generation to another. At the heart of marriage is the principle of *two sexes, one flesh,* as Scripture says: "Therefore a man shall leave his father and his mother and be united to his wife, and they shall become one flesh (Gen 2:24; Mark 10:8). The principle, deeper still, serves as a sign of the mystery of Christ and His Bride, the Church (Eph 5:31).

The promotion of homosexuality and same-sex marriage is a blatant attack on God's design in creation and redemption. (Let me clarify here that it is the *normalizing* of homosexuality that is the offence; the Church needs to minister God's love to all people, including those struggling with homosexual desires.) The repudiation of the biblical norm by Anglican churches in North America has led to the breakup of the Anglican Communion, and all the equivocations from Canterbury will not put this Humpty Dumpty back together again.

The Church of Nigeria has been a leader in standing for the truth in this matter. I want now to challenge you to go one step further. I am convinced that a corollary to the biblical principle of two sexes, one flesh in marriage is the complementary roles of man and woman in the family and in the church. St Paul teaches: "I want you to understand that the head of every man is Christ, the head of a wife is her husband, and the head of Christ is God" (1 Cor 11:3).

The blurring of the male-female distinction has been part and parcel of the attack on marriage. After all, so the logic goes, if there is no real difference between men and women, why shouldn't men marry men and women marry women if they are so inclined. The blurring of this distinction is the root issue in the ordination of women bishops. This issue has threatened the unity of the Anglican Communion for thirty-plus years and now it threatens the unity of the GAFCON movement.

I suspect much of what I have just said seems like common sense to you here in Nigeria. After all, you have a church culture of strong male bishops and strong women exercising ministry through Mother's Union. You have maintained the tradition – not to mention the gorgeous dress to go along with it – you inherited from the historic church and from traditional culture. Beware lest you lose it. I appeal to you now to defend it theologically in the wider Communion. Egalitarian secularism has made deep inroads around the world, even in Africa. It is not enough to say: "That's our culture." Culture can change; I have seen it change within my lifetime in America. It can happen to you as well. So be ready to make a defense, as St. Peter exhorts us, for the hope that is within you (1 Peter 3:15).

BASIC TRAINING FOR THE WORLDVIEW WAR

Our primary weapon in the worldview battle is the sword of the Spirit, which is the Word of God (Eph 6:17). We must know and teach the faith to our children and to our congregations, and this education must go on at all levels.

Let me begin with basic catechesis. I was involved at the GAFCON meeting in drafting the Jerusalem Declaration, a confession of basic Anglican belief. I know you are familiar with this statement. Shortly afterward, I worked with colleagues at Uganda Christian University to produce a short catechism based on the Jerusalem Declaration and we posted it on the internet (Essay 7). It was written for East Africans and was translated into six local languages. I would like to urge you to adapt this and translate it for your churches, or if not, write one of your own. Our people must be trained up in the way they should go, especially given the prevalence of other worldviews available in the electronic marketplace.

Basic education is necessary, but professionally educated Christians must go deeper still. Let me interject here a concern. As many of you know, fifteen years ago I accepted a call to help start Uganda Christian University. I accepted the call on the one condition that the Anglican Church of Uganda intended to found a Christian university not in name only but in substance. Several years ago I made a visitation to Crowther Graduate Theological College in Abeokuta and Ajay Crowther University in Oyo. In my report back, I noted many impressive things about these institutions. However, I was concerned that there was little communication between the theological college and the university and I feared that as a result, university students would not graduate with a strong intellectual and spiritual foundation in the faith.

Universities were originally founded by Christians, and there are still many fine Christian institutions. Hence when Boko Haram attacks "Western education," it sees itself as attacking Christianity as well. Ironically, many universities in the West are as hostile to Christianity as Boko Haram is, and they seek to inculcate in their students an anti-Christian worldview, which then gets reflected by the politicians and the so-called cultural elite. Many Nigerian academics have studied at these universities and bring that worldview back with them. So I want to challenge you to resist the Satanic denial of truth which comes from both fronts of the worldview war. The church here needs to invest in education at all levels and also be careful that education is integrated with the truth of God that is found in Scripture and the Christian tradition.

GOVERNMENT IS A FRIEND AND A FOE

God's Kingdom is now and not yet. The King has come and been exalted to the right hand of power on high. But even now, after His enthronement, Jesus' words before Pilate apply: "My kingdom is not of this world. If my kingdom were of this world, my servants would fight" (John 18:36). In the interim period between Jesus' first and second coming, government exercises a legitimate authority.

The New Testament speaks of government in terms of "principalities and powers." As such, it can be viewed in three ways. Firstly, it is "instituted by God" and commands our obedience and respect; its legitimate purpose is to punish what is evil and to commend what is good (Rom 13:1-7). St. Paul was proud of his Roman citizenship and appealed to the Roman authorities for justice on several occasions. I believe Paul is referring in Thessalonians to government as the Restrainer that will stand against the anti-Christ in the end-times.

Secondly, government is a structure of this present darkness. As St. Paul also says: "None of the rulers of this age understood [God's plan of salvation], for if they had, they would not have crucified the Lord of glory" (1 Cor 2:8). Indeed, the Church's calling is to make known to the principalities and powers the coming Kingdom (Eph 3:10). This does not mean, I think, that the Church is to rule the State (theocracy), but rather that it keeps the state humble by reminding it that it is accountable to God.

Thirdly, government is a power of this world which can be co-opted by Satan. The beast of Revelation 12, in my opinion, is not only the final, awful fulfillment of totalitarian power but represents the power exercised by tyrants and oppressors throughout the ages. We can see the footprints of the beast in the Roman martyrdom of Christians in John's day, in the Communist suppression of Christians over the past century (which continues in full force in North Korea today) and in the *dhimmitude*, expulsion and murder of Christians under Islam wherever Sharia law has been enforced.

I feel compelled to add a note here on the persecution of God's people the Jews. They have been the target of the beast for much of their history. In previous centuries, Jews were victims of Christian pogroms. Hostility to the state of Israel and Jew hatred is a virtual article of current Muslim faith, and over the past fifty years, they have been forced out of their homelands in the Middle East and North Africa *in toto*. Now it seems the same thing is happening to Christians. Even in secular Europe, where people swore "Never again!" after the Nazi Holocaust, anti-Semitism and violence against Jews is raising its ugly head. We Christians need to pray for the political and spiritual well-being of the Jewish people and to protest their persecution especially, alongside persecution of other minority religious groups.

We see in Christianity and Islam a fundamentally different view of law and government. For Christians, "here we have no lasting city, but we seek the city that is to come" (Heb 13:14). Hence Christians can live peaceably under a number of different regimes. For Islam, at least as many interpret its scriptures, there is only one law and one caliphate, and it is the duty of Muslims to establish it, even to die and kill for it. I hesitate to recommend much on this matter to you in Nigeria except to encourage you to speak truth to the national and regional governments and to call on them to uphold the national laws, to respect the civil rights of all citizens and to wield the sword on behalf of victims of violence. Bishop Bill Atwood recently recounted the story of how Archbishop Joseph Adetiloye confronted President Abacha about his tyranny – and the latter's dramatic end. This was the same Archbishop whom I saw at Lambeth demand from the Archbishop of Canterbury a clear Resolution on Human Sexuality.

To the extent that Government fails to do its duty due to corruption or fear of reprisal, it is failing its God-given duty. From the Christian worldview, the fact that the city of this world is not the city of God is actually a blessing for both. Worldly governments have limited and manageable duties – to keep the peace and uphold justice – and God through His faithful witnesses will prepare for the Kingdom.

SUFFERING WITNESS

I come at last to the central truth of the Book of Revelation: "they have conquered him by the blood of the Lamb and by the word of their testimony, for they loved not their lives even unto death" (Rev 12:11). This word of the Risen Lord, in one sense, should not surprise us. After all, Jesus said to His disciples: "Take up your cross and follow me" (Mark 8:34); and "whoever loves his life loses it, and whoever hates his life in this world will keep it for eternal life" (John 12:25). This is what the great German theologian and martyr Dietrich Bonhoeffer calls "the cost of discipleship."

Let me note three characteristics of discipleship that apply in a time of persecution: patient endurance, expectant prayer, and deeds of love.

HOLD ON AND REPENT

In the midst of the cosmic upheavals of the Book of Revelation, the specific command which the Lord gives to His Church comes in the Letters to the churches (Rev 2-3)

310

and this advice boils down to two commands: "Hold on!" (to three churches) and "Repent!" (to four Churches). These commands reflect the situation of spiritual attack from within as well as without. The temptation in either case is to compromise the faith.

Compromise can be the result of fear or complacency or both. Bonhoeffer, writing at the dawn of the Nazi takeover in Germany, saw the church there complacently hiding behind the doctrine of grace. Hence he wrote:

> Cheap grace is the preaching of forgiveness without requiring repentance, baptism without church discipline, Communion without confession, absolution without personal confession. Cheap grace is grace without discipleship, grace without the cross, grace without Jesus Christ, living and incarnate.

Which profile of the church fits your situation? I cannot say, but it could be a mix of both as was the case of the churches in Asia Minor. Surely there are those in your Northern region today who have been faithful even unto death. Perhaps the very success and growth of the Church here in recent years, its sense of inevitable growth, has made some complacent, as if the Kingdom of God was an automatic thing. I don't know. That is a matter for you to discern.

EXPECTANT PRAYER

The Book of Revelation is interspersed with prayer and praise. We hear the voices of the martyrs under the altar crying out: "O Sovereign Lord, holy and true, how long before you will judge and avenge our blood on those who dwell on the earth?" (Rev 6:10). Let us not discount Satan's ultimate goal in persecution: to discourage the faithful and make them feel alone and abandoned.

The one common request of all the persecuted churches in the world today is for prayer. They want to know they have fellowship in God's Spirit. Prayer is the dying gasp of the martyrs, many of whom die unknown except to God. Their greatest comfort is to know that others share in their affliction, not because misery loves company, but because we are all one in Christ's body and if one member suffers, all suffer together (1 Cor 12:26).

The prayer of the persecuted is *expectant*. "Thy Kingdom come!" is the first petition our Lord taught us. When we pray that phrase, we are bold to believe God will answer it "far more abundantly than all that we ask or think, according to the power at work within us" (Eph 3:20). Prayer can move mountains. We have seen throughout history how through prayer apostles have been raised up to take the Gospel into the unlikeliest places. We can learn something from our Pentecostal brethren here in expecting the *not yet* of the Kingdom and reaching out to the "least of Christ's flock" because the time is short.

Expectant prayer is, finally, answered prayer, calling for our praise and thanksgiving. We are part not only of the church militant on earth but the church triumphant in heaven. Before long the "night of weeping will become the morn of song," the song of the redeemed in heaven: "Hallelujah! For the Lord our God the Almighty reigns. Let us rejoice and exult and give him the glory, for the marriage of the Lamb has come, and his Bride has made herself ready; it was granted her to clothe herself with fine linen, bright and pure" (Rev 19:6-8). Let us not forget to give thanks for all things, even in the midst of trouble.

DEEDS OF LOVE

Prayer without works is dead. God is preparing His Bride by washing her gown in the blood of the Lamb, and John goes on to explain that "the fine linen is the righteous deeds of the saints" (Rev 19:8). Jesus describes these righteous deeds in this way:

Then the King will say to those on his right, "Come, you who are blessed by my Father, inherit the kingdom prepared for you from the foundation of the world. For I was hungry and you gave me food, I was thirsty and you gave me drink, I was a stranger and you welcomed me, I was naked and you clothed me, I was sick and you visited me, I was in prison and you came to me." (Matt 25:34-36)

Jesus speaks of feeding, clothing and visiting His persecuted brethren. Feeding and clothing involves material and financial support. Visiting involves personal presence and may be the most difficult work of love. While there is no substitute for physically visiting our brothers and sisters in trouble, the current social media make it possible for us to be present even from a distance. As St. Paul makes clear, the imminent return of Jesus does not release us from service. Rather, as the popular chorus puts it: "If he calls me, I will answer; I'll be somewhere working for my Lord."

The final and highest deed of love is to forgive one's enemies, as Jesus taught us: "Love your enemies, do good to those who hate you, bless those who curse you, pray for those who abuse you" (Luke 6:27-28). Brothers and sisters, I know that some of you have literally obeyed this command, and I stand in awe of you. One would like to think that such acts of forgiveness of one's persecutors would shame them, open their eyes to God's love and lead them to overthrow the beasts of this age. But even if it happens that they are so hardened and blinded by Satan that they will not turn and be saved, your reward will be great in heaven (Luke 6:23).

CHRIST IS COMING SOON!

The Kingdom of God is coming. Jesus Christ is alive and reigning even now as we speak. This fact of salvation history, the final act of the drama, is as certain as His

313

Word. He will come again in glory to judge the quick and the dead. His coming will be marvelous and unexpected. When I look through the Hubble telescope at the galaxies He has made and through an electron microscope at the subatomic particles that give substance to our earthly life, I can only say

> Great and marvellous are thy works, Lord God Almighty; just and true are thy ways, thou King of saints. Who shall not fear thee, O Lord, and glorify thy name? for thou only art holy: for all nations shall come and worship before thee; for thy judgments are made manifest. (Rev 15:3-4)

The final words of the Bible are these: "He who testifies to these things says, 'Surely I am coming soon.'" To which the church responds: "Amen. Come, Lord Jesus!" And John adds his own coda, to which I shall add my voice to you in the Church of Nigeria: "The grace of the Lord Jesus be with all the saints. Amen."

BRIEF BIBLIOGRAPHY ON THE PERSECUTED CHURCH

Paul Marshall, Lela Gilbert and Nina Shea, *Persecuted: The Global Assault on Christians* (Nashville: Thomas Nelson, 2013).

Caroline Cox and Benedict Rogers, *The Very Stones Cry Out. The Persecuted Church: Pain, Passion and Praise* (London: Continuum, 2011).

Michael Nazir-Ali, *Triple Jeopardy for the West: Aggressive Secularism, Radical Islamism and Multiculturalism* (London: Bloomsbury, 2012).

ESSAY 12
CONTENDING FOR THE FAITH

A SERMON FOR THE FEAST OF SAINTS SIMON & JUDE
(2008)

October 2008 was an eventful month. I traveled back from Uganda in order to be present on October 4 for the Convention of the Diocese of Pittsburgh, which has been my canonical home since 1979. I voted with the majority to withdraw from the Episcopal Church USA, the church where I had been ordained deacon in 1971 and priest in 1972. I proceeded from Pittsburgh – now a priest of the Southern Cone of South America – to Wisconsin, where I was honored with a Doctor of Divinity degree from Nashotah House Theological Seminary. I was invited to preach to the Nashotah community on 28 October, the feast day of the apostles Simon and Jude, and I chose to preach from the Epistle of Jude.

Jude is a one-chapter gem, brilliant and sharp-edged. It is from Jude that we get the exhortation to "contend for the faith once for all delivered to the saints" (verse 3). Not surprisingly I suppose, I saw the immediate relevance of this letter to the situation of Anglicans in North America at that time, as the Common Cause Partnership, with the encouragement from GAFCON, was in the final stages of becoming the Anglican Church in North America.

Many orthodox Episcopalians and Canadian Anglicans have wrestled with the question of whether this is the time, the crisis point (*kairos* and *krisis*), for Anglican realignment. Personally, I have never regretted for a moment the decision to leave the Episcopal Church. While I am sympathetic to those who have chosen to remain, I find their position ever harder to justify and would wish them to answer more clearly the question: *how are you contending for the faith once for all delivered to the saints?*

L et me begin by thanking the faculty and trustees of Nashotah Theological Seminary for bestowing on me the honor of the Doctor of Divinity. It may be surprising to some of you to know that I interviewed for a job here thirty years ago this month. It was the road not taken, actually the road not offered, and I went on to Trinity School for Ministry, and that has made all the difference. Well, maybe not all that much difference, as I find that these roads – the evangelical and the catholic roads – have been converging in the darkening woods of North American Anglicanism over the past decade. It is my hope that together we can emerge out of this forest into a clearing of light, the light of the gospel illuminated by Scripture and the holy tradition of the Church.

Today we celebrate the Feast of St. Simon and St. Jude. These were the last-named of Jesus' Twelve apostles, save "Judas Iscariot, who betrayed him" (Luke 6:15-16). Judas Iscariot of course gained a notoriety of sorts. The same cannot be said of Simon and Jude. Simon was called "the Zealot" and that's about all we know about him. Jude is sometimes referred to as "the obscure" and the patron of lost causes because he himself is lost from the annals of history. However, as the "brother of James" he is associated with Jude, the brother of Jesus, and although they are probably different historical individuals, their honor has been conflated along with their name. One of the Judes wrote a one-chapter letter in the New Testament, and it is to that letter that I now turn.

The Letter of Jude is found in the collection of miscellaneous letters called the Catholic Epistles. These letters have generally received less attention than the Gospels or Pauline Epistles, but I think they are tracts for our times. Let me try this theory out. Each of the great theological crises in church history has focused on a particular section of the New Testament canon. The Trinitarian and Christological crisis of the first five centuries was focused on the Gospels, especially the Gospel of John, in spelling out how God could exist as three Persons and Jesus Christ as Very God and Very Man. The Reformation focused on the question of the reception of salvation by grace and faith alone, and the Reformers' key texts were the major Pauline Epistles. The current crisis, in the Anglican Communion at least, is about ecclesiology, and the Catholic Epistles (along with Ephesians and the Pastoral Epistles of Paul) are the locus of authoritative teaching in this area. That this is so should not be surprising, as these letters reflect a transitional period to the age in which the authority of the apostles was being passed on to others and the order of the church and its leadership had become a matter of intense debate and conflict.

This is what we find in Jude's letter:

> Jude, a servant of Jesus Christ and brother of James, To those who are called, beloved in God the Father and kept for Jesus Christ: May mercy, peace, and love be multiplied to you. Beloved, being very eager to write to you of our common salvation, I found it necessary to write appealing to you to contend for the faith which was once for all delivered to the saints. For admission has been secretly gained by some men who long ago were designated for this condemnation, ungodly persons who pervert the grace of our God into licentiousness and deny our only Master and Lord, Jesus Christ. (Jude 1-4)

Allow me to make four quick comments on these first verses. First, *salvation requires vigilance, even militancy.* Jude states that he wishes to speak to them about salvation, but in their context he can do so only by a call to defend the faith. In our day, few who have followed the conflicts in the Episcopal Church and Anglican Communion can fail to miss the phrase "contend for the faith once for all delivered

319

to the saints." A year ago I set up a website called "Stephen's Witness" and gathered my writings over the past twenty years. They are not light reading, I must confess. I have considered editing them into a book titled "Contending for Anglicanism." But who would read such a book? I suspect a book of polemics would be about as hot as a copy of "Fordyce's Sermons" was in Jane Austen's day. At least Jude was brief in this polemical epistle. Nevertheless, it is a necessary part of preaching the gospel of salvation that we defend it as well.

Secondly, *contending for the faith is a task for the whole people of God.* Jude is not addressing bishops or clergy but all "who are called... and kept for Jesus Christ." To be sure, bishops in our tradition are particularly charged to guard the faith, which makes the situation in the Episcopal Church sadly ironic, since, as Philip Turner has pointed out more than once, most Episcopal bishops have put on the mantle of prophetic pioneers rather than the shield of faith. Many clergy have decided that it is not their duty to inform or equip the laity for the struggles in the church, either out of a desire to protect their tender consciences or for fear of losing them. This, I believe, is most unfortunate. Let's be honest: being contentious is never popular, especially in protracted conflicts. Witness the loss of public ardor for the war on terrorism since September 11, 2001. Willingness to contend is nevertheless, if we take Jude seriously, a general obligation of discipleship. To shield lay people from this obligation is to deny them a part of their calling.

Thirdly, *the danger to the church comes from real flesh and blood individuals.* Jude mentions "some persons" (they could be men or women) who are troubling the church, and he refers repeatedly to "these persons" throughout the epistle. This is not a war of false teachings, but a war with false teachers. He goes on to specify that they are dangerous precisely because they are in the church but not in the faith. They are wolves in sheep's clothing. Too often in the past years, many in the Episcopal Church have been willing to extend the right hand of fellowship to those whom they know to be undermining the Gospel and the church. The apostles had a much less tolerant attitude toward heretics, as epitomized in Polycarp's story of St. John fleeing out of a bathhouse "because the heretic Cerinthus is within." I don't think John stopped to pass the Peace as he went out! There are indeed bonds of affection which we as Anglicans should have for those in our tradition; because these bonds are precious, we should be careful not to stretch them like bungee cords over the chasm between us.

Fourth and finally, note that *doctrine and morals cannot really be separated.* The danger Jude confronts is not, strictly speaking, doctrinal but moral, what he calls "perverting the gospel into licentiousness." The heretics were no doubt teaching something about how freedom in Christ and the Spirit liberates believers from moral rules; hence these teachings would become grounds for justifying sinful behavior. In the trial of Bishop Walter Righter in 1996, his defenders claimed that morality was an "indifferent" matter, whereas I argued that moral behavior is part of the apostolic rule, and hence one cannot put moral teaching, especially in matters of sexual purity, in a second rank. Therefore those who practice immorality are in mortal danger, those who justify immorality even more so (Matthew 5:18).

In the body of the epistle (verses 5-19), Jude moves to an act of remembrance of scriptural teaching about heresy. He does this by free prophetic exegesis of Scriptural types, in which each example refers back to "these men" who are corrupting the church.

His first two examples are painted on a two-storied cosmic canvas: *the rebellion of the people of Israel in the wilderness and the revolt of the angels in heaven.* For Jude the watchword in these examples is: "those who stand, beware lest you fall" (cf. 1 Corinthians 10:1-12). The people saved through the Red Sea had seen and tasted that the Lord is good, yet before long many were worshipping the golden calf. In the angelic realm, Jude looks to the story, alluded to in Genesis 6:1-4 and expanded in the Book of Enoch, of the "sons of God" or "watchers," the guardian angels who "fell" for the "daughters of men" and were imprisoned until the Last Judgment. Jude reflects a common theme in the apostolic writings that the primal sins are idolatry and sexual immorality (note the exhortation to *flee* idolatry and fornication – not, I might add, to *free* them or *feel* them – see 1 Corinthians 10:14; 6:18). These sins are joined at the hip – or joined at the loins – as misdirected desire leads to misdirected worship. In the case at hand, Jude sees the unnatural sin of Sodom as typifying his opponents' "dreamings that defile the flesh, reject authority and revile the glorious ones" (verse 8). For Jude, these persons are not merely differing on a secondary matter but rebelling against nature and the heavenly host who oversee it.

Jude follows the examples from Scripture with what we might call *an argument from the hierarchy of reason.* He cites a legend of the archangel Michael arguing with Satan over the body of Moses, in which Michael submits his great power to the final judgement of God. When it comes to matters of Christian doctrine and morals, Jude says, the authority of God trumps any reason of man. Too often man's reason turns out to be rationalization of wrong desire, which is rebellion against God's sovereign wisdom. "These men," he says, "revile what they do not understand, and they are destroyed by those things that they know by instinct as irrational animals do" (verse 10). The end state of such rationalization, Jude says, is destruction, although like Michael we are to leave that final judgment to God.

Jude's next set of bad examples has to do with the danger of so-called "prophetic" individualism to true Christian community. He cites Cain, who wandered before God, Balaam the loner prophet for hire, and Korah, who tried to splinter the unity of the people under Moses and Aaron. Likewise Jude claims that his opponents are "blemishes on your agape meals" (verse 12). In Jude's view, *false prophecy is heresy and heresy is schism.* False teaching causes a break in communion, whether that leads to a formal division or not. This is also the view of the Protestant Reformers but directly contrary to various statements recently by some Anglican leaders that "schism is worse than heresy."

Jude's final example comes from *tradition* about the mysterious patriarch Enoch, who "walked with God and was not, for God took him" (Genesis 5:24). The legend of Enoch was extremely popular in late Judaism and early Christianity, and the Book of Enoch (*1 Enoch*) carried considerable prophetic authority. Enoch himself was thought to be a figure of such godliness that he was raptured into heaven, studied the book of providence, and came back to warn of coming judgment in the days before Noah. Jude seems to accept this version of the Enoch legend and links it to the false teachers of his day. This extra-biblical reference demonstrates that early Christians expected to find inspired guidance from prophecy outside what came to be the canon of Scripture. Having said this, we should note that the supreme authority, as Jude concludes his catena of witnesses, comes from the predictions of Jesus and the apostles themselves who stated: "In the last time there will be scoffers, following their own ungodly passions" (verses 17-18).

It is worth remembering in our time that the idea that there will be false teachers in the church is found throughout the New Testament (cf. Matthew 24:4ff.; 2 Timothy 3:1-9; 2 John 7-11; Revelation 2-3). It is not an occasional or accidental feature of church life but a constant, which explains why contending for the faith is a regular and expected duty. We may find this truth unpleasant to accept, but we do so at our own risk – and the church's. The presence of heresy is an ongoing eschatological sign. All Christians, and particularly Christian leaders, live constantly before the judgment seat of Christ and in the light of his coming. It is therefore of utmost importance to keep one's conscience clear. In certain circumstances, conscientiousness may lead two individuals to differ as to how to respond to heresy, but if so, they should be careful to maintain the spirit of unity in the bond of peace with each other.

As the epistle draws to a close, Jude turns to pastoral guidance for the congregation in the midst of serious conflict over the faith delivered to the saints.

> But you, beloved, build yourselves up on your most holy faith; pray in the Holy Spirit; keep yourselves in the love of God; wait for the mercy of our Lord Jesus Christ unto eternal life. And convince some, who doubt; save some, by snatching them out of the fire; on some have mercy with fear, hating even the garment spotted by the flesh. (verses 20-23)

The good pastor or good parishioner is called on to "discern the spirits" within the church. Again as Philip Turner has pointed out, a "conciliar economy" of mutual submission within the communion of the church requires spiritual virtues: faith, prayer and patience, "waiting for the mercy" of Christ. Not all those who may appear to be under the sway of false teaching are themselves false or fallen. Some are genuinely perplexed; they should be encouraged and exhorted to think again, to repent. Some are lured by temptation to practice what others preach; they should be pulled out of the fire of temptation. In these cases, the pastor or friend must be prepared to stand the heat of the fire itself by patient listening but should also be clear that sin is unacceptable before the holy God. It is this God alone who can keep all of us from falling and present us without blemish. But finally, some are truly false prophets and teachers and must be avoided like the "garment spotted by the flesh."

Jude concludes with a typical doxology but one particularly focused on the problem at hand.

> Now to him who is able to keep you from falling and to present you without blemish before the presence of his glory with rejoicing, to the only God, our Savior through Jesus Christ our Lord, be glory, majesty, dominion, and authority, before all time and now and for ever. Amen. (verses 24-25)

The God whom he praises is the powerful God who saves us through his Son, the holy God who purifies us by his Spirit, and the almighty Father whose authority is established before all time and to the end. It is this God who has loved his Church from all eternity so that the gates of hell cannot withstand it. It is this Christ who has kept his Bride pure and spotless so as to present her before his Father. It is this Spirit who unites the saints of God in heaven and on earth in one Body.

Today few would deny that the Episcopal Church and Anglican Communion worldwide have been undergoing a profound crisis of identity, faith and mission, so much so that many of the eschatological warnings in the New Testament, Jude's included, seem to apply. There are some here today who have felt conscience-bound to depart from the Episcopal Church – or have been given an assist by the powers-that-be to that end. Others have felt conscience-bound to stay in. Does Jude have anything to say specifically to our situation?

I think the answer is No and Yes. Jude does not give us specific guidance on whether to stay or go. Were the saints Jude was addressing a majority or a minority? Were the false teachers bishops or prophets with some kind of official stamp of approval? We do not know. So the answer is No, we do not know exactly what he might say to our specific situation. Was he calling the saints to come out, or the heretics to go out (cf. 2 Corinthians 6:17; 1 John 2:19)?

But at the same time, I think Yes, we can find concrete guidance for our day. Jude clearly warns that the church and by extension the wider communion will be torn at its deepest level by conflict over the truth of the "faith once for all delivered to the saints." He also makes clear that believers, all believers, must be prepared to contend for the true faith, which includes calling a spade a spade, indeed calling particular persons heretics. In looking back at the decline of the Episcopal Church, I wonder if we cannot identify one key moment to be the recommendation of the Bayne Commission in 1967, which was investigating Bishop James Pike, that "heresy" is an unhelpful category in church affairs.

Secondly, I think Jude would argue that in contending for the faith we must use all the tools: Scripture, tradition, from the Book of Enoch to the Church fathers to the Reformers and on, and godly reason based on nature. At the same time, Jude's reference to the fallen angels reminds us that we are engaged in spiritual warfare and that we cannot expect to remain faithful or to conquer without the godly virtues of prayer, patience and humility, waiting on

326

the sovereign judgment of God.

Thirdly, we should note that Jude speaks as a pastor and to pastors, who are to discern the situation of their people. Some folks need to be challenged to grow up and take their full responsibility as disciples (I think this applies to a lot of Episcopalians who just want the present unpleasantness to go away). Others, particularly those trapped in the bondages of sin, need to be loved and cared for so that they may change their minds. Others need to be identified as heretics with whom one should have nothing to do (2 Timothy 3:5; Titus 3:10). As for this last group, the question is: how does one do this when they are in control of the official structures of the church?

Let me conclude with one final observation, with special reference to you who are graduating today. We do not know the fate of Saints Simon and Jude. There is good though brief evidence that "the Lord's brothers" – and this would include Jude the Lord's brother – were traveling evangelists (1 Corinthians 9:5). Tradition has it that Simon and Jude were missionaries to Persia where they were martyred, reminding us of those today whose blood cries out around the world. Those who are commissioned today will certainly have to contend for the faith in our churches and in our culture. My point is this: whatever trouble we may find ourselves in in our particular church, the mission of Christ to take the Gospel to the ends of the earth cannot be neglected. Indeed it may well be, in the providence of God, that help may be coming for our church and our communion from those very missionaries and martyrs like James Hannington and the Ugandan converts who paid the ultimate price for their faith remembered in the American cycle of saints on October 29. Let us not therefore cease to remember our brothers and sisters around the world and the Anglican Communion, and to do good for them.

May God have mercy on our church and our communion! May he light the path ahead through his Word and Spirit and the witness of saints and martyrs and equip present-day witnesses like those going out today. May he bring us to that upland where with all the saints in light we may offer praise and glory through Jesus Christ our Lord. To him be glory in the church and in Christ Jesus for ever and ever. Amen.

About the Author

The Rev. Dr. Stephen Noll was born and raised in Arlington, Virginia. He graduated with a B.A. (Phi Beta Kappa) from Cornell University in 1968 and received the Master of Arts degree from the Graduate Theological Union in 1970 and the Master of Divinity degree from Church Divinity School of the Pacific in Berkeley, California. He studied under Professors F. F. Bruce and Barnabas Lindars at University of Manchester (UK) where he received the Ph.D. in Biblical Studies in 1979. In 2008, he was awarded the Doctor of Divinity degree from Nashotah House Theological Seminary.

Stephen became a Christian and was baptized in the Episcopal Church in 1966. He was ordained deacon and priest in 1971 and 1972 and served as Assistant and Priest-in-Charge of Truro Episcopal Church from 1971-1976.

In 1979, he joined the faculty of Trinity (Episcopal) School for Ministry, where he served for 21 years as Professor of Biblical Studies and Academic Dean, and is now Professor Emeritus.

In 2000, he was appointed the first Vice Chancellor [President] of Uganda Christian University in Mukono, Uganda, where he served two terms, retiring in 2010. Stephen continues to serve the Anglican Church in North America (ACNA) as Archbishop's Advisor for the Global Anglican Future and also as Chairman of the ACNA Task Force on Marriage, Family and the Single Life. He has been active in the Gafcon movement and serves as Convener of its Task Force on Women in the Episcopate.

In addition to the writings in this volume, Dr. Noll has written a book on *Angels of Light, Powers of Darkness: Thinking Biblically About Angels, Satan, and Principalities*

(InterVarsity Press, 1998). He maintains a website of miscellaneous writings at *www.stephenswitness.org*.

Stephen Noll has been married to his wife Peggy since 1967, and they have five children and seven grandchildren. They live in Sewickley, Pennsylvania.

Notes

ESSAY 1: READING THE BIBLE AS THE WORD OF GOD

1. In his recent worldview analysis, *Culture Wars: The Struggle to Define America* (New York: Basic Books, 1991), 44-45, James Davison Hunter distinguishes two main views of authority. "Orthodoxy" involves the *"commitment on the part of adherents to an external, definable, and transcendent authority."* "Progressives," by contrast, share the *"tendency to resymbolize historic faiths according to the prevailing assumptions of contemporary life."* As an example of the latter strategy, see John Shelby Spong, *Born of a Woman: A Bishop Rethinks the Birth of Jesus* (San Francisco: Harper, 1992), 173: "Like all theological statements, the creeds are filled with symbolic words and time-distorted meanings.... The only way to keep symbols alive forever is to crack them open periodically so that they can be filled with new meanings."

2. See the general cultural analysis of George Steiner, "The Retreat from the Word," in *George Steiner: A Reader* (New York: Oxford University Press, 1984), 283-304.

3. For the background of fundamentalism in Baconian science, see George Marsden, *Fundamentalism and American Culture: The Shaping of Twentieth-century Evangelicalism 1870-1925* (Oxford: Oxford University Press, 1980), 55-62.

4. I have been sent numerous articles in Episcopal publications attacking what Bishop Spong refers to as the "beast of literalism" in *Rescuing the Bible from Fundamentalism* (San Francisco: Harper, 1991), 215. The tip-off to caricature is the use of "-ism," which reminds me of the epigram that "tradition is the living faith of the dead, traditionalism is the dead faith of the living."

5. Many theological friends warned me against using the term *literal* to define a distinct hermeneutical position. When I asked them for an adequate substitute, they could not agree on one. So I followed the advice of Jean Cocteau when he said, "Listen carefully to first criticisms made of your work. Note just what it is about your work that critics don't like - then cultivate it. That's the only part of your work that's individual and worth keeping."

6. I argue in my responses to my co-authors Price, Norris, and Wondra that they share common presuppositions of biblical

meaning as ineffable and hence governable by human consciousness, over against my view that the Divine Logos determines the "logic" of the literal sense of scripture, which in turn governs the response of the believer.

7. See the fine meditation on John 1:1-18 in T. F. Torrance, "The Word of God and the Response of Man," in *God and Rationality* (London: Oxford University Press, 1971), 137-53.

8. Wolfhart Pannenberg, *Systematic Theology* (Grand Rapids, Mich.: Eerdmans, 1991), 1:3 Torrance, "Word of God," 149.

9. Torrance, "Word of God," 149.

10. Augustine, *On Christian Doctrine* 1.39.43; Calvin, *Institutes* 1.6.1.

11. J. L. Kugel, "Early Interpretation: The Common Background of Late Forms of Biblical Exegesis," in *Early Biblical Interpretation,* ed. J. L. Kugel and R. A. Greer (Philadelphia: Westminster, 1986), 70-71.

12. Luke 24:44-49. Cf. C. H. Dodd, *According to the Scriptures: The Sub-Structure of New Testament Theology* (London: Nisbet, 1952), 28-60.

13. B. A. Pierson, "Use, Authority and Exegesis of *Mikra in Gnostic Literature," Mikra, Text, Translation, Reading and Interpretation of the Hebrew Bible in Ancient Judaism and Early Christianity.* CRINT 2.1 (Assen: Van Gorcum, 1988), 635-52.

14. R.P.C. Hanson, *Tradition in the Early Church* (Philadelphia: Westminster, 1962), 124-29.

15. R. A. Greer, "The Christian Bible and Its Interpretation," in Kugel and Greer, *Early Biblical Interpretation*, 184-85.

16. Maurice Wiles's comment on Origen is revealing: "Despite the great range of his intellectual gifts, Origen was totally lacking in poetic sensitivity. The literal sense of scripture is for him the literally literal meaning of the words." See "Origen as Biblical Scholar" in *The Cambridge History of the Bible* (Cambridge: Cambridge University Press, 1970), 1:470. The Antiochenes in reacting against allegory likewise tended to restrict the meaning of Scripture to its "narrative sense" (*historia*).

17. The starting point of Augustine's doctrine of scripture is the clarity of the canonical text: "Anyone who understands in the Scriptures something other than that intended by them is deceived, although they do not lie" (*On Christian Doctrine* 1.36.41). At times he can refer to this intentional reading as "the literal sense." He can also make distinction between "literal" and "figurative" signs; the literal signs have a primary verbal referent

("ox" = the animal), while figures refer to something else, as in 1 Cor. 9:9 (*On Christian Doctrine* 2.10.15). In most cases figures turn out to be Old Testament types.

18. Cf. Raymond Brown's case for sensus plenior as a second meaning of the text, in "What the Biblical Word Meant and What It Means," *The Critical Meaning of the Bible* (New York: Paulist, 1981), 23-44.

19. See J.A. Preus, *From Shadow to Promise: Old Testament Interpretation from Augustine to the Young Luther* (Cambridge: Harvard University Press, 1969), 267-68.

20. "For as God alone is a fit witness of himself in his Word, so also the Word will not find acceptance in men's hearts before it is sealed by the inward testimony of the Spirit." *Institutes* 1.7.4.

21. See esp. *Laws of Ecclesiastical Polity* 1.14, 2.8, 3.8, and 5.59.2; E. Grislis, "The Hermeneutical Problem in Hooker," in *Studies in Richard Hooker* (Cleveland: Case Western, 1972), 193-96.

22. See survey and evaluation in B. S. Childs, *Introduction to the Old Testament as Scripture* (Philadelphia: Fortress, 1979), 34-41.

23. A. C. Thiselton, *New Horizons in Hermeneutics* (Grand Rapids, Mich.: Zondervan, 1992), 209-16, limits "romantic" hermeneutics to Schleiermacher and his contemporaries; however, he does show how Schleiermacher has set the agenda for all subsequent "post-modern" hermeneutics.

24. Thiselton, *New Horizons,* 226-27, credits Schleiermacher's attention to the semantic aspect of a text. Nevertheless, for Schleiermacher it is possible to understand a text better than the author because the author's historical perspective is particular and primitive, while the interpreter brings a mature and universal modern consciousness.

25. "Historicist experience" is fundamentally opaque, whereas in classical thought common-sense experience or opinion is the beginning of true insight (Aristotle, *Nicomachean Ethics* 1.4). This is why "experience" is such a loaded term in current discussions about authority.

26. Leo Strauss, *Natural Right and History* (Chicago: University of Chicago Press, 1953), 25.

27. Note the wry comment of Oliver O'Donovan in *Resurrection and Moral Order* (Grand Rapids, Mich.: Eerdmans, 1986), 161: "Cultural foreignness, which we meet in our contemporaries daily, is not a final barrier to understanding, but a warning against shallow understandings."

28. "The Sensus Literalis of Scripture: An Ancient and Modern Problem," in H. Donner et al., eds., *Beiträge zur Alttestamentlichen Theologie* (FS Zimmerli; Göttingen: Vandenhoeck und Ruprecht, 1977), 80-93.

29. Childs, "The Canonical Approach and the New Yale Theology," in *The New Testament as Canon* (Philadelphia: Fortress, 1984), 541-46; E. V. McKnight, *Post-Modern Use of the Bible* (Nashville: Abingdon, 1988), 74-79.

30. See, e.g., the philosophical theology of Carl F. H. Henry, *God, Revelation, and Authority* (Waco: Word, 1976); and the hermeneutical essays in *Hermeneutics, Authority, and Canon*, ed. D. A. Carson and J. D. Woodbridge (Grand Rapids, Mich.: Zondervan, 1986).

31. "The Centrality of Hermeneutics Today," in D. A. Carson and J. D. Woodbridge, ed., *Scripture and Truth* (Grand Rapids, Mich.: Zondervan, 1983), 333, 349-50.

32. William J. Abraham, *The Divine Inspiration of Holy Scripture* (Oxford: Oxford University Press, 1981), 67. This family debate demonstrates the ongoing vitality of the Calvinist-Arminian strands of classic Protestantism.

33. Clark H. Pinnock, *The Scripture Principle* (San Francisco: Harper, 1984), 78.

34. Abraham, *Divine Inspiration*, 106, explains New Testament references to the whole Old Testament as the Word of God in this way: "Recognizing that God has spoken his word [on occasion] and that this is recorded in the Old Testament they happily talk of all of it being the Word of God." I think he mistakes the mode of verbal revelation (e.g., God speaking to prophets) with the character of all scripture as verbally inspired.

35. Postmodernism claims to be a third way but has not really demonstrated its coherence as a worldview except by negation.

36. Pannenberg, *Systematic Theology*, 1:313, sees the essential intratrinitarian relations as the "handing over" of lordship by the Father to the Son and the Son's "handing back" of that lordship.

37. Older commentators observed a necessary link between the literal and figurative senses. So Patrick Fairbairn writes: "All languages are more or less figurative; for the mind of man is essentially analogical ... and in regard to things lying beyond the reach of sense or time, it is *obliged* to resort to figurative terms..." *Hermeneutical Manual: Introduction to the Exegetical Study, Exegetical Study of the Scriptures of the New Testament* (Philadelphia: Smith,

English, 1859), 158.

38. Cf. Northrop Frye in *The Great Code: The Bible and Literature* (New York: Harcourt Brace Jovanovich, 1982), 61-62: "The Bible means literally just what it says, but it can mean it only without primary reference to a correspondence of what it says to something outside what it says."

39. E. D. Hirsch quips in *The Aims of Interpretation* (Chicago: University of Chicago Press, 1976), 6: "Whenever I am told by a Heideggerian that I have misunderstood Heidegger, my still unrebutted response is that I will readily (if uneasily) concede that point, since the concession in itself implies a more important point, namely that Heidegger's text *can* be interpreted correctly, and has been so by my accuser."

40. Gerhard von Rad, *Old Testament Theology* (New York: Harper, 1965), 2:319-35; and Austin Farrer, *The Rebirth of Images: The Making of St. John's Apocalypse* (Westminster: Dacre, 1949), 13-22.

41. Childs, *Introduction,* 78-79; Douglas Moo, "The Problem of Sensus Plenior," *Hermeneutics, Authority, and Canon,* ed. Carson and Woodbridge, 204-9.

42. *The Poetics of Biblical Narrative: Ideological Literature and the Drama of Reading* (Bloomington: Indiana University Press, 1985), 50-51. Note the attack on "foolproof composition" by D. N. Fewell and D. M. Gunn, "Tipping the Balance: Sternberg's Reader and the Rape of Dinah," *JBL* 110 (1991): 193-211; and his rebuttal, "Biblical Poetics and Sexual Politics: From Reading to Counter-Reading," *JBL* 111 (1992): 463-88.

43. K. J. Vanhoozer, "The Semantics of Biblical Literature: Truth and the Scripture's Diverse Literary Forms," in *Hermeneutics, Authority, and Canon,* ed. Carson and Woodbridge, 99-100, points out that "illocutionary speech" is effective "simply in the hearer understanding the utterance of the speaker." Sinful human beings, apart from God's grace, can reject a clear message of scripture.

44. Both Origen and John Cassian supported the threefold distinction among the sense of scripture by references to Prov. 22:20 (LXX): "Write these things triply in your heart..." Among modern commentators, Sternberg, *Poetics,* 41, makes a triple distinction among ideological, historiographic, and aesthetic principles of biblical narrative.

45. Thiselton, *New Horizons,* 597-99, points out a major distinction in speech acts between promises and authorizations, which communicate commitments on the part of the author, and prayers and confessions, that call for a commitment on the readers' part.

46. The power of Handel's *Messiah* derives from a similar synthesis of texts and music. Cf. Hans Urs von Balthasar, *Truth Is Symphonic: Aspects of Christian Pluralism* (San Francisco: Ignatius, 1987), 7-9.

47. The classic description of mimesis in the Bible is that of Erich Auerbach, *Mimesis: The Representation of Reality in Western Literature* (Princeton: Princeton University Press, 1953). I am indebted to a development of Auerbach's case by A. D. Nuttall, *A New Mimesis: Shakespeare and the Nature of Reality* (London: Methuen, 1983).

48. Nuttall, *New Mimesis,* 181-93.

49. Cf. Stephen Prickett, *Words and the Word: Language, Poetics and Biblical Interpretation* (Cambridge: Cambridge University Press, 1986), 4-36.

50. On the use of literary omniscience and omnipotence, see Sternberg, *Poetics,* 100.

51. See David L. Bartlett, *The Shape of Biblical Authority* (Philadelphia: Fortress, 1983), 43-81.

52. *Evangelical Commentary on the Bible,* ed. W. A. Elwell (Grand Rapids, Mich.: Baker, 1989), 326-28. Cf. C. S. Lewis's letter to E. J. Carnell (4/4/53): "In what sense does the Bible 'present' the Jonah story 'as historical'? Of course, it doesn't say 'This is fiction' but then neither does our Lord say that the Unjust Judge, Good Samaritan, or Prodigal Son are fiction. (I would put *Esther* in the same category as Jonah for the same reason.) How does a denial, a doubt of their historicity lead logically to a similar denial of New Testament miracles?"

53. See, for instance, his 1535 commentary on Galatians 3:2: "all the patriarchs, prophets, and devout kings of the Old Testament were righteous, having received the Holy Spirit secretly on account of their faith in the coming Christ."

54. W. G. Dever, "Archaeology," *IDBSup* (1976): 51.

55. See critiques by Sternberg, *Poetics,* 2-35; and Baruch Halpern, *The First Historians: The Hebrew Bible and History* (San Francisco: Harper, 1988), 3-32.

56. Sternberg, *Poetics,* 34: "Omniscience in modern narrative attends and signals fictionality, while in the ancient tradition it not only accommodates but also guarantees authenticity."

57. Frye, *Great Code,* 206.

58. It may be objected that the conclusions of Job and Ecclesiastes are pious deflections of the skeptical questions within the books. Even if this were true, the canonical framing sets the books within

336

the larger wisdom tradition, without denying their radical thrust. Similarly, Shakespeare can bring Fortenbras on stage to restore the kingdom of Denmark without undoing the radical disorder that Hamlet's questioning has caused.

59. O'Donovan, *Resurrection and Moral Order,* 25: "Only God expresses love by conferring order upon the absolutely orderless, and he has contented himself with doing it but once."

60. For the term, see Frederick H. Borsch, *Many Things in Parables: Extravagant Stories of New Community* (Philadelphia: Fortress, 1988), 12-13.

61. See R. H. Fuller, "Scripture," in The *Study of Anglicanism,* ed. S. Sykes and J. H. Booty (London: SPCK, 1988), 79-91.

62. "The Official Position of the Episcopal Church on the Authority of Scripture. Part I: Present Teaching and Historical Development," *ATR* 74 (1992): 350.

63. Oliver O'Donovan, *On the Thirty-nine Articles: A Conversation with Tudor Christianity* (Exeter: Paternoster, 1986), 51, notes that *reading* of the Bible in the Tudor church took logical priority over exposition because "the way of knowing any given thing is dictated in large measure by *what the thing is,* and not only (or mainly) by the situation of the person who has come to know it."

64. As Wright notes ("Official Position," 355-56), the 1983 statement of the Episcopal House of Bishops apparently intended (!) to espouse this view by omitting the familiar phrase "to be the Word of God" in alluding to the Oath and by adding the statement that "God's Word is a Person, not a book." This view is apparently also behind the revising of the 1982 Hymnal (see esp. the revisions to Hymn 632 and the new hymns 629 and 630).

65. Anglican Church of Canada, *Book of Alternative Services* (1985), 9. I find curious Robert Wright's comment ("Official Position," 350) that the ordination oath "does not expressly deny the existence of some further Word or word(s) of God beyond or above the Sacred Page." If he means to extend this higher authority of other Word/words to matters of salvation, how can scripture contain all things necessary to it?

66. The Episcopal Church's Teaching Series claims: "What we mean by calling the Scriptures authoritative is simply that we know that the church has experienced the presence and power of God through the Bible." R. A. Bennett and O. C. Edwards, *The Bible for Today's Church* (New York: Seabury, 1979), 72. For Philip Culbertson, "Known, Knower, and Knowing: The Authority of Scripture in the Episcopal Church," *ATR* 74 (1992): 172, the

common experience is the constancy of change." For Bishop Spong, *Rescuing the Bible*, 243, it is the call "to love, to live, and to be."

67. Note how the orthodox intention of Charles Gore in the original *Lux Mundi* in asserting the inspiration of the church alongside the inspiration of scripture has become radicalized in the identification of the Holy Spirit and "experience" in the centenary update of his position. D. N. Power, "The Holy Scripture, Tradition, and Interpretation," in *Keeping the Faith: Essays to Mark the Centenary of Lux Mundi* (Philadelphia: Fortress, 1988), 153.

68. *Evangelical Essentials: A Liberal-Evangelical Dialogue* (Downers Grove: IVP, 1988).

69. Cf. Bartlett, *Shape of Scriptural Authority,* 131-54.

70. Robert Alter points out that not only have ordinary people given up reading, but students of literature have as well. See *The Pleasures of Reading in an Ideological Age* (New York: Simon and Schuster, 1989), 11.

71. St. Augustine *(Confessions* 3.5.9) describes scripture as "a text lowly to the beginner but, on further reading, of mountainous difficulty and enveloped in mysteries." Sternberg's *Poetics* is a tour de force in demonstrating the "key strategy" of biblical discourse: "the art of indirection or, from the interpreter's side, the drama of reading" (pp. 43-44).

72. Richard B. Hays, *Echoes of Scripture in the Letters of Paul* (New Haven: Yale University Press, 1989), 178-92, has shown how this method underlies Paul's reading of the Old Testament in the light of Christ. George Herbert enunciates the classic Reformation principle, based on 1 Cor. 2:13, in his second sonnet on "The Holy Scriptures": "This verse marks that, and both do make a motion/Unto a third, that ten leaves off doth lie."

73. Cranmer's sense of "digesting" scripture surely reflects the precritical assumption, as explained by Hans Frei, *The Eclipse of Biblical Narrative: A Study in Eighteenth and Nineteenth Century Hermeneutics* (New Haven: Yale University Press, 1974), 3, that "since the world truly rendered by combining biblical narratives into one was indeed the one and only real world, it must in principle embrace the experience of any present age and reader." In like fashion, Herbert can go on to say in his scripture sonnet: "Such are thy secrets, which my life makes good,/ And comments on thee: for in ev'rything /Thy words do find me out, and parallels bring..."

74. Cf. David T. Shannon, "'An Ante-Bellum Sermon': A Resource

for an African American Hermeneutic," in *Stony the Road We Trod: African American Biblical Interpretation,* ed. C. H. Felder (Minneapolis: Fortress, 1991), 98-123.

75. I know of no more convincing demonstration of this truth than Chana Bloch's eloquent exposition of George Herbert's poetics in *Spelling the Word: George Herbert and the Bible* (Berkeley: University of California Press, 1984), 30-31:

> Writing about Scripture, Herbert sets before us the mind and heart of the Christian who reads and interprets. Precisely where we might expect to find the self humbled and subordinated, we find it instead vigorously at work and conscious of its own motions in bringing the text to life.... The delighted play of the mind, so characteristic of *The Temple,* belies Stanley Fish's picture of Herbert, martyrlike, building his poetry into a pyre of self-immolation. In Herbert's poetry the self is not effaced but improved.

76. See Colin Brown, *Miracles and the Critical Mind* (Grand Rapids, Mich.: Eerdmans; 1984); and Gary Habermas and Anthony Flew, *Did Jesus Rise from the Dead? The Resurrection Debate* (San Francisco: Harper, 1987).

77. Raymond Brown's *The Virginal Conception and Bodily Resurrection of Jesus* (New York: Paulist, 1973), sums up the evidence from historical criticism.

78. See Childs, *The New Testament as Canon,* 157-65.

79. Karl Barth, *CD* 2.1.207; P. E. Hughes, *The True Image: The Origin and Destiny of Man in Christ* (Grand Rapids, Mich.: Eerdmans, 1989), 213-23.

80. The charge of illegitimacy was of course raised by Jesus' opponents (John 8:41). See the tendentious revival of this case argued by Jane Schaberg in *The Illegitimacy of Jesus: A Feminist Theological Interpretation of the Infancy Narratives* (San Francisco: Harper, 1987).

81. Cf. Bishop Spong, *Rescuing the Bible,* 217, for the *ex cathedra* pronouncement of the new orthodoxy: "The virgin birth tradition of the New Testament is not literally true. It should not be literally believed."

82. *Dirt, Greed, and Sex: Sexual Ethics in the New Testament and Their Implications for Today* (Philadelphia: Fortress, 1988).

83. Ibid., 265: "The few pertinent verses in Genesis 1 and 2, for example, are brief and allusive in their language, which leaves them open to a variety of speculative interpretations." By not

beginning in the beginning, he fails to see the natural law logic behind the purity code and behind Hebrew marriage and family law, a logic that Mary Douglas calls "keeping distinct the categories *of creation"* (my italics); *Purity and Danger: An Analysis of Concepts of Pollution and Taboo* (London: Routledge, 1966), 53.

84. Cf. H. W. House, ed., *Divorce and Remarriage: Four Christian Views* (Downers Grove: IVP, 1990).

85. "Relations Natural and Unnatural: A Response to John Boswell's Exegesis of Romans 1" *Journal of Religious Ethics* 14 (1986): 184-215.

86. "Awaiting the Redemption of Our Bodies," *Sojourners* (July 1991): 17-21. Cf. *Issues in Human Sexuality: A Statement by the House of Bishops of the General Synod of the Church of England, December 1991* (Harrisburg, Pa.: Morehouse, 1991). This report certainly takes the first step in identifying the "ultimate biblical consensus" about monogamy and celibacy (p. 18), and it refuses to grant homosexual practice the status of a "parallel or alternative form of human sexuality" (p. 40). Where the report falters (p. 41) is in granting autonomy to individual conscience over the clear teaching of scripture, thus selling short the transforming power of grace.

ESSAY 2: TWO SEXES, ONE FLESH

1. Cf., Edward Stein, *The Mismeasure of Desire: The Science, Theory, and Ethics of Sexual Orientation* (Oxford: Oxford University Press, 1999).

2. For a standard definition, see "Sex and Sexuality" in *Encyclopaedia Britannica*, Macropaedia (15th ed., 1986) 27.245.

3. *The Transformation of Intimacy: Sexuality, Love and Eroticism in Modern Societies* (Stanford: Stanford University Press, 1992).

4. Tim Stafford, *The Sexual Christian* (Wheaton, Ill.: Victor Books, 1989) 15-19.

5. See Christopher R. Seitz, "Repugnance and the Three-Legged Stool: Modern Use of Scripture and the Baltimore Declaration," in *Reclaiming Faith: Essays on Orthodoxy in the Episcopal Church and the Baltimore Declaration* (Grand Rapids: Eerdmans, 1993) 87.

6. Countryman, *Dirt, Greed, and Sex: Sexual Ethics in the New Testament and Their Implications for Today* (Philadelphia: Fortress Press 1988) 243.

7. "Finding a Way to Talk: Dealing with Difficult Topics in the Episcopal Church," in *Our Selves, Our Souls and Bodies: Sexuality and the Household of God,* ed. Charles Hefling (Cambridge, Mass.: Cowley, 1996) 11-12.

8. Cf. Hays, *Moral Vision*, 399: "Only because the new experience of Gentile converts proved hermeneutically illuminating of Scripture was the church, over time, able to accept the decision to embrace Gentiles within the fellowship of God's people.

9. *Biblical Ethics and Homosexuality: Listening to Scripture*, ed. Robert L. Brawley (Louisville: Westminster John Knox Press, 1996). We note *causa honoris* one essay in this volume by Ulrich Mauser that upholds the plain sense of Scripture. The General Assembly of the Presbyterian Church U.S.A., meeting in July 1996, did not follow the direction suggested by the rest of these essays.

10. Oliver O'Donovan, "Transsexualism and Christian Marriage," *Journal of Religious Ethics* 11 (1983) 146.

11. Roger Scruton, *Sexual Desire: A Moral Philosophy of the Erotic* (New York: Free Press, 1986) 339.

12. Dietrich Bonhoeffer, *Letters and Papers from Prison* (New York: Macmillan, 1971) 42.

13. Germain Grisez, "The Christian Family as Fulfillment of Sacramental Marriage," in *Studies in Christian Ethics* 9 (1996) 30. A view similar to Grisez's was articulated by Otto Piper, *The Biblical View of Sex and Marriage* (New York: Scribner's, 1960) 137-138.

14. See Wendy Shalit, *A Return to Modesty: Discovering the Lost Virtue* (New York: Free Press, 1999).

15. See Edward Stein, ed., *Forms of Desire: Sexual Orientation and the Social Constructionist Controversy* (New York: Routledge, 1990).

16. Scruton, *Sexual Desire*, 307-309.

17. David F. Greenberg, *The Construction of Homosexuality* (Chicago: University of Chicago Press, 1988).

18. Alasdair MacIntyre, *Whose Justice? Which Rationality?* (South Bend: University of Notre Dame, 1988).

19. Dennis Prager, "Judaism's Sexual Revolution," *Crisis* (Sept. 1993) 29. The original version of Prager's essay appeared in *Ultimate Issues* 6/2 (Apr./Jun. 1990) 1-24.

20. Scruton, *Sexual Desire*, 356.

21. *Second Treatise on Government*, sec. 78.

22. *Emile or On Education*, ed. Allan Bloom (New York: Basic Books, 1979) 357-358.

23. *Democracy in America* 3.12.

24. *The War over the Family: Capturing the Middle Ground* (Garden City, N.Y.:

Doubleday Anchor, 1983) 172.

25. Sigmund Freud, *Civilization and Its Discontents* (New York: Norton, 1961) 51.

26. *Touching Our Strength: The Erotic as Power and the Love of God* (San Francisco: Harper, 1989) 152.

27. Paula L. Ettelbrick, "Marriage Is Not a Path to Liberation," in *Homosexuality: Opposing Viewpoints* (San Diego: Greenhaven Press, 1993) 180-181.

28. John Spong, *Living in Sin: A Bishop Rethinks Human Sexuality* (San Francisco: Harper Collins, 1988) 208-218; Andrew Sullivan, *Virtually Normal: An Argument about Homosexuality* (New York: Vintage, 1996) 202.

29. *Touching Our Strength*, 3.

30. "Limited Engagements," in Philip Turner, ed., *Men and Women: Sexual Ethics in Turbulent Times* (Cambridge, Mass.: Cowley, 1989) 55.

31. *The Pilgrim's Progress* (2nd ed.; Oxford: Clarendon, 1960) 292.

32. C. S. Lewis, *Perelandra* (New York: Macmillan, 1943) 200.

33. Book of Common Prayer (Episcopal Church U.S.A., 1979) 423.

ESSAY 4: THE DECLINE AND FALL (AND RISING AGAIN) OF THE ANGLICAN COMMUNION

1. In this line, I have included more personal anecdotes and references to my work than might normally be expected in a scholarly paper. Many of my writings during this period are collected at www.stephenswitness.org. [Note: my original website of stephenswitness.com was stolen.]

2. Philip Turner, "The End of a Church and the Triumph of Denominationalism: On How to Think about What is Happening in the Episcopal Church," in Ephraim Radner and Philip Turner, *The Fate of Communion: The Agony of Anglicanism and the Future of a Global Church* (Grand Rapids: Eerdmans, 2006) pp. 15-24; see also *idem*, "Episcopal Oversight and Ecclesiastical Discipline: A Comment on the Concordat of Agreement between the Episcopal Church USA and the Evangelical Lutheran Church in America," in *Pro Ecclesia* 3 (1994) pp. 436-454; and "Episcopal Authority in a Divided Church," *Pro Ecclesia* 8 (1999).

3. Later Williams came out against monogamy, was forced to resign from the Episcopal "Oasis" ministry (not defrocked, however), authored a book *Just As I Am: A Practical Guide to Being Out, Proud,*

Christian (1993), and died from AIDS on Christmas Eve 1992.

4. "The Righter Trial and Christian Doctrine," *Churchman* 110 (1996) pp. 198-216; "The Righter Trial and Church Discipline," *Churchman* 110 (1996) pp. 295-324.

5. In my opinion, "holding" a doctrine was intended according to the canon to include actions that would proceed logically from that doctrine. Hence even if Righter had not openly advocated homosexual practice (which he did), by his action in ordaining Stopfel, he "held" that teaching. The Court never affirmed or denied this meaning of the canon since it chose to redefine "teaching" itself.

6. "Righter Trial and Christian Doctrine," p. 215.

7. "Righter Trial and Church Discipline," p. 320.

8. The same Humpty-Dumpty-esque hermeneutic of the Righter judges was applied to the Bible ten years ago by Bishop Charles Bennison: "…we wrote the Bible and we can rewrite it. We have rewritten the Bible many times." More recently, this hermeneutic has been taken up by the Queen of Hearts, a.k.a. the Presiding Bishop of The Episcopal Church, in her treatment of Bishops Robert Duncan and Jack Iker. Pronouncing sentence on the former before he had committed the crime, she reasoned: "In these circumstances, I concur with my Chancellor and Parliamentarian that any ambiguity in the canon [actually there is none] should be resolved in favor of making this important provision [his deposition] work effectively…" In the case of the latter, she accepted his resignation in the absence of, and indeed his refusal to give, the actual letter of resignation required by the canons. Lewis Carroll said it all: "The Queen had only one way of settling difficulties, great or small: 'Off with his head!' she said, without even looking around." For a less literary analysis, see Philip Turner, "Subversion of the Constitution and Canons of the Episcopal Church: On Doing What It Takes to Get What You Want," at http://www.anglicancommunioninstitute.com/?p=326; and Christopher Seitz et al, "Descent into Canonical Chaos: The Presiding Bishop's Response to Bishop Iker," at http://www.anglicancommunioninstitute.com/?p=338.

9. See *Theological Freedom and Social Responsibility* (New York: Seabury Press, 1967) p. 22. For extended commentary on this trend, see C. Fitzsimmons Allison, "The Episcopal Church: The Canary in the Culture's Coal Mine" (November 2008) at http://www.wordalone.org/pdf/Allison-keynote-1.pdf.

10. Exhibit A of this fact is Bishop John Shelby Spong, who after having denied virtually every article of the Christian Creeds, continued to serve as a member and chairman of the House of Bishops Theology

Committee and remains to this day a bishop in good standing (retired).

11. For my thoughts on the subject of "Broken Communion," see http://www.stephenswitness.org/1999/03/broken-communion.html.

12. See Miranda K. Hassett, *Anglican Communion in Crisis: How Episcopal Dissidents and Their African Allies Are Reshaping Anglicanism* (Princeton: Princeton University Press, 2007) p. 60. For the Kuala Lumpur Statement on Human Sexuality, see www.globalsouthanglican.org/index.php/comments/the_kuala_lum pur_statement_on_human_sexuality_2nd_encounter_in_the_south_ 10/.

13. *The Handwriting on the Wall: A Plea to the Anglican Communion* (Solon, OH: Latimer Press, 1998). Prior to the Conference, I had sent a copy of this pamphlet to Presiding Bishop Frank Griswold, imploring him to take action to avert the impending crisis. Never having received a reply, I approached him after a press conference at Lambeth and asked if he had received it. Before his handler could whisk him away, he said "No." Later that day, I had a copy slipped under the door of his room at the University of Kent. This is merely one vignette demonstrating that calls for dialogue by revisionist leaders are a mere tactic. Like an army on the move, they are all for dialogue when it comes to unconquered territory, but behind their lines, it's all about suppression. The cultural bolshevists have learned their lessons well.

14. In my role at the Conference as a stealth "journalist," I had a pink name badge along with real journalists like Ruth Gledhill. For her take on the media manipulation, see "My Lambeth Hell" at http://justus.anglican.org/resources/Lambeth1998/articles/980815a .html. In 2008, the Communion Office made sure that the Franciscan Centre at the University of Kent was unavailable for any repeat subversion by conservatives.

15. "Lambeth Speaks Plainly" in *Mixed Blessings: A Response to the Report and Resolution of the Episcopal Church's Standing Commission on Liturgy and Music* (Dallas: American Anglican Council, 2000) pp. 30-37.

16. "Lambeth Speaks Plainly," p. 33.

17. *Two Sexes, One Flesh: Why the Church Cannot Bless Same-Sex Marriage* (Solon, Oh.:Latimer Press, 1997). Copies of this book were sent to all bishops and deputies to the 1997 General Convention. None of the bishops and deputies calling for dialogue bothered to respond to me, except for Bishop Herbert Thompson, then a candidate for Presiding Bishop, who thanked me and said he agreed with my conclusions.

18. *Two Sexes, One Flesh*, p. 45.

19. So I argue in "Look Not to Cantuar: A Friendly Rejoinder to Michael Poon" (2006) at http://www.globalsouthanglican.org/index.php/blog/comments/look_not_to_cantuar.

20. "Lambeth Speaks Plainly," pp. 33-34.

21. O'Donovan, *Church in Crisis: The Gay Controversy and the Anglican Communion* (Eugene, Or.: Cascade Books, 2008) pp. 115-116. Generous though O'Donovan's offer of serious dialogue is, it will never be seriously taken up by gay activists in the Communion. To do so would require stepping down from positions and actions that have led to political success in the Episcopal Church and elsewhere. The tacticians who propelled women's ordination from forbidden to mandatory in 25 years are hardly going to step back into the closet for a tête-à-tête with Oliver O'Donovan, or Rowan Williams for that matter.

22. Richard B. Hays, "Awaiting the Redemption of Our Bodies," *Sojourners* (July 1991) pp.17-21.

23. The "St. Andrew's Day Statement" can be found at http://www.ceec.info/st-andrews-day-statement.html. As a principal author, O'Donovan comments further on this Statement in "Reading the St. Andrew's Day Statement," *EFAC Bulletin* 48 (1997) pp. 9-16.

24. Later in this essay I criticise the role of Archbishop Rowan Williams in failing to exercise proper discipline. The same can be said as well of his predecessor, George Carey. Although Archbishop Carey did facilitate and publicly advocate the passage of Resolution 1.10, he allowed the Anglican Communion Office to continue to set the agenda of post-Lambeth affairs, most notably the Primates' Meetings at Oporto and Kanuga in 2000 and 2001, respectively. Likewise the many conservative American bishops who voted for Resolution 1.10 failed to organize a strong defense of it in the face of public protests against it within the Episcopal Church.

25. So from the Archbishop's Advent Letter of 14 December 2007: "Insofar as there is currently any consensus in the Communion about [blessing homosexual unions], it is not in favour of change in our discipline or our interpretation of the Bible."

26. The phrase "unchangeable standard of marriage" comes from Resolution 66 of Lambeth 1920. If the standard can change or has changed, then the Resolution was false. As to the meaning of No, Ephraim Radner, "Truthful Language and Orderly Separation" (9 Sep 2008) at http://www.anglicancommunioninstitute.com/?p=262, makes much the same case about the meaning of a "moratorium" on same-sex blessings and gay bishops. To the Left, the word means a

slight delay until conservatives adjust to the new situation. Radner suggests that conservatives should use the word "cessation" instead.

27. On a number of occasions, I have used the analogy with child-rearing. If a parent looks the child in the eye and says "Don't do that!" and the child looks right back and does it anyway and the parent then walks out of the room, the parent has in effect communicated, "I did not really mean what I said."

28. In December, 1998, the Association of Anglican Congregations in Mission (AACOM) produced a "Petition to the Primates' Meeting and the Primates of the Anglican Communion for Emergency Intervention in the Province of the Episcopal Church in the United States of America," including two lengthy appendixes, which documented at length the widespread rejection of Lambeth 1.10. See http://www.freerepublic.com/focus/f-religion/1694593/posts.

29. http://episcopalarchives.org/cgibin/acts_resolution.pl?resolution= 2000-D039

30. For those wanting to understand the nature of "conversation" in the Episcopal Church, I refer again to Lewis Carroll, "The Walrus and the Carpenter," in *Through the Looking-Glass.*

31. See my article, "The Official Position of the Episcopal Church on Sex Outside Marriage," at http://www.stephenswitness.org/2000/08/official-position-of-episcopal-church.html.

32. Chadwick, "Introduction," in Roger Coleman, ed., *Resolutions of the Twelve Lambeth Conferences 1867-1988* (Toronto: Anglican Book Centre, 1992) p. viii. Note that Bishop George Selwyn and Robert Gray had both served as missionary bishops (in New Zealand and South Africa respectively) and had had to deal with problems resulting from the particular polity of the Established Church when it moved overseas.

33. Report of Committee IV, Lambeth 1930, sec. I,8. See *Lambeth Conference 1930: Encyclical Letter from the Bishops with Resolutions and Reports* (London: SPCK) pp. 154-155.

34. Roger Beckwith, "The Limits of Anglican Diversity," *Churchman* 117 (2003) pp. 347-362.

35. *To Mend the Net: Anglican Faith and Order for Renewed Mission*, eds. Drexel W. Gomez and Maurice W. Sinclair (Carrollton, Tx.: Ekklesia Society, 2001). The Proposal is found on pages 9-23.

36. *To Mend the Net*, p. 12.

37. Resolution 11 at http://www.lambethconference.org/resolutions/1978/. The

presenting issue in 1978 was the ordination of women to the priesthood in the Episcopal Church. Resolution 13 (1978) makes clear that the guardianship of the faith is a collegial responsibility of the "whole episcopate" (Lambeth Conference), the Primates, and the Archbishop of Canterbury. These entities, along with that of the Anglican Consultative Council, came to be known as the "Instruments of Unity."

38. Resolution 18. The Resolution calls for the Primates to be consulted "on the appointment of the Archbishop of Canterbury" and comments that the decennial Conference could be held elsewhere than Canterbury.

39. Explanatory Note on clause 2. Another note on clause 5 makes clear that the Primates are meant to exercise oversight, whereas the Anglican Consultative Council is merely advisory.

40. *To Mend the Net*, pp. 20-22. The following summary is a paraphrase, drawing out the implications of the proposal.

41. The word used in step 8 of "To Mend the Net" is that "communion be suspended," which seems merely a polite way of saying "excommunicated." Presumably the new jurisdiction now becomes the territorial province, and if the former province were to repent, it would need to be incorporated into the new jurisdiction.

42. *Communion, Conflict and Hope: The Kuala Lumpur Report of the Third Inter-Anglican Theological and Doctrinal Commission* (London: Anglican Communion Office, 2008) at http://www.anglicancommunion.org/media/107653/Communion-Conflict-and-Hope-the-Kuala-Lumpur-Report.pdf. In an earlier Report, "The Communion Study" (2002), Chairman Stephen Sykes offered a "yes, but…" evaluation of "To Mend the Net": "It would be important to bear in mind the strong voluntary character of communion in the Anglican Communion and to be meticulous about seeking consent to the strengthening of international canonical procedures."

43. *To Mend the Net*, p. 87.

44. Although "To Mend the Net" was scuttled at the Primates' Meeting chaired by George Carey, Rowan Williams as Archbishop of Wales was present at that meeting and no doubt consented to its demise. Cf. his comments on the March 2000 Primates' Meeting in Portugal: "Anglicanism has always been wary of a central executive power…. The primates' meeting showed no signs of wanting to become a ruling synod."

45. For my evaluation of the Windsor process, see "Put Not Your Trust in Windsor" at http://www.stephenswitness.org/2008/12/put-not-

your-trust-in-windsor.html. As for the indaba process, Archbishop Williams has announced that future Primates' Meetings will be conducted with the indaba format.

46. In the understatement of the Conference, they say: "Our discussions have drawn us into a much more detailed response than we would have thought necessary at the beginning of our meeting." Indeed, the toe-to-toe confrontation went on past the official closing of the meeting.

47. See the text of the Communiqué at https://www.ireland.anglican.org/news/343/communique-issued-by-the-primates.

48. She was inspired no doubt by the example of her predecessor, Frank Griswold, who had joined the "unanimous" decision of the Primates in October 2003 "not to take act precipitately on these wider questions" and then presided over the consecration of Gene Robinson less than three weeks later.

49. For the Panel of Reference Report, see http://www.anglicancommunion.org/media/100360/The-Panel-of-Reference.pdf: "The Panel published its report on 27 February 2007, recommending a form of extended episcopal ministry. Since then a civil action in relation to ownership of church property has been resolved in favour of the diocese, and the parish appears to have decided that it cannot in conscience continue in communion with the Diocese or The Episcopal Church." For further documentation, see http://www.virtueonline.org/florida-documents-detail-por-redeemer-and-bishop-howard.

50. For this reason, Archbishop Henry Orombi, one of the five members of the JSC, refused to attend. Archbishop Mouneer Anis did attend and wrote a highly critical assessment of the General Convention at http://www.globalsouthanglican.org/index.php/blog/comments/bishop_mouneer_anis_reflections_on_the_joint_standing_committee_jsc. His view was largely ignored in the final Report.

51. Other signs of the relegation of the Primates include: dropping the Primates from the disciplinary process in the St. Andrew's Covenant draft; the absence of any significant role of the Primates who did attend Lambeth (compare their role at GAFCON); and the reply as to why he had called a Primates' Meeting by saying: "I haven't called it with any agenda, except to have a Primates' meeting. It's time we had one…" The final blow was his announcement that he planned to employ the indaba method for future Primates' Meetings as well.

52. For the full text of "The Road to Lambeth," see http://www.globalsouthanglican.org/index.php/comments/the_roa

d_to_lambeth_presented_at_capa/. My colleagues in drafting the statement were Archbishop Nicholas Okoh of Nigeria and Bishop Zac Niringiye of Uganda. We exchanged drafts by email and then met in May to finish the final draft. Archbishop Akinola himself added certain key phrases, all of which made the document even more pointed in its message. The statement was received by the CAPA Primates in Kigali in September 2006, but some Primates said they would need individual approval from their House of Bishops or Provincial Synod. It was later endorsed by the House of Bishops of Uganda, Nigeria, Rwanda and Kenya.

53. Radner, "Wheels Within Wheels: The Promise and Scandal of Anglican Conciliarism," (The Inaugural Lecture at Wycliffe College, Toronto and SEAD Conference 9-10 October 2007) pp. 22-23, at http://www.anglicancommunioninstitute.com/wp-content/uploads/2008/08/conciliarism.pdf.

54. Some former students may remember with chagrin my lectures on the prophetic *rib*, fashioned after a legal indictment, with God functioning as prosecutor and Israel in the dock.

55. Though a remnant in terms of official power structures of the Communion, the churches represented at Jerusalem number about half the practicing Anglicans in the world.

56. The Statement refers to "a fellowship of confessing Anglicans." The first Primates' Council in August 2008 (http://www.gafcon.org/index.php?option=com_content&task=view&id=89&Itemid=31) raised the status of the term to "Fellowship of Confessing Anglicans" (FCA), although "GAFCON movement" may well persist as a memorable marker.

57. In all honesty, the ultimate intention is to form a replacement, not a parallel province. Pragmatically, a two-track province in North America is inevitable, whether recognized by Canterbury or not.

58. "Wheels within Wheels," p. 20.

59. See http://www.globalsouthanglican.org/index.php/comments/statement_on_lambeth_conference_2008/.

60. See Andrew Goddard's proposed a typology of four Anglican groups: federal conservatives, communion conservatives, federal liberals and communion liberals. For a summary see http://www.globalsouthanglican.org/index.php/blog/comments/shechem_corinth_and_columbus_ecusas_choices_graham_kings. My argument holds that the Global Anglican Future Statement contains elements both of "confessionalism" and "conciliarist catholicity." In this sense it might merge two of Goddard's final categories. See

Robert Munday, "Confessional or Conciliar: the GAFCON Dilemma" at http://toalltheworld.blogspot.com/2008/06/confessional-or-conciliar-gafcon.html.

61. See my "The Future of the Anglican Covenant in the Light of the Global Anglican Future Conference" at http://www.stephenswitness.org/2009/01/future-of-anglican-communion-covenant-blueprint.html.

62. See my "The Global Anglican Communion: A Blueprint" at http://www.stephenswitness.org/2007/06/global-anglican-communion-blueprint.html.

63. Sec. 3.2.5 states: "However, commitment to this Covenant entails an acknowledgement that in the most extreme circumstances, where a Church chooses not to adopt the request of the Instruments of Communion, that decision may be understood by the Church itself, or by the resolution of the Instruments of Communion, as a relinquishment by that Church of the force and meaning of the covenant's purpose, until they re-establish their covenant relationship with other member Churches." There is no final separation and no provision for an alternative jurisdiction. In my opinion, this is the way the Communion ends, not with a bang but a whimper.

64. "Truthful Language," p. 5. In the service of truthful language, I think it fair to say that "reconciliation" in the case of those who have torn the Communion apart means "repentance." It is also hard to see how those who have caused such damage would be allowed to continue in positions of leadership.

65. This was an address given to a conference on primacy sponsored by the Fellowship of St. Alban and St. Sergius at St. Vladimir's Seminary in New York City on 5 June 2008. See http://rowanwilliams.archbishopofcanterbury.org/articles.php/1357/rome-constantinople-and-canterbury-mother-churches.

66. In "Whither the Branch Theory?" (see http://archive.li/SN6m7), Fr. Gregory Mathewes-Green, who converted from the Episcopal Church to Orthodoxy, concludes that this theory is "theologically defective, resting as it does on a non-Biblical, non-Patristic ecclesiology, very late in development and believed by a minority of those for whom it was devised."

67. Resolutions 6-10.

68. Williams cites the Anglican-Orthodox Statement "The Church of the Triune God" (2006) sec. V, para. 19-23 in support of his view. Para. 21 states: "The theological argument for primacy begins with local and moves on to regional and global leadership. Primacy thus

receives increasingly wide expression through Episcopal representation of the Church's life. This ensures a proper balance between primacy and conciliarity; and the primate is the first among equals in synods of bishops. Primacy should not be seen as the prerogative of an individual, but of a local church. In the case of the universal primacy this would mean the primacy of the Church of Rome." While it may well be true that a regional primate is first among equals in a synod of bishops, it is not clear that there is a place for a "branch" primate of primates who is of distinctively different status. For the Dublin statement, see http://www.anglicancommunion.org/media/103818/The-Church-of-the-Triune-God.pdf.

69. See Mark D. Chapman, "The Dull Bits of History: Cautionary Tales for Anglicanism," in *idem*, ed., *The Anglican Covenant: Unity and Diversity in the Anglican Communion* (London: Mowbray, 2008) pp. 81-99. Chapman's "caution" about the failure of conciliarism at the Council of Constance seems to prove the point that it is difficult to mix polities, in this case primacy and conciliarity. The Eastern churches seem to have a purer model. Even the Ecumenical Patriarch of Constantinople has only the power of influence and representation, and even that is disputed by some of the Orthodox. Thus the *Dublin Agreed Statement* (1984) para. 28, says: "Thus, even though the seniority ascribed to the Archbishop of Canterbury is not identical with that given to the Ecumenical Patriarch, the Anglican Communion has developed on the Orthodox rather than the Roman Catholic pattern, as a fellowship of self-governing national or regional Churches."

70. I intentionally leave out the Anglican Consultative Council. The ACC is the weakest of the Instruments of Unity, being granted no authority in matters of doctrine and discipline. It is intended, according to its constitution, to share information and to coordinate Anglican ecumenical efforts. But the ACC has developed a secretariat which has exercised power over the other Instruments far beyond its charter and is more an arm of Canterbury and its Anglo-American financiers than the Communion as a whole. If a Communion bureaucracy is desired, it should be accountable to the Primates through the President of the Primates' Council. There may be an argument for a Primates Council with lay and clergy representation, which is the direction taken recently by adding the Primates to the ACC, but if so the Primates and Consultative Council should function in tandem – wheels within wheels.

71. If the Episcopal Church were to split off from the Canterbury Communion, it would of course expose the deep fissure in the Church of England itself. That fate, I believe, lies ahead for the Mother Church no matter what Canterbury does or does not do.

Select Bibliography

I have included a "Select Bibliography" of books which cover Anglicanism during this quarter-century period. Readers will find, I think, that these books cover a variety of viewpoints. As is generally the case today, I think you will find "conservatives" tend to read "liberal" authors, but the reverse is not true. In fact, liberals are frequently illiberal, whereas orthodox Anglicans value true liberality (see e.g., the 2008 pre-GAFCON book, *The Way, the Truth, and the Life*, page 36). While they talk a lot about "listening," they listen very selectively, and certain viewpoints are simply dismissed out of court.

Let me cite Paul Avis's new book *The Vocation of Anglicanism* as an example of illiberal "selectivity." [*N.B.* The $90 price tag will select out most readers in the Global South]. Avis begins by acknowledging the "predicament" of Anglicanism over the past 25 years and the "*Angst*" it has caused, but he is convinced that his own version of Anglican "peaceableness" possesses the resources to smooth any ruffled feathers. He does not see the new pansexual ethos as a doctrinal problem (it's not addressed in the Creeds or the Articles), and he thinks that each autonomous province can deal with any disciplinary matters through its canons.

Avis does devote a brief passage (pages 81-87) to those who do not see matters his way. Unfortunately, he shows very little understanding of the Gafcon movement or the rationale that links the Jerusalem Declaration (which he calls "moderate" and "unexceptionable" – did he read clause 13?) to the diagnosis of the problem facing the Communion and the subsequent actions of the meeting.

He complains that the Gafcon leaders were not even

willing to *confer* in 2008 at Lambeth. What does he think the Global South Primates were doing between 1998 and 2008? Even those bishops like Mouneer Anis who did take part in the Lambeth indaba and subsequent Communion meetings concluded that there was no way the challenge to orthodoxy by the Episcopal Church would be dealt with.

The unwillingness of Avis and others like him – with the notable exception of Miranda Hassett – to even try to understand the developments of the last quarter century displays a Sadducean aloofness to the seriousness of the threat posed by heresy in the Anglican Communion today. It is also, in my opinion, a strategy of "avoiding closure" in the belief that the dissidents will eventually melt or go away and all will return to normalcy (in this regard, see Charles Raven's insightful analysis of Rowan Williams's thought and practice [*Shadow Gospel*]).

Ashey, Phil. *Conciliarism: The Church Meeting to Decide Together*. Newport Beach, CA: Anglican House, 2017.

Atherstone, Andrew and Andrew Goddard, eds. *Good Disagreement: Grace and Truth in a Divided Church*. Oxford: Lion, 2015.

Avis, Paul. *The Identity of Anglicanism: Essentials of Anglican Ecclesiology*. London: T&T Clark, 2008.

Avis, Paul. *The Vocation of Anglicanism*. London: Bloomsbury T&T Clark, 2016.

Barnum, Thaddeus. *Never Silent: How Third World Missionaries Are Now Bringing the Gospel to the US*. Colorado Springs: Eleison Publishing, 2008.

Bray, Gerald. *Heresy, Schism and Apostasy*. Latimer Studies 67. London: Latimer Trust, 2008.

Chapman, Mark, ed. *The Hope of Things to Come: Anglicanism and the Future*. London: Mowbray, 2010.

Coleman, Roger, ed. *Resolutions of the Twelve Lambeth Conferences*, with an Introduction by Owen Chadwick. Toronto: Anglican Book Centre, 1992.

Davie, Martin. *The Gospel and the Anglican Tradition.* West Knapton UK: Gilead Books, 2018.

Doe, Norman. *An Anglican Covenant: Theological and Legal Considerations for a Global Debate.* Norwich: Canterbury Press, 2008.

Doe, Norman. *Canon Law in the Anglican Communion: A Worldwide Perspective.* Oxford: Oxford University Press, 1998.

Francis, Peter, ed. *Rebuilding Communion: Who Pays the Price? From the Lambeth Conference 1998 to the Lambeth Conference 2008 and Beyond.* Hawardan, Flintshire: Monad Press, 2008.

Gagnon, Robert. *The Bible and Homosexual Practice: Texts and Hermeneutics.* Nashville: Abingdon Press, 2002.

Gomez, Drexel W. and Maurice W. Sinclair, eds. *To Mend the Net: Anglican Faith and Order for Renewed Mission.* Carrollton, TX: The Ekklesia Society, 2001.

Hassett, Miranda K. *Anglican Communion in Crisis: How Episcopal Dissidents and Their African Allies Are Reshaping Anglicanism.* Princeton: Princeton University Press, 2007.

Jensen, Michael P. *Sydney Anglicanism: An Apology.* Eugene, OR: Wipf & Stock, 2012.

Kaye, Bruce. *An Introduction to World Anglicanism.* Cambridge: Cambridge University Press, 2008.

Markham, Ian S., et al. *The Wiley-Blackwell Companion to the Anglican Communion.* Chichester: Wiley-Blackwell, 2013.

Middleton, Arthur. *Restoring the Anglican Mind.* Leominster, Herefordshire: Gracewing, 2008.

Nazir-Ali, Michael. *How the Anglican Communion Came To Be and Where It Is Going.* London: Latimer Trust, 2013.

O'Donovan, Oliver. *Church in Crisis: The Gay Controversy and the Anglican Communion.* Eugene, OR: Cascade Books, 2008.

Podmore, Colin. *Aspects of Anglican Identity.* London: Church Publishing House, 2005.

Radner, Ephraim, and Philip Turner. *The Fate of Communion: The Agony of Anglicanism and the Future of a Global Church.* Grand Rapids: Eerdmans, 2006.

Raven, Charles. *Shadow Gospel: Rowan Williams and the Anglican Communion Crisis.* London: Latimer Trust, 2010.

Raven, Charles, ed. *The Truth Shall Set You Free: Global Anglicanism in the 21ˢᵗ Century.* London: Latimer Trust, 2013.

Rosenthal, James M., and Nicola Currie, eds. *Being Anglican in the Third Millennium: The Official Report of the 10ᵗʰ Meeting of the Anglican Consultative Council, Panama 1996.* Includes the Virginia Report and the Dublin Liturgical Report. Harrisburg, PA: Morehouse, 1997.

Sachs, William L, ed. *Global Anglicanism c. 1910-2000.* The Oxford History of Anglicanism, vol. V. Oxford: Oxford University Press, forthcoming in 2018.

Sachs, William L, *Homosexuality and the Crisis of Anglicanism.* Cambridge Cambridge University Press, 2009.

The Way, the Truth and the Life: Theological Resources for a Pilgrimage to a Global Anglican Future. Prepared by the Theological Resource Team of GAFCON. London: Latimer Trust, 2008.

Valliere, Paul. *Conciliarism: The History of Decision-Making in the Church.* Cambridge: Cambridge University Press, 2012.

Ward, Kevin. *A History of Global Anglicanism.* Cambridge: Cambridge University Press, 2006

Index of Scripture References

Author and Subject Index

Two Sexes, One Flesh (Noll), 48, 54, 134

Uganda Christian University, 8, 307-308
unchangeable glory of marriage, 94–95
unholy trinity, 298–299

Valliere, Paul, 233
Vanhoozer, K. J., 335
variations in marriage, 72
vigilance, 319–320
Virgin Birth, 39–41
Virginia Report, 165, 236
The Vocation of Anglicanism (Avis), 353–354

Watts, Isaac, 113
Welby, Justin, 227-228, 269–270, 276-278
Wesley, Charles, 32, 113
Westminster Confession, 55, 105
Westminster Larger Catechism, 62
Westminster Shorter Catechism, 86
Wiles, Maurice, 332
Williams, Robert, 128–129
Williams, Rowan
    generally, 8, 342–343, 354
    conciliarity and, 158–160
    Dar es Salaam Communiqué and, 148–149, 264

discipline and, 345
Global South Movements and, 261–262
Primates and, 347–348
Resolution I.10 and, 135, 137, 277
"To Mend the Net" and, 145–146
Windsor Report and, 259
Windsor Report, 98, 123, 146, 236, 258, 260, 262, 277, 283
women, 63–65
Wondra, Ellen, 13, 331–332
Word of God, 16–20, 303
worldview war, 300–303, 306–308
worship, 111–113
Wright, J. Robert, 35, 337

Zadok, 205
Zechariah, 59
Zizioulas, John, 158